# EVALUATING ECONOMIC LIBERALIZATION

CASE-STUDIES IN ECONOMIC DEVELOPMENT

General Editor: **David Greenaway**, *Professor of Economics and Director of the Centre for Research in Economic Development and International Trade (CREDIT), University of Nottingham*

*Published*

Volume 1: POLICY ADJUSTMENT IN AFRICA
Chris Milner and A. J. Rayner (*editors*)

Volume 2: TOPICS IN POLICY APPRAISAL
V. N. Balasubramanyam and John Maynard Bates (*editors*)

Volume 3: POVERTY, INEQUALITY AND RURAL DEVELOPMENT
Tim Lloyd and Oliver Morrissey (*editors*)

Volume 4: EVALUATING ECONOMIC LIBERALIZATION
Mark McGillivray and Oliver Morrissey (*editors*)

**Case-Studies in Economic Development**
**Series Standing Order ISBN 0–333–71463–6**
(*outside North America only*)

You can receive future titles in this series as they are published by placing a standing order. Please contact your bookseller or, in case of difficulty, write to us at the address below with your name and address, the title of the series and the ISBN quoted above.

Customer Services Department, Macmillan Distribution Ltd
Houndmills, Basingstoke, Hampshire RG21 6XS, England

# Evaluating Economic Liberalization

## Case-Studies in Economic Development

## Volume 4

Edited by

Mark McGillivray
*Associate Professor of International Development*
*RMIT University*
*Melbourne*
*Australia*

and

Oliver Morrissey
*Director of the Centre for Research in Economic Development and International Trade (CREDIT), and*
*Senior Lecturer*
*School of Economics*
*The University of Nottingham*

First published in Great Britain 1999 by
**MACMILLAN PRESS LTD**
Houndmills, Basingstoke, Hampshire RG21 6XS and London
Companies and representatives throughout the world

A catalogue record for this book is available from the British Library.

ISBN 0–333–67829–X

First published in the United States of America 1999 by
**ST. MARTIN'S PRESS, INC.,**
Scholarly and Reference Division,
175 Fifth Avenue, New York, N.Y. 10010

ISBN 0–312–22569–5

Library of Congress Cataloging-in-Publication Data
Evaluating economic liberalization : case-studies in economic development, volume 4 / edited by Mark McGillivray and Oliver Morrissey.
p. cm.
Includes bibliographical references (p. ) and index.
ISBN 0–312–22569–5 (cloth)
1. Rural poor—Developing countries—Case studies. 2. Rural development—Developing countries—Case studies. 3. Agriculture––Economic aspects—Developing countries—Case studies. 4. Developing countries—Rural conditions—Case studies. I. Lloyd, Tim. II. Morrissey, Oliver.
HC59.72.P6P684 1994
362.5'09173'4—dc20 93–47023
CIP



This book is printed on paper suitable for recycling and made from fully managed and sustained forest sources.

10 9 8 7 6 5 4 3 2 1
08 07 06 05 04 03 02 01 00 99

Printed and bound in Great Britain by Antony Rowe Ltd, Chippenham, Wiltshire

# Contents

# List of Tables and Figures

**Tables**

**Figures**

# General Editor's Foreword

Development economics is a core sub-discipline of economics and an area where there has been growing interest in the application of economic theory and the tools of applied economics to understand development processes better. The award of the 1998 Nobel Prize in Economics to Professor Amartya Sen is an indicator of the growing centrality of this area of our discipline.

Case-study material is especially useful in this sub-discipline given the diversity of developing countries. This particular series was initiated as a response to the need to provide good-quality case-study material around particular themes. Volume 4 in the series, *Evaluating Economic Liberalization*, focuses on the experience of developing countries with liberalization. Since the 1980s over 100 developing countries have undergone liberalization programmes. The evidence on the success of those programmes is somewhat mixed. The papers in this volume look at ways of evaluating liberalization and include case-studies of actual experiences.

Many of the papers were presented at meetings of the Structural Adjustment Forum (SAF) at the University of Nottingham, a joint initiative between the Department for International Development (ODA at the time of initiation) and CREDIT. The series of SAF workshops have run since 1993, and we are particularly grateful to Sean Conlin (then of ODA) for supporting and encouraging the initiative. I am very grateful to the editors, Mark McGillivray and Oliver Morrissey, for selecting the papers, editing them and providing such a useful overview.

David Greenaway
University of Nottingham

# Notes on the Contributors

**Tony Addison** is Lecturer in Economics at the University of Warwick, on secondment to UNU/WIDER, Helsinki, for 1998–99.

**Prema-chandra Athukorala** is Senior Fellow in the Division of Economics, Research School of Pacific and Asian Studies, Australian National University, Canberra.

**Clara de Sousa** is Lecturer in Economics at the University of Maputo. She was at the University of Warwick at the time the chapter was written.

**David Greenaway** is Professor of Economics and Pro-Vice Chancellor at the University of Nottingham. He was Chairman of CREDIT from 1995 to 1998.

**Karel Jansen** is Associate Professor of Economics at the Institute of Social Studies, The Hague. He was based at the University of Economics, Ho Chi Minh City, Vietnam, at the time of writing his contribution to this volume.

**Steve Leybourne** is Reader in Econometrics at the University of Nottingham.

**Mark McGillivray** is Associate Professor of International Development in the School of Social Science and Planning at RMIT University in Melbourne, Australia, and an External Fellow of CREDIT at the University of Nottingham.

**Andrew McKay** is Lecturer in Economics and an Internal Fellow of CREDIT at the University of Nottingham.

**Chris Milner** is Professor of International Economics and Head of Department and an Internal Fellow of CREDIT at the University of Nottingham.

**Oliver Morrissey** is Senior Lecturer in Economics and Director of CREDIT, University of Nottingham.

**David Sapsford** is Professor of Economics at the Business School, University of Lancaster.

# 1 Evaluating Economic Liberalization: Issues, Concepts and Approaches

Mark McGillivray and Oliver Morrissey

## 1.1 INTRODUCTION

The early 1980s witnessed a profound change in attitude towards economic policy in developing countries. Increased oil prices, higher rates of interest, a slump in real commodity prices, significant reductions in private capital inflows, an associated international recession and reduced access to foreign markets each contributed to extremely serious balance of payments problems and other forms of macroeconomic instability in many developing countries. This imposed debilitating foreign exchange constraints and spiraling foreign debts and contributed to significant declines in overall economic performance. It also drove home the realization that fundamental and decisive policy interventions were required, manifested in World Bank structural adjustment policies (Greenaway and Morrissey, 1993). While donors such as the World Bank may not now engage in the types of adjustment programmes that were prevalent in the 1980s, economic policy reform is still an issue of great importance in developing (if not also developed) economies. In nearly all cases the types of economic reforms proposed and advocated are of the liberalizing type, measures to reduce government-induced distortions so as to render the economy more market-based, i.e. more responsive to market-determined price incentives. It is in this sense that we refer to economic liberalization.

This volume contributes to the literature on liberalization, not only by reviewing and summarizing previous literature, nor by offering yet another simple set of evaluations but, we hope, by distilling from the literature a set of principles regarding the appropriate methods to employ in the evaluation of the process and impact of economic liberalization. The first five chapters are concerned with general issues, in particular how to quantify liberalization. Existing approaches to evaluating the effects of reform are reviewed, and appropriate quantitative techniques suggested. Quantitative evaluations are not without problems. The difficulties of actually measuring liberalization are discussed, in the context of trade policy, the complex ways in which reforms can impact on individuals and groups are illustrated in the context of poverty, and the qualitative importance of political concerns are addressed. The final four chapters offer case-studies, two of which employ the types of quantitative techniques recommended. However, many of the poorest countries have insufficient data to warrant econometric evaluations, and two case-studies address economies of that type.

Major aid donors, most notably the World Bank, responded to the economic crisis in developing countries in the late 1970s with a major change in aid policy that involved a move towards tying financial inflows to changes in domestic economic policies in recipient countries. The rationale for this was not only that something had to be done to attack the problems that many developing countries were facing, but that many previous policy interventions had actually exacerbated these problems. In essence, it was thought that poor macroeconomic performance in developing countries was due to poor economic policies, and that external assistance was doomed to failure unless appropriate domestic policies were in place. Excessively distortionary state intervention (including such measures as price controls, subsidies, regulation of interest rates and the imposition of tariffs), too large a public sector, inefficient parastatals and discrimination against export sectors (especially agriculture) were held to blame. Reforms were therefore required, with aid inflows being conditional upon stabilization and subsequent structural adjustment to the supply sides of recipient economies. Stabilization (the removal of public sector fiscal and current account deficits) was regarded as a prerequisite for successful adjustment. These adjustments were generally of a type that reduced the extent of government intervention in the economy and relied more on the efficacy of market forces in a more liberal economic environment. For this reason the overall package of reforms have commonly been described as economic liberalization, at the root of which is changes to relative prices.

Economic liberalization has since become almost the *sine qua non* of economic development policy since the first World Bank-sponsored adjustment programme was implemented in 1980. By the mid-1990s, one can only identify a small, disparate group of developing countries that had *not* followed an economic liberalization programme of some form (for example, Afghanistan and Liberia, both war-ravaged throughout much of the period; Myanmar, Sudan and so on). Most liberalizing economies have followed a programme designed and implemented under the guidance of either the World Bank, the International Monetary Fund or both of these agencies. However, there is also a group of countries which has independently embarked on economic liberalization of the general type that would be sponsored by the Bank or Fund, without the direct involvement of either agency. These countries include China, India, Malaysia and Vietnam.

There is now a very large literature assessing and evaluating economic liberalization, especially World Bank and IMF structural adjustment programmes (SAPs). Individual chapters in this volume will refer to some of this literature in detail, but it is appropriate here to note some of the general reviews. General evaluations include World Bank (1988, 1990b, 1992), Mosley *et al.* (1991a, 1991b), Thomas *et al.* (1991), Corbo *et al.* (1992) and Greenaway and Morrissey (1993). There is a large literature on adjustment in Africa, with recent contributions including Elbadawi *et al.* (1992), Aderanti (1993), Cornia and Helleiner (1994), Husain and Faruqee (1994), Sahn (1994), Simon *et al.* (1995) and Lensink (1996). Specific trade policy reform has also attracted a large literature with evaluations including Papageorgiou *et al.* (1991), Foroutan (1993), Dean *et al.* (1994), and Greenaway and Morrissey (1994). IMF programmes have been singled out by a number of studies including Killick *et al.* (1992), Bird (1995) and Killick (1995a). There is also a rapidly growing literature on the socioeconomic implications of economic liberalization, including its impact of poverty. Studies include Cornia *et al.* (1987), Commonwealth Secretariat (1989), Elson (1991), Afshar and Dennis (1992), Rose (1995), Killick (1995b) and Stewart (1995).

Evaluations of liberalization programmes, or of liberalizing economies (LEs), to introduce an acronym we will use, take a number of forms. Of course, there are those which consider nature and timing of the programme. Key questions are whether the policies introduced are appropriate to the economy under consideration, and whether the range of policies are introduced at the appropriate time and in the right sequence. A not uncommon characteristic of these evaluations is that liberalization is necessarily good for the country under consideration. Other evaluations largely avoid this question by assessing the outcomes or impacts of liberalization, be it in terms of traditional economic variables or social, political or environmental indicators. The main questions are whether liberalization has worked in terms of meeting its own objectives and of the impacts on related variables such as health and education. There have also been studies that test for the economic behavioral relationships on which liberalization programmes are premised (for example, that there is a positive relationship between real rates of interest and investment). To this extent, these evaluations consider whether liberalization can work. These evaluations use a range of methodologies (such as comparing the experience of countries with a liberalization programme to those without such a programme), most of which are discussed in Chapter 2. A key issue in most evaluations is the problem of the counterfactual; that is, what would have prevailed in the absence of a liberalization programme. Before considering issues not specifically addressed in this volume, we briefly review the contents.

## 1.2 CONTENTS OF THIS VOLUME

In Chapter 2, **Mark McGillivray** reviews the various methods that have been employed to quantitatively evaluate both the macroeconomic and socioeconomic impacts of economic liberalization programmes. The standard approaches – whether targets were achieved, before-after and with-without comparisons – are all shown to be unsound and unreliable unless rather restrictive *ceteris paribus* conditions are satisfied. Econometric techniques offer more promise, with their inherent ability to control for initial conditions and exogenous shocks, but there are profound statistical problems in identifying structural change in a complex system and attributing causality. Data requirements, in particular, are large and this poses tremendous problems when dealing with developing countries. New techniques offer promise, but the chapter shows that detailed and rigorous country case-studies are probably the most reliable method of evaluation. Econometric techniques can be employed if data allow, but such studies offer some potential in disentangling before and after liberalization trends in one country.

**Chris Milner** and **Oliver Morrissey** address the problems of measuring economic policy reforms, using the particular case of trade liberalization to illustrate their arguments. Many evaluations of SAPs are based on some measure of compliance, (to what extent) did the adjusting country actually implement the reforms required, but these are shown to often be meaningless. Values of macroeconomic variables, such as of export growth in the context of trade liberalization, can reveal trends, but these are at best only indicators of outcomes which may or may not be due to the reform. Many important reforms, notably import liberalizaton, will require changes in tax rates; while changes in scheduled rates can be observed, it is difficult to get any reliable summary measures, especially in effective tax rates. More reliable measures, which reflect results from implementing a reform, should reflect relative price changes. Commonly used examples include the real exchange rate, agricultural producer prices (especially relative to border prices), and relative domestic prices for non-tradables as a measure of trade reform. The authors conclude that it is the broad summary measures that tend to be most misleading (further undermining the reliability of cross-country comparisons) and the best information is contained in relative prices, unfortunately often very difficult to calculate.

Assuming one has reliable measures and an accepted method of evaluating the impact of reforms, there remain difficult issues of interpretation. If a SAP is seen to have failed, in the sense that a deterioration or at least no improvement in economic performance is observed, this may be for a number of reasons. It could be that the economic policy advice was wrong (an issue addressed in some of the chapters), or it could be because of the impact of exogenous shocks (which should be identified if an appropriate evaluation method is employed). Alternatively, it may be due to implementation failure, the issue addressed by **Oliver Morrissey** in Chapter 4. If an adjusting country fails to implement a reform it is important to identify why. Possibilities include that the government did not intend to implement reforms, that it was unable to push through reforms in the face of strong political opposition, or that it lacked the necessary administrative capability. Evidence for all of these possibilities is found, and economic policy advisors could predict which failures are potential if they appraised themselves of the policy environment (nature of domestic politics).

There have been widespread concerns regarding the impact of economic liberalization on poverty, especially given that significant increases in poverty levels have occurred at the same time as many countries have pursued liberal economic reforms. There is an obvious temptation to think that these phenomena are linked, but the reality is far more complex than this. That two events occur largely simultaneously need not imply a causal relationship between them. A careful analysis is required, which accounts for the possible influences on poverty of a range of factors in addition to economic reform. This issue is addressed by **Andrew McKay** in Chapter 5, which looks at methodological issues in assessing the impact of economic reform on poverty. Three main issues are highlighted: (i) the measurement of poverty; (ii) the channels by which macroeconomic reform can impact on poverty; and (iii) the methods by which these impacts can be assessed empirically in any given country.

**David Greenaway**, **Steve Leybourne** and **David Sapsford** present a particular econometric technique for identifying system changes, and illustrate its application to evaluating trade liberalization in Chapter 6. This complements Chapter 2 in offering an evaluation method of essentially three stages. First, choose an observable variable that will be an indicator of the impact of reform, such as the budget deficit, export growth, growth in real income. Second, determine if the trend value of the output variable has changed significantly. Third, assess if this change coincided with the period of reform. The approach is useful but no panacea. The data requirements are great, especially if a multivariate analysis is required, and it does not demonstrate causality.

These chapters are not intended to be a comprehensive review of all issues important in evaluating adjustment programmes. Rather the aim is to address a set of the more important issues. Thus, the contributions mentioned above cover general economic evaluation methodologies, measurement issues (with respect to trade), political dimensions, and the impact on poverty. Later in this chapter (in Sections 1.3 to 1.4) we briefly discuss some of the omitted issues, such as macroeconomic policy aspects of adjustment, public expenditure (and how this relates to social dimensions), and social impacts (although these are covered to some extent in Chapter 5).

The remaining chapters are four country case-studies of experiences of specific liberalizing economies (LEs). Two of these countries have embarked on policy reforms independently of lending agencies (Sri Lanka and Vietnam), two have done likewise but with the assistance of these agencies (Pakistan and Mozambique). One is an economy reconstructing itself after years of war (Mozambique), one has only partially implemented its intended programme of reforms (Pakistan), another (Sri Lanka) has introduced a comprehensive range of reforms, and one is a socialist economy undergoing a transition to a (more) market-based economy (Vietnam). To this extent, the case-studies provide a rich diversity of background and experiences of countries undergoing liberal economic reforms.

Many countries have experienced appreciable improvements in their macroeconomic performance following the introduction of a liberalization programme. Pakistan is one of these countries and **Mark McGillivray** looks at its experience in Chapter 7. Pakistan introduced a

World Bank and (subsequently) IMF-supported adjustment programme in late 1980. This chapter commences with a brief overview of Pakistan's macroeconomic experience under this adjustment programme and debates over its efficacy. After providing some brief insights into the approaches used and findings of empirical evaluations of the programme, Chapter 7 applies a smooth transitions model to Pakistani real GDP data for the period 1960–94. The central question under consideration is whether the adjustment programme has been the prime source of Pakistan's improved performance with respect to GDP. The evidence, as is often the case, is mixed.

Mozambique faces the enormous task of rebuilding its economy and society after a bloody fifteen-year war which destroyed much of the rural economy's infrastructure. **Tony Addison** and **Clara de Sousa** look in Chapter 8 at attempts to both rebuild and reform Mozambique's economy. Their analysis is essentially qualitative, as the quality of the data available is poor. Economic reform in Mozambique began over a decade ago and has involved dismantling the system of state intervention and planning introduced soon after independence in 1975. While Mozambique is not alone in introducing such reforms, few countries have implemented them in such difficult circumstances. Chapter 8 highlights important issues concerning these reforms, especially concerning fiscal policy, which has seen major disagreements between the IMF and other donors, and agricultural policy, which is important for rural poverty reduction (and so provides a link to Chapter 5). Revitalizing agriculture is seen to be central both to liberalization and to poverty-reduction. This study illustrates the problems faced by many countries attempting reconstruction after war and civil strife.

The liberalization programmes of some countries involve a transition from a centrally controlled to a market economy. This often involves the creation of an entirely new structure of institutions, within which the freedom of economic agents is considerably increased. Vietnam is one such country and **Karel Jansen** looks at its liberalization experience in Chapter 9. The chapter looks at the background to Vietnam's liberalization programme, the nature of the reforms and their apparent results, in as much as one can tell from a simple comparison of pre- and post-liberalization data. As for Mozambique, agriculture is seen to be a key sector (and also data are of poor quality). The chapter points to some rather impressive results. There has been a rapid growth in exports, agricultural production has increased, GDP growth is high (despite low investment levels), foreign investment is high and inflation has decreased. A qualitative evaluation of Vietnam's programme of reforms is then given. Its focus is on the long-term growth potential of the Vietnamese economy and it draws on the experience of other countries, China especially. It is argued that the nature of the reforms and the gradual way they have been introduced (here linking to some of the arguments in Chapter 4) generally bodes well for future growth, although a combination of the presence of state enterprises and bureaucratic meddling may limit such prospects.

A number of developing countries which have embarked on liberalization reforms over the past two decades have experienced improvements in export performance, especially with respect to manufactured exports. While it is agreed that export success has contributed to both the sustainability and economic success of reforms (especially the expansion of manufacturing output and employment), the driving forces behind rapid export expansion remain a matter of debate. In Chapter 10, **Prema-chandra Athukorala** contributes to this debate through a case-study of the Sri Lankan experience with liberalization reforms over the past two decades. Given the decisive policy shift in 1977 and policy continuity during the ensuing years, Sri Lanka provides a valuable laboratory for the study of this issue. Chapter 10 traces the evolution of trade and industry policy in Sri Lanka since independence. A discussion of the key elements of the market-oriented reforms initiated in 1977 is followed by an examination of the pattern of overall incentives for manufactured exports. The emphasis is on the pivotal role played by export-oriented foreign direct investment in transforming a classical primary commodity-dependent economy into a 'new exporting country'. It then turns to an econometric analysis of the determinants of manufactured exports. Athukorala concludes by stressing the importance of institutions and investment, rather than trade policy reforms alone, in promoting export expansion (echoing the arguments of Chapter 3).

## 1.3 MACROECONOMIC STABILIZATION

The single most important area of liberalization that we do not specifically review is reform of macroeconomic policy. In principle, stabilization involves three core elements: liberalization and realignment, usually devaluation, of the exchange rate to achieve external balance; restrictions on the domestic money supply to reduce inflation and achieve internal balance; and fiscal reforms to reduce the budget deficit. Conventionally, stabilization should precede adjustment, so that some macroeconomic stability is in place before the microeconomic (price) reforms associated with adjustment are implemented (Edwards, 1990; Greenaway and Morrissey, 1993). As mentioned above, there is a large literature on stabilization, especially evaluating IMF programmes, and it is not an issue addressed specifically in this volume (although it is addressed in many chapters). This is not to say we consider it less important than the issues addressed. Rather, we choose to focus on adjustment in general rather than macroeconomic policy reforms. Some of the most salient aspects of stabilization, and the related issues in public sector reform, are outlined here (Tarp, 1993, provides an eminently readable review of stabilization and how it relates to adjustment).

Stabilization responses require expenditure reducing and/or expenditure switching policies. Expenditure reducing policies typically involve quite drastic cuts in public investment and public sector wages, which impact quickly and impose heavy costs to restore internal balance. Often, a large proportion of the formal sector suffers reductions in real income. Donor funds can usefully be directed towards alleviating the social costs of expenditure reductions. Expenditure switching policies are designed to encourage a shift in preferences towards domestic rather than imported goods, and so restore external balance; as such, they should be part of trade and other price liberalization components of SAPs.

The lessons of Latin America suggest an appropriate reform sequence (Edwards, 1995: 58–9). First, public sector deficits must be controlled if macro stability is to be achieved. There are a number of means of reducing budget deficits. Tax reforms can be implemented to increase efficiency and revenue, but this poses a problem for countries heavily dependent on trade taxes (Greenaway and Milner, 1991). Administrative reforms will generally be required to increase collection efficiency. Cost recovery and expenditure reductions can be attempted but generally have a detrimental impact on social sectors and public investment. In some cases privatization proceeds can provide a useful source of revenue, but these are of limited immediate relevance in most LEs.

Second, the external sector should be exposed to competition. This is achieved by trade liberalization in conjunction with attaining external balance (exchange rate liberalization). Third, it is often desirable to reduce the role of the state, through privatization and deregulation, which of course links with budgetary reforms. The available evidence suggests that, on balance, LEs that have had some success in implementing these stages of reform have performed better than countries that failed to establish core macroeconomic stability. For overviews see Greenaway and Morrissey (1993) and Mosley *et al.* (1991a); for Latin America, see Edwards (1995); for Africa, see Elbadawi *et al.* (1992), Husain and Faruqee (1994). As the cited studies also show, many countries failed to achieve macroeconomic stability and continue to face excessive current account and budget deficits; no such countries have achieved successful adjustment.

**Public Sector Reforms**

Fiscal reforms are elements of macroeconomic reform because an objective of stabilization is reducing the budget deficit. It is the difficulties facing most low income LEs in implementing reforms that reduce the deficit which provide the justification for aid support in the form of deficit financing. Such reforms can be implemented, but they will only impact over the medium to long term. Typically, LEs have limited capacity to reduce expenditure. Cutting public capital spending or 'consumption' spending on health and education (human capital) is myopic. Such a strategy reduces public investment, and tends to discourage private investment also, as infrastructure (human and physical) is inadequate. Reducing military spending is difficult to enforce. Reducing the public sector wage bill is a typical response, but imposes high costs on those whose real incomes fall or who become unemployed (and tends to reduce domestic demand). A major form of expenditure, debt servicing, is difficult to reduce (unless the donors forgive the debt). An effective form of expenditure reduction is privatization. Loss-making enterprises are no longer a burden on the budget, and the proceeds represent (temporary) revenue. However, privatization is a slow process and typically only the profitable, or least costly, parastatals can be privatized early; effective privatization requires efficient financial markets, typically absent in low income LEs, which take time to develop. There is no easy form of expenditure reduction for LEs undergoing stabilization.

The implication is that revenue enhancing reforms are required. However, there are few means of mobilizing domestic resources that appear to act quickly. VAT was of some benefit to Latin American countries (Edwards, 1995), but the administrative requirements for full implementation suggest it is of limited relevance to poor LEs. Income tax revenue tends to fall during stabilization (as public sector employment, a large component of the tax base, shrinks), and corporate profits tax is a minor source of revenue. Taxes on agriculture are undesirable as one wants to encourage expanded production there. Furthermore, many LEs are heavily reliant on trade taxes (Greenaway and Milner, 1991), implying a need for carefully designed revenue-enhancing trade liberalization. For example, Tanzania combined significant devaluation with moderate tariff reductions and doubled tariff revenue as aid inflows were available to finance imports (Morrissey, 1995); converting QRs to tariffs also increases revenue. In sum, the potential for quick increases in domestic taxes are slim (Patel, 1997, provides a number of case-studies on the fiscal impact of adjustment in low-income countries).

Put simply, macroeconomic stability is difficult to achieve, and the process of trying to achieve it tends to impose high costs on the economy, especially on vulnerable groups (see below). Nevertheless, the desirability of stability and the macroeconomic policies required to achieve it are relatively well known. The practical difficulties are in how to implement the policies, how to soften detrimental impacts, on sectors and vulnerable groups, and what other policies (such as regarding trade and public expenditure) to put in place to ensure that stability provides a platform for growth and development. It is with these types of difficulties that we are concerned in this volume. While stabilization is not addressed in detail, issues of policy implementation and distributional impact are.

## 1.4 SOCIAL IMPACTS

The social impact of adjustment is both a contentious and important area of research and is an issue that must be considered in evaluating liberalization. It is a contentious issue in the sense that there is often wide disagreement over the social impact. Indeed, it is probably *the* most controversial aspect of liberalization with evaluations often providing conflicting conclusions. It is an important area of research on the grounds that the ultimate test of any economy is to provide ongoing and sustained improvements in the quality of human life of all of its inhabitants. It follows that a liberalization programme can hardly be considered successful if it has resulted in a deterioration in the quality of human life, however positive its impact on traditional macroeconomic variables. While many of the most salient issues are addressed in Chapter 5, some general issues deserve discussion here. Liberalization programmes have been widely criticized over possible adverse effects on social welfare. Zuckerman (1991) identifies a number of characteristics of SAPs which may have adverse social impacts:

(i) *currency devaluation and export promotion* – it is argued that these measures cause the prices of non-tradable goods to fall in relative terms, which in turn hurt farmers growing non-exportable crops and others engaged in non-tradable activities such as services and informal sector output;

(ii) *liberalization of prices and the removal of subsidies* – these measures will severely affect the poor if applied to food, public transport, energy and water, and the rural poor if applied to farm inputs such as fertilizer;

(iii) *reduction of public sector staffing and cuts in public sector salaries* – while not causing the individuals involved to become destitute, these measures will tend to lower standards of living, especially if they are unsuccessful in finding comparably-paid new jobs or if compensation schemes built into adjustment programmes fail; and,

(iv) *cuts in public sector social services and increases in cost recovery for the provision of such services* – these measures will adversely affect all income groups, but especially poorer groups which cannot afford to pay for health, education and other services.

There are valid concerns that females may be over-represented in all groups adversely effected by SAPs (Afshar and Dennis, 1992). Two specific concerns have been expressed, both of which are consistent with the gender blindness of the models underpinning the design of many liberalization programs (Elson, 1991, 1995). The first relates to cuts in public sector spending. Cornia *et al.* (1987), Nzomo (1992) and Lensink (1996) argue that it was mainly female teachers, nurses and civil servants who lost their jobs due to efforts to reduce recurrent expenditure. More serious is the reduction or charging for the provision of social services. It is argued that these cuts create particular difficulties for women as they are primarily responsible for the survival and well-being of the family (Senapaty, 1994; Commonwealth Secretariat, 1989). These measures have pushed women into the labour market, taking unpleasant and lowly paid jobs and without commensurate reductions of home duties (Çatay and Özler, 1995). Such cuts may even see women having to sacrifice there own consumption of health and education services, for example, in order to help maintain that going to other family members. The second concern relates to biases in liberalization programmes favouring the formal and tradable goods sectors at the expense of the informal and non-tradable goods sectors. Women suffer disproportionately from these biases as they are mainly engaged in the latter sectors (Senapaty, 1994, Commonwealth Secretariat, 1989).

Notwithstanding the validity of the preceding concerns, there are some aspects of SAPs, including some of those just identified, which may indeed be social welfare enhancing and pro-poor. Killick (1995b) notes that import liberalization is likely to benefit many groups through the increased availability and quality of imported supplies, while World Bank (1990a) and Zuckerman (1991) suggest that devaluation will help poor farmers who produce tradable goods. The World Bank (1990a) also points out that the removal of ceilings on agricultural prices will benefit those who are net producers of food. More fundamentally, Stewart (1995) and White (1996) point out that SAPs will positively impact on a range of primary and secondary incomes if they lead to higher economic growth rates. There are also reasons for expecting that SAPs will have no significant impact on social welfare or poverty in either direction. Killick (1995b) argues that liberalization measures are not for the most part addressed to the prime determinants of poverty, such as unequal distributions of wealth or inadequate access to social services, hence they will not impact strongly on poverty. These issues are elaborated comprehensively in Chapter 5.

## 1.5 CONTEXT

We will not attempt to refer to all other issues in liberalization not addressed in this volume, such as general equilibrium approaches to evaluation (but see Chapter 5) and the impact of adjustment on investment, savings and consumption. Such issues are touched on in some of the studies cited here, or in some of the chapters. Rather, we will conclude by explaining the background to the volume.

In 1993, the Overseas Development Administration (ODA, since 1997 the Department for International Development, DFID) agreed to fund the Centre for Research in Economic Development and International Trade (CREDIT) to run the Structural Adjustment Forum (SAF). SAF was envisaged as a series of workshops, to be held at the University of Nottingham, each addressing specific issues in adjustment. The proceedings of each workshop were summarized and disseminated in a series of SAF Newsletters. Initially, the funding was for five workshops over three years, but this was extended in 1996 for another five workshops. To date (August 1998), there have been nine workshops and associated Newsletters. These have addressed topics such as trade policy reform, political dimensions of adjustment, poverty, gender, health, grassroots experiences of macroeconomic reforms, and approaches to evaluating adjustment. In total, there have been some fifty papers presented at workshops.

SAF workshops, by intention, have attracted participants from a wide range of disciplines and affiliations. These have included economists, political scientists, sociologists and social anthropologists, representatives from donor agencies (notably but not only ODA and the World Bank) and from a variety of NGOs. The aim was to encourage dialogue and inter-disciplinary discussion, and in this there was some success. Another concern was to encourage dissemination. This was largely achieved through the Newsletters and three papers in a Policy Arena on 'Micro-Macro Linkages' (*Journal of International Development*, Vol. 9, No. 5, 1997). This volume is also a part of the dissemination activities of SAF, which is in part a reason for the specific focus adopted. All of the chapters in Part I were originally presented at SAF workshops, as were the case-studies on Pakistan and Mozambique, although the current versions may bear little resemblance to those presentations. The chapters on Sri Lanka and Vietnam were invited so that we could include case-studies of a country that had reformed without World Bank support and of one in transition.

Finally, some expressions of gratitude. This volume has been rather long in gestation. We thank the contributors for their patience. Some have had to wait a long time after initial submission before receiving our requests for revisions; if any chapter appears dated, we must assume responsibility. We also thank Macmillan for being patient, and David Greenaway for encouraging us to compile this volume. Most of all, however, we wish to thank Sean Conlin. When he was in ODA it was he who initiated SAF, and who actively supported the endeavour through its early years. Without him, neither SAF nor this volume may have appeared. We also thank ODA, and now DFID, for continued funding, and all the many people who contributed to SAF workshops. Finally we should thank our respective partners, Sul and Vera, for their perseverance. Many absences from home have been attributed to this volume, and now we will have to think of a new excuse.

**References**

Aderanti, A. (ed) (1993), *The Impact of Structural Adjustment on the Population of Africa*, London: James Currey.
Afshar, H. and C. Dennis (1992), *Women and Adjustment Policies in the Third World*, London: Macmillan.
Bird, G. (1995), *IMF Lending to Developing Countries*, London: Routledge.
Corbo, V., S. Fischer and S. Webb (eds) (1992), *Adjustment Lending Revisited: Policies to Restore Growth*, Washington, DC: The World Bank.
Cornia, G.A., R. Jolly and F. Stewart (eds) (1987), *Adjustment with a Human Face: Protecting the Vulnerable and Promoting Growth*, Oxford: Clarendon Press.
Cornia, A.V. and G. Helleiner (ed) (1994), *From Adjustment to Development in Africa*, London: Macmillan.
Çatay, N. and S. Özler (1995), 'Feminization of the Labour Force: The Effects of Long-term Development and Structural Adjustment', *World Development*, 23: 11, pp. 1883–1894.
Commonwealth Secretariat (1989), *Engendering Adjustment for the 1990s*, Report on the Commonwealth Expert Group on Women and Structural Adjustment, Commonwealth Secretariat, London.
Dean, J., S. Desai, and J. Riedel (1994), 'Trade Policy Reform in Developing Countries Since 1985: A Review of the Evidence', *World Bank Discussion Papers 267*, Washington, DC: The World Bank.
Edwards, S. (1990), 'The Sequencing of Economic Reform: Analytical Issues and Lessons from Latin America', *The World Economy*, 13, pp. 1–14.
Edwards, S. (1995), *Crisis and Reform in Latin America: From Despair to Hope*, Washington, DC: Oxford University Press for the World Bank.
Elbadawi, I., D. Ghura and G. Uwujaren (1992), 'World Bank Adjustment Lending and Economic Performance in Sub-Saharan Africa in the 1980s', *Country Economics Department WPS 1000*, Washington, DC: The World Bank.
Elson, D. (1991), 'Male Bias in Macroeconomics: The Case of Structural Adjustment', in D. Elson (ed), *Male Bias in the Development Process*, Manchester University Press, Manchester, pp. 164–190.
Elson, D. (1995), 'Gender Awareness in Modeling Structural Adjustment', *World Development*, 23: 11, pp. 1851–1869.
Foroutan, F. (1993), 'Trade Reform in Ten Sub-Saharan African Countries: Achievements and Failures' *Policy Research WPS 1222*, Washington, DC: The World Bank.
Greenaway, D. and C. Milner (1991), 'Fiscal Dependence on Trade Taxes and Trade Policy Reform', *Journal of Development Studies*, Vol. 27, pp. 95–132.
Greenaway, D. and O. Morrissey (1993), 'Structural Adjustment and Liberalisation in Developing Countries: What Lessons Have We Learned?', *Kyklos*, 46, pp. 241–261.
Greenaway, D. and O. Morrissey (1994), 'Trade Liberalisation and Economic Growth in Developing Countries', in S. M. Murshed and K. Raffer (eds), *Trade Transfers and Development*, London: Edward Elgar.
Husain, I. and R. Faruqee (1994), *Adjustment in Africa: Lessons from Country Case Studies*, Washington, DC: The World Bank, Regional and Sectoral Studies.

Killick, T. (1995a), *The Design and Effect of IMF Programmes in Developing Countries*, London: Routledge.

Killick, T. (1995b), 'Structural Adjustment and Poverty Alleviation: An Interpretative Survey', *Development and Change*, 26: 2, pp. 305–331.

Killick, T., M. Malik and M. Manuel (1992), 'What can we know about the effects of IMF Programmes?', *The World Economy*, Vol. 15 (5), pp. 575–598.

Lensink, R. (1996), *Structural Adjustment in Sub-Saharan Africa*, London: Longman.

Morrissey, O. (1995), 'Political Commitment, Institutional Capacity and Tax Policy Reform in Tanzania', *World Development*, Vol. 23 (4), pp. 637–649.

Mosley, P., J. Harrigan and J. Toye (1991a), *Aid and Power: The World Bank and Policy-based Lending. Volume 1*, London: Routledge.

Mosley, P., J. Harrigan and J. Toye (1991b), *Aid and Power: The World Bank and Policy-based Lending. Volume 2: Case Studies*, London: Routledge.

Nash, J. (1993), 'Implementation of Trade Reform in sub-Saharan Africa', *Policy Research Working Paper 1218*, Washington, DC: The World Bank.

Nzomo, M. (1992), 'Beyond Structural Adjustment Programs: Democracy, Gender, Equity, and Development in Africa, with Special Reference to Kenya', in J.E. Nyangoro and T.M. Shaw (eds), *Beyond Structural Adjustment in Africa: The Political Economy of Sustainable and Democratic Development*, Praeger, New York, pp. 99–117.

Papageorgiou, D., M. Michaely and A. Choksi (1991), *Liberalizing Foreign Trade*, 7 vols, Oxford: Basil Blackwell.

Patel, C.K. (ed) (1997), *Fiscal Reforms in the Least Developed Countries*, Cheltenham: Edward Elgar.

Rose, P. (1995), 'Female Education and Adjustment Programs: A Cross-country Statistical Analysis', *World Development*, 23: 11, pp. 1931–1949.

Sahn, D. (ed) (1994), *Adjusting to Policy Failure in African Economies*, Ithaca: Cornell University Press.

Senapaty, M. (1994), 'Gender, Health and Education in the Context of Structural Adjustment: A Follow Up to the Findings of the Commonwealth Expert Group Report', *Gender Analysis and Development Economics Working Paper No. 7*, University of Manchester.

Simon, D., W. van Spengen, C. Dixon and A. Närman (1995), *Structurally Adjusted Africa: Poverty, Debt and Basic Needs*, London: Pluto Press.

Stewart, F. (1995), *Adjustment and Poverty*, London: Routledge.

Tarp, F. (1993), *Stabilization and Structural Adjustment*, London: Routledge.

White, H. (1996), 'Adjustment in Africa', *Development and Change*, 27, pp. 785–815.

Thomas, V., A. Chhibber, M. Dailami and J. De Melo (eds) (1991), *Restructuring Economies in Distress: Policy Reform and the World Bank*, Oxford: OUP.

World Bank (1988), *Report on Adjustment Lending*, Document R88–199, Country Economics Department, Washington, DC: The World Bank.

World Bank (1990a), *World Development Report 1990: Poverty*, Washington, DC: The World Bank.

World Bank (1990b), *Report on Adjustment Lending II: Policies for the Recovery of Growth*, Washington, DC: The World Bank, Document R90–99.

World Bank (1992), *Adjustment Lending and Mobilization of Private and Public Resources for Growth*, Washington, DC: The World Bank.

World Bank (1993), *The East Asia Miracle: Economic Growth and Public Policy*, New York: OUP for the World Bank.

Zuckerman, E. (1991), 'The Social Costs of Adjustment', in Thomas *et al.* (1991), pp. 247–271.

# 2 Assessing the Impact of Economic Liberalization Programmes: A Survey of Empirical Methodologies

Mark McGillivray*

## 2.1 INTRODUCTION

There have been many attempts to evaluate the impact of economic liberalization, especially that resulting from IMF- and World Bank-sponsored structural adjustment programmes. Evaluations have focused mainly on macroeconomic performance indicators such as GDP growth, investment, inflation, exports and domestic saving. This is understandable given the main objective of most programmes: to restore economic growth. Other evaluations have been more concerned with what loosely can be described as the socioeconomic impacts of liberalization and have looked, therefore, at a range of indicators of educational and health status, the incidence of poverty and extent of gender discrimination. Many different evaluation techniques have been applied, which vary from simple data inspection to more complex econometric modelling. Most involve comparison of actual country experience in the presence of a liberalization programme to counterfactual non-programme scenarios.

This chapter critically surveys variants of the two techniques most extensively used in evaluations of the economic and socioeconomic impacts of economic liberalization programmes: simple data inspection and econometric estimation. A number of studies are highlighted as examples of the application of a particular evaluation technique. While it attempts to provide a comprehensive coverage of the specific evaluation techniques falling under the above categories, the chapter does not attempt such a coverage of the general literature on liberalization and its findings.[1] It looks at the above techniques in a relatively non-technical manner, in as much as this is possible. The main concerns are the way the economic and social impacts of liberalization are conceptualized, the relative merits of the different approaches and how to interpret results emerging from them, including the caveats that ought to be applied to these results. There are of course many other issues one could look at, such as the theoretical frameworks, assumptions regarding the underlying properties of the data, diagnostic testing and measurement error. As valid as these questions may be, we largely leave them to more specialized works. As such, the chapter attempts to cater for the statistical and econometric non-specialist, including end users of evaluations.

The chapter commences, in Section 2.2, with a survey of data inspection techniques popular in social and early economic evaluations. The chapter then surveys the different types of econometric evaluations in Section 2.3. These surveys not only explain how the various techniques are applied and identify their relative merits, but they serve as a basis for identifying properties of a desirable evaluation technique. This is considered more explicitly in Section 2.4, in which these properties are consolidated and used to suggest possible directions for future research. A number of basic properties are emphasized, the most fundamental being the ability to tell us whether liberalization has *caused* a particular outcome, rather then merely being associated with it.[2] The constraints imposed by developing country data sets are also emphasized.

## 2.2 DATA INSPECTION TECHNIQUES

Data inspection techniques may be described as those which compare, in a fairly simple way, actual country experience in the presence of an adjustment programme(s) to various counterfactual scenarios. As Mosley (1991) points out, these scenarios (should) typically represent a 'best guess' of what would have happened in the absence of a programme.[3] Two specific approaches have been popular: 'before and after' and 'with and without' (or control group) comparisons.

The before and after popular approach involves comparison of the value of a variable before and after the occurrence of some event, in this case the introduction of a liberalization programme. The counterfactual is a continuation of the pre-liberalization period experience. If the value of the variable has improved following the introduction of a programme, then one is tempted to conclude that liberalization has had a beneficial impact. The with and without approach involves comparing the performance of liberalization and non-liberalization programme (control group) countries over the same period. The counterfactual is that adjustment programme countries would exhibit similar performance to the non-liberalization programme countries. If the former countries show significantly better performance, one could conclude that liberalization has been successful.

Some well known before and after comparisons are shown in Tables 2.1 to 2.6. We observe from World Bank's study that adjustment programmes seemed to be generally associated with declines in investment, growth, the current account balance and private consumption per capita and increases in debt servicing (see Table 2.1). With respect to individual countries, studies by Dailami (1991) and Ahmed (1991) indicate that the presence of a liberalization programme seems to be good for growth, inflation and the current account in South Korea and good for inflation and investment but bad for growth in Indonesia (see Tables 2.2 and 2.3).

Turning the social aspects of liberalization, the World Bank's before and after comparisons indicate that 30 recipients of adjustment loans experienced, on average, higher calorie supplies, lower infant mortality rates, longer life expectancies and higher primary school enrolment ratios following the receipt of these loans (see Table 2.4).[4] In short, these results would suggest that some of the widespread concerns for the social impact of adjustment programmes had not been realized. These results are seemingly contradicted by the work of the Commonwealth Secretariat, which shows that a smaller sample of adjustment loan recipients has on average experienced higher infant and child mortality rates and lower primary school enrolment ratios since receiving these loans (see Tables 2.5 and 2.6). These results hold for both low- and middle-income countries.[5]

A widely cited study which used with and without comparisons is Corbo and Rojas (1992). It examined the macroeconomic performance of three country groups: early-intensive adjustment lending countries (EIALs), other less intensive adjustment lending countries (OALs) and non-adjustment lending countries (NALs).[6] Although not stated explicitly in Corbo and Rojas, the latter serve as the control group for both the EIALs and OALs, and as such the counterfactual is the NAL group performance. The OALs also serve as an additional control group for the EIALs. Performance was judged on the basis of the 1981–84 and 1985–88 average values of a range of macroeconomic indicators compared to those in the pre-adjustment loan period of 1970–80. Results are shown in Table 2.7. The most consistent results are those for saving and exports. For saving, the EIAL, OAL and NALs groups

Table 2.1 Before and After Comparison of Macroeconomic Indicators for 30 Adjustment Loan Recipients

| Indicator | Period | Low-income | Middle-income | Sub-Saharan Africa | Highly Indebted | Manufacturing Exporters |
|---|---|---|---|---|---|---|
| Investment (% of GDP) | Before | 19.2 | 24.7 | 20.6 | 23.1 | 25.0 |
| | After | 18.1 | 19.2 | 17.1 | 17.9 | 22.2 |
| GDP Growth (%) | Before | 3.0 | 2.3 | 2.7 | 1.2 | 2.9 |
| | After | 2.3 | 2.2 | 1.8 | 1.9 | 4.9 |
| Government Budget Deficit (% of GDP) | Before | –7.6 | –6.0 | –6.5 | –4.2 | –4.4 |
| | After | –7.6 | –5.7 | –7.5 | –7.0 | –3.4 |
| Current Account (% of GDP) | Before | –9.0 | –7.2 | –9.4 | –6.9 | –5.0 |
| | After | –7.0 | –4.5 | –6.5 | –3.7 | –2.6 |
| Debt Service (% of Exports) | Before | 20.6 | 27.6 | 17.5 | 34.6 | 29.0 |
| | After | 22.6 | 30.9 | 23.4 | 36.5 | 28.0 |
| Private Consumption Growth (per capita) | Before | –0.8 | 2.1 | –0.7 | 1.5 | 3.0 |
| | After | –0.5 | 0.0 | –0.7 | –0.9 | 2.2 |

*Source:* World Bank (1988).

*Table* 2.2 Before and After Comparison of Macroeconomic Indicators for South Korea

| Indicator | 1975–79 Average | 1980 | 1985 | 1986 | 1987 | 1988 | 1985–87 Average |
|---|---|---|---|---|---|---|---|
| GNP Growth (%) | 9.8 | –5.2 | 5.4 | 12.3 | 12.0 | 12.2 | 10.5 |
| CPI Inflation (%) | 16.7 | 28.7 | 2.5 | 2.8 | 3.0 | 7.1 | 3.9 |
| Current Account Balance (% of GDP) | –3.8 | –9.4 | –1.0 | 4.7 | 8.3 | n.a. | 3.0 |
| Foreign Debt (% of GDP) | n.a. | 29.8 | 48.0 | 45.1 | 35.6 | 32.0 | 40.2 |

*Source:* Dailami (1991).

display the worst, second worst and least worst performances, respectively, in both adjustment loan periods. The reverse was the case with exports. Mixed results were obtained for investment and GDP growth, although in 1985–88 the EIAL group displayed the best (or least worst) growth performance, the OAL group the second best and the NAL group the worst. This contrasts with the findings of Table 2.1.

Other with and without comparisons of economic performance are shown in Tables 2.8 and 2.9. While we return to the former below, the results in Table 2.9, taken from the very well known study of Mosley *et al.* (1991), are of interest as they show non-recipients of adjustment loans doing better in terms of GDP than their adjustment loan counterparts. While this is inconsistent with the results of Corbo and Rojas (1991), there is consistency between this study and that of Mosley *et al.* over investment: both show the adjustment loan countries

*Table* 2.3 Before and After Comparison of Macroeconomic Indicators for Indonesia

| Indicator | 1970–79 Average | 1981–88 Average |
|---|---|---|
| CPI Inflation (%) | 15.3 | 8.4 |
| Investment (% of GDP) | 2.8 | 7.8[a] |
| GDP Growth (%) | 7.5 | 3.3 |

a: average relates to 1982–85.
*Source:* Ahmed (1991).

*Table* 2.4 Before and After Comparison of Social Indicators for 30 Adjustment Loan Recipients

| Indicator | 1970–79 Average | 1980 | 1981 | 1982 | 1983 | 1984 | 1985 | 1986 | 1980–86 Average |
|---|---|---|---|---|---|---|---|---|---|
| Daily Calorie Supply (% of requirements) | 101.3 | 104.5 | 104.9 | 104.3 | 102.9 | 103.6 | 104.2 | n.a. | 104.1[a] |
| Infant Mortality Rate | 99.5 | 87.8 | 86.1 | 84.6 | 81.3 | 79.6 | 78.0 | 76.2 | 81.9 |
| Life Expectancy | 54.2 | 56.2 | 56.5 | 56.9 | 57.3 | 57.6 | 58.0 | 58.4 | 57.3 |
| Primary School Enrolment Ratio | 83 | 88 | 92 | 90 | 92 | 90 | 97 | n .a. | 92[a] |

a: average based on data for 1980–95.
*Source:* World Bank (1988).

*Table* 2.5 Before and After Comparison and Infant and Child Mortality Rates for 14 Adjustment Loan Recipients

| Country | Infant Mortality Rate 1980 | 1985 | % Change | Child Mortality Rate 1980 | 1985 | % Change |
|---|---|---|---|---|---|---|
| Low-income | | | | | | |
| Ethiopia | 146 | 168 | 15.1 | 32 | 38 | 18.8 |
| Mali | 154 | 174 | 13.0 | 34 | 43 | 26.5 |
| Madagascar | 71 | 109 | 53.5 | 11 | 21 | 90.9 |
| Uganda | 97 | 108 | 11.3 | 18 | 21 | 16.7 |
| Tanzania | 103 | 110 | 6.8 | 19 | 22 | 15.8 |
| Somalia | 146 | 152 | 4.1 | 32 | 33 | 3.1 |
| Kenya | 87 | 91 | 4.6 | 15 | 16 | 6.7 |
| Haiti | 115 | 123 | 7.0 | 18 | 22 | 22.2 |
| Average | 115 | 129 | 13.4 | 22 | 27 | 25.1 |
| Middle Income | | | | | | |
| Indonesia | 93 | 96 | 3.2 | 11 | 12 | 9.1 |
| Philippines | 14 | 48 | 242.9 | 4 | 4 | 0.0 |
| Zimbabwe | 74 | 77 | 4.1 | 12 | 7 | –41.7 |
| Jamaica | 16 | 20 | 25.0 | (a) | 1 | n.a. |
| Peru | 88 | 94 | 6.8 | 9 | 11 | 22.2 |
| Panama | 22 | 25 | 13.6 | 1 | 1 | 0.0 |
| Average | 51 | 60 | 49.3 | 6.2 | 6 | –2.1 |

(a): less than smallest unit shown.
*Source:* Commonwealth Secretariat (1989).

outperforming the non-adjustment loan countries with respect to this variable.

Comparisons of social indicators are shown in Tables 2.10 to 2.12. Rose (1995) looks at gender gaps in enrolment ratios for the EIAL, OAL and NAL country groups (see Table 2.10). Results indicate that gender gaps have narrowed to a generally greater extent in EIAL and OAL groups than in the NAL group, and that female/male ratios have improved to a largely greater extent in the NAL group than in others. These results notwithstanding, the experiences of all groups of countries shown in Table 2.12 are, however, broadly similar. Maasland and van den Gaag (1992) found that while expenditure on education had fallen between 1970–80 and 1985–87 in the EIAL and OAL groups, it had risen between these periods in the NAL group (see Table 2.11). In contrast, they found that health and other social expenditures had risen to a greater extent in both the EIAL and OAL groups than in the NAL

*Table* 2.6 Before and After Comparison of Primary School Enrolment Ratios for Countries with IMF and/or World Bank Adjustment Programmes during 1981–85

| | Total | | | Female | | |
|---|---|---|---|---|---|---|
| Country | 1980 | 1985 | Change (%) | 1980 | 1985 | Change (%) |
| Low-income Countries | | | | | | |
| Ethiopia | 43 | 36 | –16.3 | 30 | 28 | –6.7 |
| Nepal | 91 | 79 | –13.2 | 53 | 47 | –11.3 |
| Bangladesh | 62 | 60 | –3.2 | 47 | 50 | 6.4 |
| Mali | 27 | 23 | –14.8 | 20 | 17 | –15.0 |
| Mozambique | 93 | 84 | –9.7 | 79 | 74 | –6.3 |
| Tanzania | 104 | 72 | –30.8 | 98 | 85 | –13.3 |
| Togo | 116 | 95 | –18.1 | 89 | 73 | –18.0 |
| Somalia | 41 | 25 | –39.0 | 29 | 18 | –37.9 |
| Rwanda | 70 | 64 | –8.6 | 67 | 63 | –6.0 |
| Kenya | 108 | 94 | –13.0 | 101 | 91 | –9.9 |
| Sudan | 51 | 49 | –3.9 | 43 | 41 | –4.7 |
| Pakistan | 57 | 47 | –17.5 | 30 | 32 | 6.7 |
| Ghana | 69 | 66 | –4.3 | 60 | 59 | –1.7 |
| Guinea | 33 | 30 | –9.1 | 22 | 19 | –13.6 |
| Laos | 96 | 91 | –5.2 | 88 | 79 | –10.2 |
| Vietnam | 116 | 100 | –13.8 | 109 | 94 | –13.8 |
| Average | 74 | 63 | –13.8 | 60 | 54 | –9.7 |
| Middle-income Countries | | | | | | |
| Yemen, PDR | 72 | 66 | –8.3 | 51 | 35 | –31.4 |
| Philippines | 110 | 106 | –3.6 | 108 | 106 | –1.9 |
| Nigeria | 98 | 92 | –6.1 | n.a. | 81 | n.a. |
| El Salvador | 74 | 70 | –5.4 | 74 | 70 | –5.4 |
| Colombia | 128 | 117 | –8.6 | 130 | 119 | –8.5 |
| Chile | 117 | 109 | –6.8 | 116 | 106 | –8.6 |
| Costa Rica | 108 | 101 | –6.5 | 106 | 100 | –5.7 |
| Jordan | 108 | 99 | –8.3 | n.a. | 99 | n.a. |
| Mexico | 120 | 115 | –4.2 | 116 | 114 | –1.7 |
| Portugal | 118 | 112 | –5.1 | 116 | 119 | 2.6 |
| Yugoslavia | 99 | 96 | –3.0 | 98 | 96 | –2.0 |
| Panama | 113 | 105 | –7.1 | 111 | 102 | –8.1 |
| Argentina | 116 | 108 | –6.9 | 116 | 108 | –6.9 |
| Korea, Rep. | 107 | 96 | –10.3 | 96 | 105 | 9.4 |
| Romania | 101 | 98 | –3.0 | 101 | 97 | –4.0 |
| Average | 106 | 99 | –6.2 | 103 | 98[a] | –5.6 |

a: excludes Nigeria and Jordan.
*Source:* Commonwealth Secretariat (1989).

*Table* 2.7 With and Without Comparison of Macroeconomic Performance

| Country Group | GDP Growth (%) | | | Domestic Saving (% of GDP) | | | Investment (% of GDP) | | | Exports (% of GDP) | | |
|---|---|---|---|---|---|---|---|---|---|---|---|---|
| | 1970–80 | 1981–84 | 1985–88 | 1970–80 | 1981–84 | 1985–88 | 1970–80 | 1981–84 | 1985–88 | 1970–80 | 1981–84 | 1985–88 |
| EIAL Average | 4.6 | 1.3 | 4.2 | 18.7 | 14.8 | 17.2 | 24.3 | 19.9 | 18.6 | 24.7 | 25.1 | 28.1 |
| OAL Average | 3.9 | 2.3 | 3.0 | 13.9 | 12.7 | 13.3 | 23.6 | 22.0 | 29.1 | 24.7 | 24.4 | 23.6 |
| NAL Average | 5.5 | 3.1 | 2.7 | 14.6 | 14.0 | 14.4 | 22.6 | 24.1 | 20.0 | 29.9 | 26.1 | 24.6 |

*Source:* Corbo and Rojas (1992).

*Table* 2.8 With and Without Comparison of Imports as a Percentage of GDP

| Country Group | Percentage Change in Group Averages Between: 1984–86 and 1980–82 | 1985–87 and 1981–83 |
|---|---|---|
| Intensive Trade Adjustment Loan Recipients (*n* = 10) | –2.9* | –0.1* |
| Trade Adjustment Loan Recipients (*n* = 26) | –9.3* | –3.8* |
| Trade Adjustment Loan Recipients (*n* = 40) | –7.7* | –5.5* |
| Non-Recipients of Trade Adjustment Loans (*n* = 47) | –14.6 | –14.0 |

*: significantly different from non-recipient group change for the given period at the 90% level or greater.
*Source:* Thomas (1991).

*Table* 2.9 With and Without Comparison of Macroeconomic Performance, 1982–86

| Indicator | Averages for 20 Recipients of World Bank Structural Adjustment Loans | Averages for 20 Non-recipients of World Bank Structural Adjustment Loans |
|---|---|---|
| GDP Growth[a] | 2.0 | 2.7 |
| Consumption (% of GDP) | 85.7 | 84.4 |
| Investment (% of GDP) | 19.3 | 20.5 |
| Current Account Balance (% of GDP) | –4.8* | –6.7 |
| Exports (% of GDP) | –0.4 | –1.3 |

*: significantly different from non-recipient average. a: period is 1980–86.
*Source:* Mosley *et al.* (1991).

group. Maasland and van den Gaag also looked at changes in child mortality rates between pre- and post-adjustment programme implementation periods (see Table 2.12). They found that these rates declined to a greater average extent among the EIAL group than in the

*Table* 2.10 With and Without Analysis of Gender Gaps in Combined First- and Second-Level Gross Enrolment Rates

| | Male-Female Difference in Group Averages | | | Female/Male Ratio of Group Averages | | |
|---|---|---|---|---|---|---|
| Country Group | 1970 | 1980 | 1990 | 1970 | 1980 | 1990 |
| EIAL Countries | | | | | | |
| Full Sample ($n$ = 23) | 12 | 12 | 9 | 0.72 | 0.81 | 0.85 |
| Low-income ($n$ = 12) | 16 | 17 | 13 | 0.60 | 0.71 | 0.78 |
| Middle-income ($n$ = 11) | 8 | 6 | 4 | 0.85 | 0.91 | 0.93 |
| OAL Countries | | | | | | |
| Full Sample ($n$ = 18) | 12 | 12 | 9 | 0.69 | 0.73 | 0.78 |
| Low-income ($n$ = 11) | 14 | 15 | 13 | 0.55 | 0.61 | 0.65 |
| Middle-income ($n$ = 7) | 7 | 6 | 2 | 0.90 | 0.93 | 0.98 |
| NAL Countries | | | | | | |
| Full Sample ($n$ = 18) | 13 | 11 | 10 | 0.72 | 0.80 | 0.86 |
| Low-income ($n$ = 6) | 14 | 18 | 20 | 0.55 | 0.61 | 0.71 |
| Middle-income ($n$ = 12) | 13 | 8 | 5 | 0.80 | 0.89 | 0.94 |

*Source:* Rose (1995).

NAL group. This of course paints a somewhat different picture of the impact of liberalization on child mortality to that provided by Commonwealth Secretariate (see Table 2.5).

The before and after and with and without approaches are of considerable appeal to the evaluation of liberalization and policy reform in general on the grounds of expediency and simplicity: their results are easy to interpret, they do not involve complicated statistical work and are often not overly data intensive. But they suffer from a rather fundamental weakness: extremely restrictive *ceteris paribus* assumptions. If these assumptions are violated then one cannot ascribe causation to the introduction of a liberalization programme.

*Table* 2.11 With and Without Comparison of Social Expenditures

| Country | Education (%)[a] 1970–80 | Education (%)[a] 1985–87 | Health (%)[a] 1970–80 | Health (%)[a] 1985–87 | Other[b] (%)[a] 1970–80 | Other[b] (%)[a] 1985–87 |
|---|---|---|---|---|---|---|
| EIAL | | | | | | |
| Chile | 15.0 | 13.7 | 7.8 | 6.4 | 34.4 | 46.7 |
| Costa Rica | 29.5 | 19.2 | 13.4 | 23.2 | 25.2 | 26.7 |
| Korea | 16.8 | 19.7 | 1.3 | 1.9 | 7.6 | 8.7 |
| Mauritius | 15.7 | 16.9 | 9.0 | 9.6 | 26.5 | 24.8 |
| Mexico | 19.8 | 19.3 | 4.5 | 2.6 | 25.6 | 20.0 |
| Morocco | 16.9 | 20.1 | 4.2 | 3.4 | 8.2 | 8.7 |
| Pakistan | 2.3 | 3.4 | 1.6 | 1.1 | 6.6 | 13.3 |
| Thailand | 22.3 | 23 | 4.4 | 7.0 | 7.7 | 6.2 |
| Togo | 10.7 | 13.5 | 5.1 | 4.0 | 15.2 | 11.8 |
| Turkey | 19.6 | 13.1 | 3.1 | 2.4 | 4.9 | 4.3 |
| EIAL Average | 16.9 | 16.2 | 5.4 | 6.2 | 16.2 | 17.1 |
| OAL | | | | | | |
| Hungary | n.a. | 1.9 | n.a. | 3.7 | n.a. | 27.9 |
| Indonesia | 8.7 | 10.8 | 2.2 | 2.3 | 2.4 | 2.8 |
| Panama | 18.7 | 19.6 | 15.5 | 19.5 | 14.8 | 22.1 |
| Uruguay | 10.7 | 7.4 | 4.4 | 4.8 | 48.3 | 54.8 |
| Zimbabwe | 14.5 | 23.7 | 6.4 | 7.1 | 8.1 | 7.7 |
| OAL Average | 13.5 | 12.7 | 7.1. | 7.5 | 18.4 | 23.0 |
| NAL | | | | | | |
| India | 2.5 | 2.6 | 2.2 | 2.4 | 3.9 | 6.0 |
| Oman | 3.5 | 10.1 | 3.4 | 4.9 | 3.0 | 3.8 |
| Sri Lanka | 11.9 | 9.7 | 6.6 | 5.2 | 26.0 | 13.0 |
| Venezuela | 17.3 | 22.1 | 10.2 | 10.7 | 10.5 | 12.9 |
| Yemen Arab Rep | 8.2 | 19.9 | 3.2 | 4.2 | 2.3 | 2.2 |
| NAL Average | 8.7 | 12.9 | 5.1 | 5.5 | 9.1 | 7.6 |

a: percentage of total consolidated central government expenditure (less interest payments). b: 'Other' expenditures are those on social security and welfare, housing and community affairs, and recreational, cultural and religious affairs. *Source:* Maasland and van der Gaag (1992).

The before and after approach requires that all other variables affecting the chosen indicator have remained unchanged between the two periods. The control group approach requires that the programme and control group countries can be differentiated only in terms of having, or not having, a liberalization programme. In short, it requires that the control group is valid. Specifically, it requires that each group has experienced the same external environment over the period of

*Table* 2.12 With and Without Comparison of Child Mortality Rates (% Change)

| Country | 1970–75 to 1975–80 | 1975–80 to 1980–85 |
|---|---|---|
| EIAL | | |
| Brazil | –14.4 | –19.6 |
| Chile | –34.2 | –46.2 |
| Colombia | –28.1 | –34.4 |
| Costa Rica | –45.3 | –31.4 |
| Ghana | –13.8 | 6.7 |
| Mexico | –13.0 | –11.5 |
| Philippines | –11.9 | –6.7 |
| Senegal | –12.0 | –13.2 |
| Thailand | –23.1 | –21.4 |
| Turkey | –13.6 | –11.3 |
| Average | –20.1 | –18.9 |
| OAL | | |
| Argentina | –17.2 | –12.5 |
| Bangladesh | –3.1 | –2.7 |
| Ecuador | –14.7 | –22.4 |
| Indonesia | –16.6 | –16.4 |
| Mali | –7.1 | –9.9 |
| Panama | –30.9 | –21.3 |
| Uganda | –5.0 | 8.8 |
| Uruguay | –5.8 | –30.6 |
| Average | 12.6 | 13.4 |
| NAL | | |
| Botswana | –21.1 | –33.3 |
| Dominican Rep. | –25.8 | –10.2 |
| Egypt | –18.3 | –15.3 |
| Guatemala | –14.2 | –15.1 |
| Haiti | –10.8 | –8.7 |
| Jordan | –17.4 | –19.7 |
| Liberia | –11.6 | –9.5 |
| Malaysia | –25.8 | –10.9 |
| Peru | –7.5 | –23.9 |
| Trinidad and Tobago | –13.5 | –12.5 |
| Average | 16.6 | 15.9 |

*Source:* Maasland and van der Gaag (1992).

analysis and that they share the same basic economic structure.[7] Moreover, if we accept that current macroeconomic performance is a function of past performance, it also requires that each country group exhibit highly similar performance in the pre-policy reform period.[8] Satisfying each these and many other pertinent requirements is in practice a difficult and necessarily problematic task and for these reasons all of the results shown in Tables 2.1 to 2.12 ought be treated with extreme caution, especially those based on before and after comparison.[9]

A main implication of the preceding remarks is that the counterfactual is only a valid basis for comparison if the relevant *ceteris paribus* assumption is correct. If this assumption is not correct, the counterfactual is an invalid representation of what would have happened in the absence of a liberalization programme.[10] One would need to allow for the influence of non-liberalization factors, thus ensuring that the only difference between the counterfactual and the scenario to be evaluated is the presence of a liberalization programme. If this cannot be done, before and after and with and without comparisons are at best a useful descriptive, but not explanatory, statistical tools. As Goldstein (1986) notes, they can be 'used to show what happened in programme countries, but not why it happened'.[11]

One further point remains with respect to before and after and with and without analysis. If they are to be used for descriptive purposes, it is essential that one tests for statistically *significant* differences between the counterfactual and actual scenarios. Two simple and appealing tests involve evaluating the null hypotheses that: (i) the average outcome associated with a liberalization programme is the same as some outcome in the absence of such a programme; and (ii) that there is no difference between average liberalization and average non-liberalization outcomes. The formal representations of these hypotheses are, respectively:

$$H_o : \bar{x}_l = \bar{x}_{nl}$$
$$H_1 : \bar{x}_l \neq \bar{x}_{nl}$$

and

$$H_o : \bar{x}_l - \bar{x}_{nl} = 0$$
$$H_1 : \bar{x}_l - \bar{x}_{nl} \neq 0$$

where $\bar{x}_l$ and $\bar{x}_{nl}$ are mean values of the chosen indicator for the liberalization and non-liberalization samples. The null hypotheses are evaluated using the following statistics:

$$t = \frac{\bar{x}_l - \bar{x}_{nl}}{s_{\bar{x}_l}} \tag{2.1}$$

and

$$t = \frac{(\bar{x}_l - \bar{x}_{nl}) - 0}{s_{\bar{x}_l - \bar{x}_{nl}}} \tag{2.2}$$

where the denominators of the ratios are the standard error of liberalization programme sample means and the standard error of the difference between liberalization and non-liberalization sample means, respectively. Both statistics have $t$ distributions for $n_l - 1$ degrees of freedom (where $n_l$ is the liberalization sample size) and $n_l - n_{nl} - 2$ degrees of freedom (where $n_{nl}$ is the non-liberalization sample size), respectively.

Only two of the nine studies for which results were reported in Tables 2.1 to 2.12 report results for significant differences. Those studies are Mosley *et al.* (1991) and Thomas (1991) (see Tables 2.8 and 2.9, respectively). The first of the above tests was applied in both instances. Applying both tests, where it was possible, to the other means in Tables 2.1 to 2.12 produces some interesting results.[12] Null hypotheses cannot be rejected at the 95 per cent level in a number of instances for the means and their differences in Tables 2.10 and 2.11.[13] In contrast, neither null hypothesis is rejected, at the 95 per cent level, for the results shown in Tables 2.2, 2.4, 2.5, 2.6 and 2.12. Not only does this invalidate a number of the conclusions of the corresponding studies, but it follows that some of the apparent conflicts between the results are removed. Specifically, adjustment is not associated with significantly lower or higher child mortality rates which do not appear to be significantly different from rates existing prior to or without liberalization.

## 2.3 ECONOMETRIC MODELLING

The main conclusion of the preceding section is that data inspection techniques should be treated with caution since they cannot adequately control for extraneous, non-adjustment factors. It is on both grounds that multivariate econometric modelling – the widely used (and often abused) technique in applied economic research – comes into play. Econometric modelling has the ability to both control for a range of factors and to shed light on the adjustment process as it affects a given indicator. One should, however, apply a number of caveats. Principal among them is that the econometric model is correctly specified, containing the major determinants of the chosen indicator, and is estimated using an appropriate method. This largely turns on the model being based on an appropriate theoretical framework, which accounts (directly or indirectly) for both endogenous and exogenous determinants of the chosen indicator.

We now consider three categories of econometric studies in turn:

(i) those which look at the extent of reform;
(ii) those which look at underlying behavioural relationships; and
(iii) those which look at the presence of a liberalization programme *per se*.

A fourth, smooth transitions modelling, is touched upon, but only briefly as it is covered in depth elsewhere in this volume.

**Modelling the Extent of Reform**

Studies falling under the first of the above categories seek to explain variables of interest (usually indicators of macroeconomic performance) using a vector of indicators of the extent of reform, along with one or more vectors of extraneous variables. Three indicators of the extent of reform have been used: the level of adjustment lending, the number of policies implemented under a liberalization programme and the number of months in a given year in a programme.

An example of this type of study, and one of the most widely-cited econometric analyses of adjustment, is that by Mosley *et al.* (1991).[14] They attempted to model (explain) GDP growth, export growth, import growth, investment as a share of GDP and inflows of private foreign finance under regimes of adjustment in 19 SAL recipients. Cross country data, pooled for the years 1980–86, were used. Three groups of potential determinants of the above indicators were identified: (i) financial flows (including the level of SALs); (ii) the extent of compliance with the conditions on which adjustment loans were advanced; and (iii) a range of relevant extraneous variables.[15] The econometric model applied to GDP growth, for example, was:

$$\begin{aligned} gGDP_{i,t} = \alpha &+ \beta_1 IMF_{i,t} + \beta_2 SAL_{i,t} + \beta_3 SAL_{i,t-1} + \beta_4 SAL_{i,t-2} \\ &+ \beta_5 INV_{i,t} + \beta_6 CI_{i,t} + \beta_7 CI_{i,t-1} + \beta_8 CI_{i,t-2} + \beta_9 W_{i,t} \\ &+ \beta_{10} ToT_{i,t} + \beta_{11} gEX_{i,t} + \mu_{i,t} \end{aligned} \tag{2.3}$$

$gGDP_{i,t}$ is real GDP growth in country $i$ in year $t$; $IMF_{i,t}$ is the level of IMF finance as a percentage of GDP drawn by $i$ in year $t$; $SAL_{i,t}$ is the level of SAL and SECAL loans as a percentage of GDP in year $t$; $SAL_{i,t-1}$ and $SAL_{i,t-2}$ are the levels of these loans as a percentage of GDP one and two years prior to year $t$, respectively; $INV_{i,t}$ is the level of investment as a share of GDP in $i$ in year $t$; $CI_{i,t}$, $CI_{i,t-1}$ and $CI_{i,t-2}$ are indices of $i$'s compliance with SAL policy conditions in years $t$, $t-1$ and $t-2$, respectively; $W_{i,t}$ is an index of weather in $i$ in year $t$; $ToT_{i,t}$ is $i$'s year $t$ terms of trade, and; $gEX_{i,t}$ is growth in $i$'s exports in year $t$. By lagging the SAL and compliance variables, Mosley *et al.* allow for a delayed impact of adjustment on growth. $\alpha$ is an intercept term, $\beta_1$ through to $\beta_{11}$ are regression coefficients which measure the impact on GDP growth of a one unit change in their respective variables after allowing for the influence of all other explanatory variables and $\mu_{i,t}$ is a residual term picking up random variation in GDP growth not accounted for by the other explanatory variables. It follows that $\beta_2$ to $\beta_4$ and $\beta_6$ to $\beta_8$ provide the most crucial information on the impact of adjustment on growth. Numerical estimates of these coefficients and their counterparts show the extent and direction of influence of adjustment on the chosen indicator.

Mosley *et al.* obtained estimates of the coefficients of equation (2.3) and those for the other performance indicators using reasonably standard econometric techniques: applying the ordinary least squares (OLS) method of plotting a line of best fit (regression line) to the data which minimizes the sum total of squared residuals. As is usual practice, these coefficients were subject to hypothesis tests similar to those described earlier in this chapter. Using a variant of equation (1), the objective of these tests was to determine whether the estimated values were significantly different from a counterfactual value of zero. If a coefficient fails this test, its corresponding variable is usually judged to have no significant impact on the indicator being modelled. The essence of this test is demonstrated in Figure 2.1, which plots a hypothetical regression line (functional relationship) between SALs and GDP growth, both for the current period $t$. All other variables affecting GDP growth are held constant. Here we assume that the estimated value of $\beta_2$, which determines the slope of the regression line, is positive, sloping upward from left to right. The level SALs is thus hypothetically shown to be positively associated with growth – that is, high SAL recipients have higher growth rates and *vice versa*. The counterfactual is shown by the lower, horizontal line in Figure 2.1. Here the rate of growth among countries is independent of the level SALs and $\beta_2$ is therefore equal to

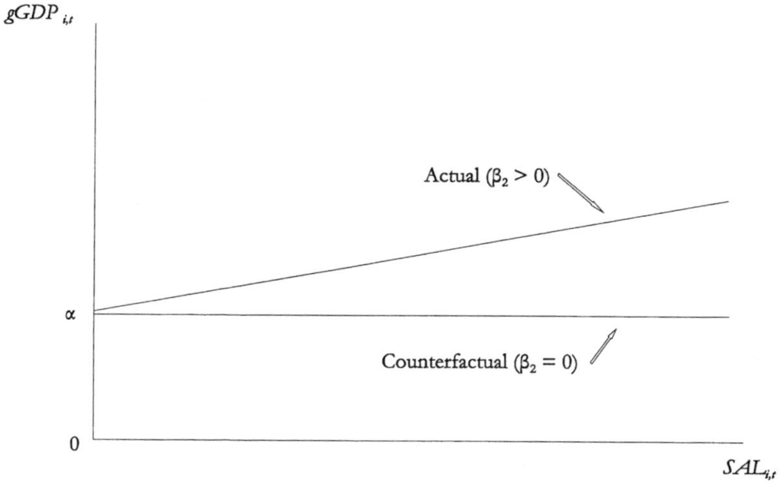


*Figure* 2.1 Growth and Adjustment Lending Regression Line (Hypothetical)

zero. The hypothesis test therefore involves ascertaining whether the upper regression line significantly departs from the lower line.

The outcome of the preceding tests produced some interesting results in the case of Mosley *et al.* In particular, in the only instances when the level of SALs was found to have a significant influence on performance, the effect was negative. That is, SALs seemed to actually *reduced* performance with a downward-sloping regression line. This was the case with GDP growth (with a one year lag) and export growth. The extent of compliance, on the other hand, was generally found to significantly influence performance in an upward direction in the majority of instances.

The econometric analysis of Mosley *et al.* is a quantum improvement over the simple data inspection techniques. Yet as Mosley *et al.* themselves acknowledge, it too is characterized by a number of limitations. Here we highlight four. The first relates to model specification. Mosley *et al.* acknowledge that there were many other extraneous variables which could be reasonably expected to influence the five performance indicators modelled. In other words, there were a number of other variables whose possible influences on these indicators have not been sufficiently accounted or controlled for in the Mosley *et al.* econometric models.[16] As such, specification bias emerges and it is likely that the estimates of the regression coefficients are biased and misleading.

The second limitation of the Mosley *et al.* econometric analysis is more fundamental and arises even if their models were more comprehensively specified. It concerns the use of cross country rather than time series data. The limitations of the former are well known among applied economics researchers. Applying an econometric model to such data assumes that the relationships between each determinant and the variable being modelled are the same for all countries included in the sample. That is, for each variable a single regression coefficient applies to each country. This means, for example, a given change in the level of SALs will cause an identical change in the GDP growth rate in each country in the sample. This is clearly a very restrictive assumption. Moreover, it is one that Mosley *et al.* are forced to make. Adjustment lending commenced in the 1980s, which for a number of years to come will rule out the use of time series data in econometric analysis. There are simply not enough time series observations of the level of adjustment loans and compliance indices to permit efficient estimation. This is an issue to which we shall return on a number of occasions throughout this paper.

The third limitation concerns the compliance indices. These indices are unweighted percentage shares of the total number of SAL and SECAL loan conditions implemented at the end of the loan period. The rationale for the use of these indices as measures of the extent of policy reform is very sound: one would certainly expect that the extent of reform would play some role in determining economic performance. The proponents of adjustment would, of course, contend that economic performance would (sooner or later) be better the greater the extent of reform. Irrespective of whether one supports this contention, it is certainly interesting and appropriate to submit it to the data as a testable hypothesis. However it is questionable whether the extent of reform is adequately measured by compliance indices of the nature used by Mosley *et al.* Is it the case that the extent of reform in a country which, for example, implements 50 per cent of adjustment loan conditions within the agreed time frame only half that in a country which implements 100 per cent of conditions?

The answer to this will depend on the nature of the reforms. It could be the case that the reforms implemented in the second country may be trivial or less strategic than those implemented in the first country. Put more succinctly, the Mosley *et al.* compliance indices make no allowance for qualitative differences in adjustment lending conditions. Nor do they account for the overall extent of reform. For example, a country may indeed fully comply with the conditions of an adjustment loan package, but this may only consist of four or five reforms. Another country may also fully comply, but implement ten or more reforms. Yet both countries would share the same compliance indices. The Mosley *et al.* use of these indices is not sensitive to this, implicitly assuming that the size of an adjustment programme is the same in all countries. These criticisms can also be made of the third above-mentioned indicator of the extent of reform: months in a given year with a programme.

The fourth limitation is reflected by the use of the OLS method of estimation. This requires that each explanatory variable is exogenous, which in turn dictates that the equations estimated by Mosley *et al.* be interpreted as reduced-form equations. The parameter of these equations show total impacts, which are a composite of direct and indirect relationships. While the former are very useful in their own right, they tell us little about the processes or channels through which a liberalization programme affects the indicator under consideration. Referring to the estimated parameters of equation (3), for example, precisely how does an adjustment loan impact on GDP? The answer will lie in a number of far more complex relationships than revealed by $\beta_2$, $\beta_3$ and $\beta_4$ and will involve a range of exogenous and endogenous variables. It could, say, be the case that SALs are used as a supplement to domestic saving by the recipient government, and as such are allocated to the capital budget, which results in a higher level of investment and in turn growth than would otherwise be the case. It might also be the case that an increase in public investment crowds out some private investment, say through an increase in the price of capital goods,[17] which in turn limits or even negates the increase in GDP. Such information is crucial for evaluating the impact of liberalization and the design of liberalization programmes. Not only do we need to know *what* the impact of a programme is, but *how* this impact has arisen.

Information on the latter, in the context of econometric modelling, can only be provided by a system of structural, rather than reduced-form, equations. Econometric efficiency requires the simultaneous estimation of these equations using far more complex methods than OLS. It is not uncommon for a system of structural equations, especially those looking at macroeconomic relationships, to contain 20 or more regression coefficients. It follows that the data requirements of such systems are especially large, requiring a large sample of time series or cross section data. This poses tremendous difficulties if the former data are used, as is appropriate. Quarterly data are not available for most developing countries; one is thus forced to use annual data. Moreover, time series extending back to the pre-1950s or even pre-1960s are often extremely difficult if not impossible to locate for the great majority of countries. In some cases, especially in Africa, pre-1970s data cannot even be obtained. In short, the reality of developing country data dictates that structural modelling as described will often not be possible, however important information of the processes by which liberalization causes certain outcome might be.

**Underlying Behavioural Relationships**

The success of a liberalization programme requires the economy to behave in a particular way. That is, it is premised on the existence of certain behavioural characteristics such as there being a positive elasticity between saving and interest rates, a negative elasticity between investment and interest rates, that the supply of agricultural commodities responds positively to price increases and so on. Some studies attempt to evaluate liberalization programmes by testing for the presence of such relationships. In this sense, they seek to test whether liberalization can work, or can have an impact.

An example of this type of study is Khan and Aftab (1994). It looked at financial sector reforms in Pakistan, seeking to ascertain whether the economy was 'likely to gain benefits from such liberalization' (p. 100). Khan and Aftab tested for a number of possible behavioural relationships, including that between saving and real interest rates. The specific rationale for looking at this relationship is that an objective of Pakistan's financial reforms was to stimulate saving by removing central controls on interest rates. These controls had, it was argued, kept nominal interest rates artificially low and on occasion had resulted in negative real rates. It was hoped that the removal of such controls would avoid this outcome and result in higher levels of saving. The following equation was therefore estimated using time series data for the period 1970–90, which covers periods both before and after the introduction of the financial sector reforms:

$$S_t = \alpha + \beta_1 OTR_t + \beta_2 R_t + \beta_3 \ln CGNP_t + \beta_4 GR_t + \mu_t \qquad (2.4)$$

where $S_t$ is gross national saving expressed as a ratio of GNP in period $t$, $OTR_t$ is inflows of official foreign transfers in $t$, $R_t$ is the average real rate of interest on scheduled bank deposits in that year, $\ln CGNP_t$ is the logarithm of GNP per capita in $t$ and $GR_t$ is GNP growth in $t$. Khan and Aftab used the two-stage least squares method of estimation owing to the assumed endogeniety of GNP growth. In estimation, therefore, $GR_t$

was replaced with its fitted value obtained from an OLS regression of this variable on a vector of exogenous variables. We return to this general issue below.

The key parameter of (2.4), given Khan and Aftab's objectives, is $\beta_2$. Their estimate of this parameter was –0.00007, which was subsequently found to be significantly different from zero. Given the extremely low value of this parameter, and the response of saving to changes in the rate of interested indicated by it, Khan and Aftab concluded that the liberalization of interest rate determination would have only a negligible impact on saving.

Khan and Aftab's approach is of intuitive appeal. But it suffers from a fundamental although not inherent problem. Liberalization is about changing behavioural relationships through the removal or reduction of structural rigidities which constrain the behaviour of rational economic agents. A financial liberalization involving the removal of artificial interest rates controls would be expected, or at least hoped, to result in a greater sensitivity of saving to changes in these rates. In equation (2.4), for example, it might lead to an increase in the absolute value of $\beta_2$. Econometric evaluations ought test for the presence and extent of such changes. Indeed, not allowing in estimation for such changes will result in misleading results. Estimates of the relevant parameters in this event will be downward biased, in absolute values, if a programme of reform has resulted in a more sensitive actual relationship. This will lead in turn to erroneous conclusions which understate the extent to which an adjustment programme can or has worked.

### Presence of a Programme

To a number of studies it is not so much the extent of reform that matters but the existence of a programme of reform *per se*. To this extent they are the econometric equivalent of either the before and after or with and without approach. Specifically, they seek to reveal the extent and, where relevant, direction of influence of the presence of a programme on various indicators of interest.

Ikhide (1993) adopted a variant of this general approach in looking at a sample of African countries which had liberalized interest rate determination.[18] The following econometric model was utilized:

$$\Delta \ln m_t = \alpha_0 + \alpha_1 \Delta (d - \pi^e)_t + \alpha_2 \Delta \ln y_t + \alpha_3 \Delta \ln m_{t-1} + \mu_t$$
$$t = 1, ..., n \qquad (2.5)$$

where $\Delta \ln m_t$ is the change in the logarithm of real money balances during period $t$ (that is, the level of this variable in period $t$ minus that in period $t-1$), $\Delta(d - \pi^e)_t$ is the change in the anticipated real rate of interest in $t$ (that is, the nominal rate, $d$, minus the anticipated rate of CPI inflation, $\pi^e$), $\Delta \ln y_t$ is the change in the logarithm of real GDP and $\Delta \ln m_{t-1}$ is the change in the logarithm of real money balances in period $t-1$.

Ikhide estimated equation (2.5) twice: once for the time period prior to liberalization and once for the period after the liberalization. That is, the equation

$$\Delta \ln m_t = \alpha_0' + \alpha_1' \Delta(d - \pi^e)_t + \alpha_2' \Delta \ln y_t + \alpha_3' \Delta \ln m_{t-1} + \mu_t' \qquad (2.5a)$$

is estimated for the period $t = 1, ..., k$ and the equation

$$\Delta \ln m_t = \alpha_0'' + \alpha_1'' \Delta(d - \pi^e)_t + \alpha_2'' \Delta \ln y_t + \alpha_3'' \Delta \ln m_{t-1} + \mu_t'' \qquad (2.5b)$$

is estimated for the period $t = k + 1, ..., n$. According to this approach one then compares the estimated parameters of the two equations. The key parameters in this case are those relating to $\alpha_1$. If liberalization has worked one would expect that $\alpha''$ would be significantly greater than $\alpha'$ in absolute values. One would therefore evaluate the null hypothesis that $\alpha'' = \alpha'$ using a ratio similar to equation (1) above.[19] Unfortunately Ikhide did not pursue this line of enquiry, focusing only on whether each was significantly different from zero.

The approach adopted by Ikhide is of considerable merit to the extent that it looks at the possible impact of liberalization on behavioural relationships. As such, it avoids the criticism levelled against the approach used by Khan and Aftab. However, its application suffers very much from not only the constraints imposed by developing country data sets but from the fact that liberalization in developing economies is a relatively recent phenomenon. The first of these points will often dictate an uncomfortably short pre-liberalization time series, while the second will dictate for many years to come an equally uncomfortably short post-liberalization time series. Not only will the efficiency of the econometric estimates be open to question, but testing alternative and possibly more complex specifications, the application of multi-equation models and evaluation of the assumptions on which accuracy of OLS estimates depend is simply not possible.

Faini *et al.* (1991a) and the World Bank (1990), in widely cited studies, tackle the issue of the extent of policy reform using a rather different approach.[20] Faini *et* al. analyzed GDP growth rates, investment rates, inflation and current account balances using a cross country sample which included both adjustment and non-adjustment programme countries. The following model was used to analyse GDP growth:

$$\Delta Y_{i,t} = \alpha + \beta_1 Y_{it-1} + \beta_2 \left(\frac{I}{Y}\right)_{i,t-1} + \beta_3 \left(\frac{CA}{Y}\right)_{i,t-1} + \beta_4 \Delta P_{i,t-1} + \beta_5 SH_{i,t} + \beta_6 CON_{i,t} + \mu_{i,t} \quad (2.6)$$

The dependent variable ($\Delta Y_{i,t}$) is country *i*'s GDP growth rate in year *t*;[21] $Y_{i,t-1}$, $(I/Y)_{i,t-1}$, $(CA/Y)_{i,t-1}$, and $\Delta P_{i,t-1}$ are *i*'s GDP, investment to GDP ratio, current account balance to GDP ratio and inflation rate, respectively, all in the previous year; $SH_{i,t}$ is an indicator of external shocks,[22] and; $CON_{i,t}$ is a binary (0,1) dummy variable taking the value of one if *i* is a recipient of IMF and/or World Bank adjustment loans or zero if otherwise.

Given the focus of the Faini *et al.* paper, the variable of most interest is the binary variable *CON*. It crudely measures policy reform, simply by observing the presence or otherwise of a programme. The effects of the programme are measured by estimates of $\beta_6$. Although not made clear in the Faini *et al.* paper, the theoretical interpretation of rests on what McGillivray *et al.* (1994) call the 'size effect' of adjustment. That is, the introduction of a programme may result in an exogenous change in the level of a determinant of the indicator under consideration. For example, as already discussed, a financial liberalization may see a fall in interest rates and this, according to simple economic behavioural relationships, would lead to an increase in investment. This, in turn, would feed through to an increase in GDP growth, as equation (2.6) would hold.

The econometrics of the Faini *et al.* procedure are reasonably straightforward. *CON* operates as an intercept dummy. For those countries in recipient of adjustment lending (that is, those countries for which $CON_{i,t} = 1$), equation (2.2) may be rewritten as

$$\Delta Y_{i,t} = (\alpha + \beta_6) + \beta_1 Y_{it-1} + \beta_2 \left(\frac{I}{Y}\right)_{i,t-1} + \beta_3 \left(\frac{CA}{Y}\right)_{i,t-1} + \beta_4 \Delta P_{i,t-1} + \beta_5 SH_{i,t} + \mu_{i,t} \quad (2.6a)$$

and in the case of non-adjustment lending countries (for which $CON_{i,t} = 0$)

$$\Delta Y_{i,t} = \alpha + \beta_1 Y_{it-1} + \beta_2 \left(\frac{I}{Y}\right)_{i,t-1} + \beta_3 \left(\frac{CA}{Y}\right)_{i,t-1} + \beta_4 \Delta P_{i,t-1} + \beta_5 SH_{i,t} + \mu_{i,t} \quad (2.6b)$$

Provided $\beta_6$ is significantly different from zero, it will either increase or decrease performance (in this case GDP growth) by a constant additive factor, depending on whether it is positive or negative. This effect is greater the larger the absolute value of $\beta_6$. The relationship is demonstrated diagrammatically in Figure 2.2. Here we focus on the functional relationship between GDP growth ($\Delta Y_{i,t}$) and the previous year's investment ratio ($(I/Y)_{i,t-1}$), holding all other relevant variables constant. We assume that both $\alpha$ and $\beta_2$ are greater than zero. In the latter case, this dictates that growth increases across countries with increases in last year's investment ratio, the rate of increase being determined by the numerical size of $\beta_2$. For presentational convenience only, we also assume that all adjustment countries have lagged investment ratios which are greater than $(I/Y)'_{i,t-1}$ and non-adjustment countries have ratios less than this value. The lower function plot in Figure 2.2 is the non-adjustment case and corresponds to equation (2.6b). What Faini *et al.* hypothesize is that the adoption of an programme exogenously shifts the function upward by the value of $\beta_6$. The counterfactual is that adjustment programme countries would remain on the lower line to the right of $(I/Y)'_{i,t-1}$, in which case $\beta_6$ would be insignificantly different from zero.[23]

Faini *et al.* reported what they considered to be a 'remarkable' result: based on estimated values of $\beta_6$, the presence of an adjustment programme does not seem to have any significant impact on GDP growth. Indeed, this also seemed the case with investment and inflation,

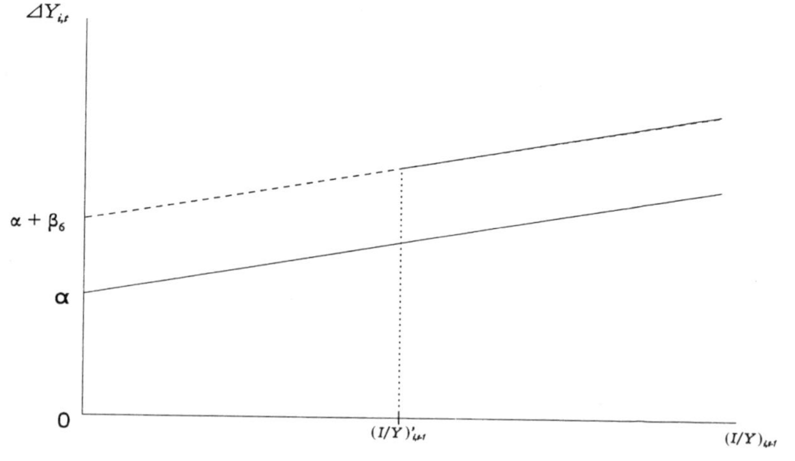


*Figure* 2.2 Size Effect of Adjustment

but not with current account performance. In the latter case, adjustment seemed to have a beneficial impact.

The World Bank (1990) also gauges the impact of a programme through the use of an intercept dummy. But it differs from the Faini *et al.* approach in two respects, as will soon become clear. The following basic equation was proposed:

$$y_i = x_i'\omega + W'\alpha + Bd_i + e_i \tag{2.7}$$

where $y_i$ is a macroeconomic performance variable, $x_i$ is a vector of variables representing macroeconomic policies that would be expected in the absence of a liberalization (in this case World Bank adjustment) programme, $W$ is a vector of variables representing the external economic environment, $d_i$ is a binary dummy taking the value of one if country $i$ has a Bank-supported programme or zero if otherwise, $\omega$ and $\alpha$ are vectors of parameters, B is a parameter and $e_i$ is an error term. $d_i$ operates in the same manner as $CON_{i,t}$ in the Faini *et al.* study. Since policies which would have prevailed in the absence of a programme cannot be observed directly, it was posited that:

$$\Delta x_i = \gamma_{oi} - \gamma y_{i,-1} + u_i \tag{2.8}$$

where $y_{i,-1}$ is the value of the given performance value in the preceding year. The World Bank (1990) argues that equation (2.8) assumes that policymakers in one period react to deviations of performance from constant target variables in the previous period. The World Bank arrives at its model for estimating the effects of the presence of a programme by subtracting $y_{i,-1}$ from each side of (2.7) and substituting equation (2.8) for $x_i$ to obtain:

$$\Delta y_i = \beta_0 + \beta_1 y_{i,-1} + \beta_2 x_{i,-1} + \beta_3 W_i + \beta_4 d_i + e_i \tag{2.9}$$

In a further departure from Faini *et al.* and other similar studies, the World Bank argues that $d_i$ should be treated as an endogenous variable. That is, it argues that a country's macroeconomic performance will determine the presence or otherwise of a programme and *vice versa*. The World Bank points out that if this is the case then failing to allow for it in estimation will almost certainly lead to biased and misleading estimates of the parameters of the equation under consideration.[24] This is potentially a major issue in the modelling the impact of liberalization and is therefore worthy of some consideration; almost all econometric evaluations published to date will have reported misleading results if the Bank is correct on this point.

The problem of endogeniety in econometric estimation usually arises if a bi-directional, contemporaneous correlation exists between the dependent and explanatory variables. Thus, the question of whether $d_i$ should be treated as an endogenous variable (as well as $CON_{i,t}$ in equation (6)) turns on whether the *decision* to introduce a programme depends on current macroeconomic performance and *vice versa*. That we emphasize the decision to introduce a programme is of central importance. The presence of a programme is the outcome of decisions made by policy-makers. Thus consideration of the likely determinants of such a presence we must look to the criteria on which these decisions are based. While these determinants are a matter of some speculation, any decision can only be based on information available at the time of the decision.

Will the decision to introduce a programme be based on information of current macroeconomic performance? This is unlikely due to the often significant time lags with the release of economic, especially macroeconomic, data. Due to these informational time lags decision-makers will simply not know the status of current macroeconomic performance when deciding to introduce a programme. They may be well aware of current information on interest rates, exchange rates, inflationary expectations and so on, but these are not usually the variables used to measure macroeconomic performance. These variables will clearly influence macroeconomic performance, but the extent of this influence will not be currently known. At best, therefore, decision makers will be aware of period $t-1$ performance, but not period $t$. Since the presence of a programme today cannot logically affect what has happened prior to its introduction, there would appear to be a strong intuitive case for the exogeniety of the variable indicating the presence of a programme. If this case is correct, which it would appear to be, then treating the variable as endogenous in estimation may itself cause misleading regression results. This argument also applies to other possible liberalization evaluations, including socio-economic, or other liberalization variables such as compliance.[25]

There would appear to be two other reasons why one should treat the presence of a programme as an exogenous variable. First, even if current information is known, it is rarely the case that a programme is introduced overnight. There needs to be agreement between a range of parties over the design and implementation of the programme, including in most cases agreement with one or more lending agencies. This is often a time-consuming process. Yet even if there are no informational of implementation lags (or the lags are short and do not extend beyond one time period), one would not often expect to observe either partially or fully the impact of the programme in the period in which it was introduced. This also tends to rule out a contemporaneous correlation. It also suggests that one ought lag the variable indicating the presence of a programme ($d_i$ and $CON_{i,t}$ above), or at least test for alternative lag structures.

Faini *et al.* and World Bank studies are useful contributions to the literature and clearly avoid the aforementioned criticism of the approach used by Ikhide (1993). Like all studies, however, they do have weaknesses. While we have already questioned the World Bank's assumed endogeniety of the variable indicating the presence of a programme, four weaknesses are for the moment worth highlighting. The first is that like Mosley *et al.*, their applications are to cross country data. The effect of adjustment is thus assumed to be the same in all programme countries. The second is that they tell us even less about the process by which liberalization impacts on growth. The use of an intercept dummy is entirely a 'black box' approach, not even being able to identify which of the explanatory variables through which the size affect operates. Thirdly, both studies overlook the argument, stated above, that successful liberalization changes the nature of behavioural relationships between variables. Testing for a size effect is perfectly valid. But if liberalization has changed these relationships with respect of any one or more the explanatory variables in (2.6) and (2.8), the equation is mis-specified and its results will almost certainly be biased and misleading. For convenience, in what follows we shall follow McGillivray *et al.* (1995) and label such a change as the *sensitivity* effect of liberalization. We shall shortly turn to a diagrammatic presentation of this effect.

A number of studies have tested for size and sensitivity effects. These include Greenaway and Sapsford (1994a) and McGillivray *et al.* (1994). In a study of Pakistan's liberalization experience from 1980, McGillivray *et al.* applied an error correction model of the general form:

$$\Delta y_t = \beta_0 + \beta_1 \Delta x_t + \gamma(y_{t-1} - \delta x_{t-1}) + \mu_t \qquad (2.7)$$

where $\Delta y_t$ is growth rate of some macroeconomic performance indicator in period $t$, $\Delta x_t$ is a determinants of this rate, $y_{t-1}$ and $x_{t-1}$ are lagged values of these variables, $\beta_0$ is a constant and $\mu_t$ is a residual term.[27] The final expression in brackets is an error correction term, which captures the long-run relationship between $y$ and $x$. The size effect is modelled by attaching a 0,1 dummy to $\beta_0$. This variable takes the value of one for the adjustment period and zero for the non-liberalization period and can be lagged one or more periods to capture the full effect of a programme. The sensitivity effect is modelled by attaching a dummies to $\delta$, $\beta_1$ and $\gamma$. If these effects are thought to be permanent one can set both dummies to one for all years from that in which a programme is introduced. Assuming the sensitivity effect is confined to $x_t$, equation (2.7) may be written as:

$$\Delta y_t = \beta_0 + \beta_1 \Delta x_t + \gamma(y_{t-1} - \delta x_{t-1}) + \beta_2 A_{1,t-j} + \beta_3 A_{2,t-j}(\Delta x_t) + \mu_t \tag{2.7a}$$

where $A_{1,t-j}$ and $A_{2,t-j}$ are the size and sensitivity dummies, respectively, lagged $j$ periods. Note that $j$ can be set to zero. After the introduction of a liberalization programme equation (2.7a) becomes

$$\Delta y_t = (\beta_0 + \beta_2) + (\beta_1 + \beta_3)\Delta x_t + \gamma(y_{t-1} - \delta x_{t-1}) + \mu_t \tag{2.7b}$$

and reduces back to equation (2.7) in the pre-liberalization programme years. Here we have assumed the size and sensitivity effects to be permanent. A diagrammatic exposition is given in Figure 2.3.

Figure 2.3 does, however, point to a problem with simultaneously modelling for the size and sensitivity effects. The size effect is given by the vertical distance between points $a$ and $b$. But due to the pivoting of

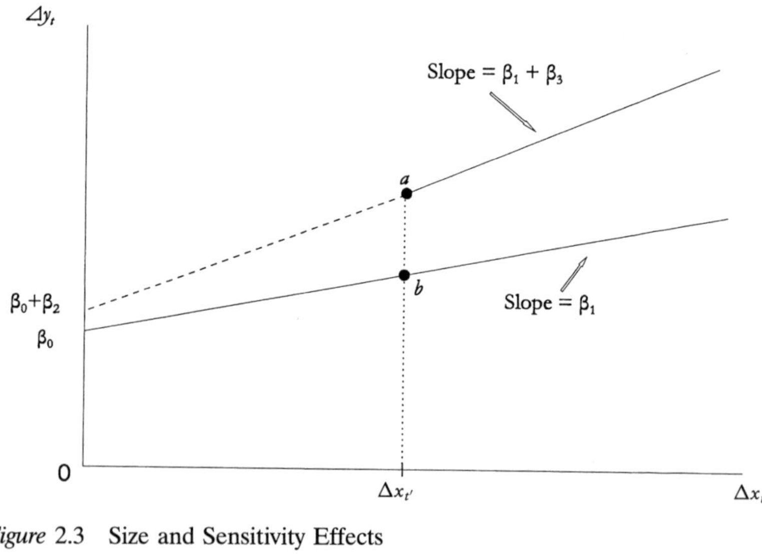


*Figure* 2.3 Size and Sensitivity Effects

the regression line (due to the sensitivity effect), the value of $\beta_2$ understates the magnitude of the size effect. Indeed, if the sensitivity effect is relatively very large, one could detect a negative size effect when the reverse is actually the case. This ambiguity is inherent to testing simultaneously for size and sensitivity effects. One could attempt to separately test for these effects by estimating separate regression equations. But this cure could be worse than the disease. That is, if both effects have actually occurred, then they ought both be included in the regression equation to minimize specification bias.

Greenaway and Sapsford (1994a) modelled GDP growth in 12 countries over periods dating from the late 1950s to middle 1980s.[28] The following econometric model was proposed:

$$N_t^* = \alpha_0 + \alpha_1 X_t^* + \alpha_2 \dot{K}_t + \alpha_3 L_t + \mu_t \qquad (2.8)$$

where (ignoring subscripts and superscripts) $N$ is the rate of growth of GDP (net of exports), $X$ is export growth, $\dot{K}$ is capita stock growth (proxied by investment ratio growth), $L$ is labour force growth, $\mu$ is a residual term. $\alpha_o$ is a constant and $\alpha_1$, $\alpha_2$ and $\alpha_3$ are regression coefficients. Greenaway and Sapsford then augmented equation (2.8) with a series of binary dummies. The interest in this study is its concern with modelling the effects of up to three separate liberalizations. Thus, up to three dummies picking up size effects and three picking up sensitivity effects were used. It was postulated that the latter would operate via liberalization's possible effect on exports. Each were assigned values of one during their corresponding liberalization period and zero in all other periods. The augmented model is as follows:

$$\begin{aligned} N_t^* = {} & \alpha_0 + \alpha_1 X_t^* + \alpha_2 \dot{K}_t + \alpha_3 L_t + \alpha_4 DI_{1,t-j} + \alpha_5 DI_{2,t-j} \\ & + \alpha_6 DI_{3,t-j} + \alpha_7 DS_{1,t-j}(X_t^*) + \alpha_8 DS_{2,t-j}(X_t^*) \\ & + \alpha_9 DS_{3,t-j}(X_t^*) + \mu_t \end{aligned} \qquad (2.8a)$$

where $DI_{1,t-j}$, $DI_{2,t-j}$ and $DI_{3,t-j}$ are size effect dummies corresponding to the first, second and third liberalizations periods, respectively. The lags assigned to each dummy of $j$ periods allows for a delayed effects. $DS_{1,t-j}$, $DS_{2,t-j}$, $DS_{3,t-j}$ are corresponding sensitivity effect dummies.

The Greenaway and Sapsford model works as follows. For convenience we assume no lagged size and sensitivity effects (that is, that $j = 0$). In those years prior to the first liberalization, for which $DI_{1,t-j} = DI_{2,t-j} = DI_{3,t-j} = DS_{1,t-j} = DS_{2,t-j} = DS_{3,t-j} = 0$, equation (2.4) applies. The following applies during the first liberalization (for which $DI_{2,t-j} = DI_{3,t-j} = DS_{2,t-j} = DS_{3,t-j} = 0$):

$$N_t^* = (\alpha_0 + \alpha_4) + (\alpha_1 + \alpha_7)X_t^* + \alpha_2\dot{K}_t + \alpha_3 L_t + \mu_t \tag{2.8b}$$

It follows that during the second liberalization (for which $DI_{1,t-j} = DI_{3,t-j} = DS_{1,t-j} = DS_{3,t-j} = 0$):

$$N_t^* = (\alpha_0 + \alpha_5) + (\alpha_1 + \alpha_8)X_t^* + \alpha_2\dot{K}_t + \alpha_3 L_t + \mu_t \tag{2.8c}$$

and during the third (for which $DI_{1,t-j} = DI_{2,t-j} = DS_{1,t-j} = DS_{2,t-j} = 0$):

$$N_t^* = (\alpha_0 + \alpha_6) + (\alpha_1 + \alpha_9)X_t^* + \alpha_2\dot{K}_t + \alpha_3 L_t + \mu_t \tag{2.8d}$$

Equations (2.4c) and (2.4d) assume that the effects of the second and third liberalizations are non-cumulative. This is the equivalent of treating the effects of a liberalization episode as being temporary; that is, it does not itself impart a permanent improvement in performance, other factors being constant. In the case of cumulative effects we would in (2.4c) replace $(\alpha_0 + \alpha_5)$ with $(\alpha_0 + \alpha_4 + \alpha_5)$ and $(\alpha_1 + \alpha_8)$ with $(\alpha_1 + \alpha_7 + \alpha_8)$. Similarly, in (2.4d) we would replace $(\alpha_0 + \alpha_6)$ with $(\alpha_0 + \alpha_4 + \alpha_5 + \alpha_6)$ and $(\alpha_1 + \alpha_9)$ with $(\alpha_1 + \alpha_7 + \alpha_8 + \alpha_9)$.

The relationships described by equations (2.4) to (2.4d) are diagrammatically depicted in Figure 2.4. It is assumed for convenience

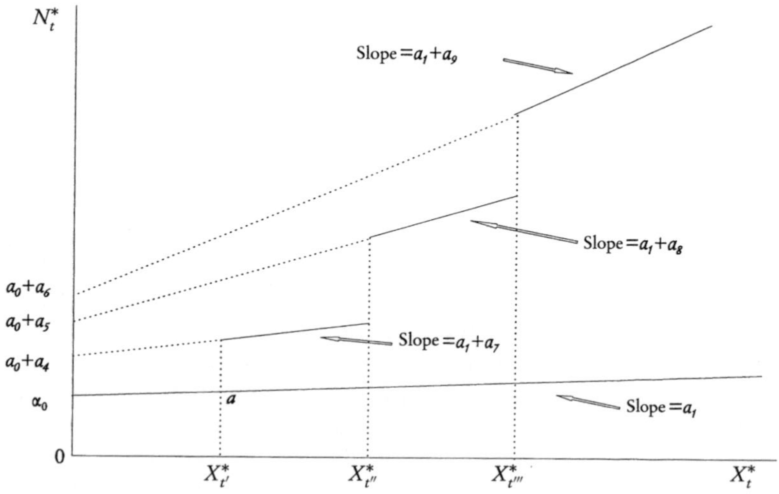


*Figure* 2.4 Sequential Size and Sensitivity Effects

that each of the coefficients attached to the size and sensitivity effect dummies are positive and increase with each liberalization (that is, $\alpha_6 > \alpha_5 > \alpha_4$ and $\alpha_9 > \alpha_8 > \alpha_7$). It is also assumed that GDP growth is an increasing function of export growth (that is, $\alpha > 0$). Figure 2.4 depicts a liberalization when export growth reaches $X^*_{t'}$ (that is, in year $t'$), and two later liberalizations in years $t'$ and $t''$. The latter liberalizations immediately follow one another. For each liberalization, the counterfactual is that the country would remain on the lower line to the right of point *a*.[29]

McGillivray *et al.*, in addition to reporting estimates of regression coefficients, conducted a number of *ex post* simulations. This involved comparing actual macroeconomic performance to that predicted by their econometric models under various counterfactual, non-liberalization programme scenarios. It follows that these simulations are a form of with and without analysis which controls for the influence of extraneous factors. One must speculate over values the explanatory variables of the econometric model would take in the absence of a programme to arrive at the counterfactual scenarios. A number of scenarios were considered for inflation and investment in the McGillivray *et al.* study. The simplest involved setting the size and sensitivity effect parameters to zero, which must be the case in theory if there is no liberalization programme. Others involved, for example, limiting a post-1981 depreciation of the nominal Pakistan rupee-US dollar exchange rate to half the actual rate (this variable was found to determine the inflation rate) and setting both above effects to zero.[30] It was assumed, therefore, that this devaluation would not have occurred in the absence of Pakistan's liberalization programme. A comparison of actual rates of inflation and those which were generated under this scenario is shown in Figure 2.5. Inflation is higher in most years in the simulated, no-liberalization scenario.

*Ex post* simulations have merit on a number of grounds. Let us consider three. First, simulations can be used to consider a range of different scenarios. For instance, in the case of the Mosley *et al.* (1991) regressions one could have considered the impact on economic performance of alternative levels of compliance. Second, in the context of the sorts of analyses conducted by McGillivray *et al.* and Greenaway and Sapsford (1994a), they avoid the problem associated with the ambiguity of the size effect in the presence of a significant sensitivity effect. This is because the simulation displays final combined outcomes, although one may not know the precise contribution of each effects on the indicator under consideration. Thus the question of whether the

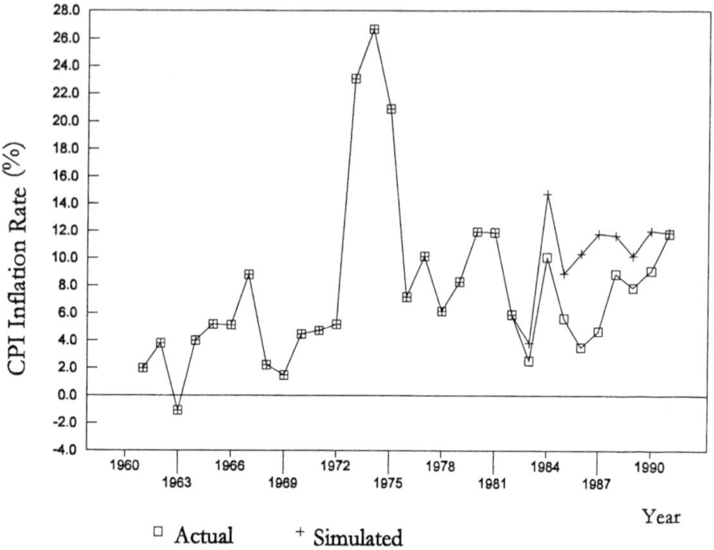


*Figure* 2.5 Simulated versus Actual Inflation Rates – Pakistan

programme has resulted in better performance than would otherwise be the case can be more accurately answered.

Third, simulations can address another arguably more important line of enquiry. It can be argued that a programme will ultimately successful only if it results in an improved position relative to that which existed prior to its introduction. We know, for example, that a stated goal of virtually all liberalization programmes is either the restoration or improvement in the rate of economic growth. Thus, according to this criterion the programme should result in a higher growth rate than that which prevailed prior to its introduction. To answer this essentially before and after (as opposed to with and without) question, one needs to consider the influence of the presence of a programme on the relevant indicator relative to that of other variables. For example, in the context of equation (4b), it could well be the case $\alpha_4$ and $\alpha_7$ are positive, implying higher growth in the liberalization period than would otherwise have been the case in that period, but that $\alpha_2$ is strongly negative and the size of $K_t$ is large relative to $X_t^*$, so much so that $N_t^*$ is lower after the introduction of the programme. This is not of course to say that liberalization has caused this outcome. It simply has not had a sufficiently strong offsetting effect. It is precisely this type of information that a simulation can convey, by taking into account not only the estimated parameters of the econometric equation but the magnitude of the variables to which these parameters are attached. For instance, from Figure 2.5 if can be inferred that without its liberalization programme, Pakistan's inflation rate would have often been higher than in the five years preceding the introduction of this programme.

Let us now return to the size and sensitivity effects. The effects shown in Figures 2.2, 2.3 and 2.5 are rather discrete changes involving sudden changes in economic performance, observed within a single year. Is it reasonable to posit such changes? Some variables may indeed respond quickly to the introduction of a programme. For example, investment might increase dramatically if the programme results in a large increase in investor confidence, or government expenditures might do likewise if the programme also involves stabilization measures. Yet in general one it would seem reasonable to speculate that the economic and social effects of a programme would be felt gradually over time. Liberalization programmes tend to be implemented in a rather gradual way, with a range of reforms implemented in sequence over a number of years. One would not therefore expect to completely observe the outcomes of this process in a single year. Nor would one if a programme is, as Greenaway *et al.* (1997) describe it, 'big bang' in its implementation. Referring to GDP growth, Greenaway *et al.* argue that any subsequent economic effects will be gradual rather than automatic with the speed of adjustment being dependent on the efficacy of markets in the economy in question.

The implication of the preceding argument for econometric studies seeking to model the presence of a programme with binary dummies is that their models are in most cases mis-specified and that at best they only pick-up part of the effects of a programme. Conclusions based on the results of these studies are thus open to serious question. Methodologically, one should perhaps attempt in most cases to model liberalization as a smooth transition between initial and final states using an appropriate econometric model. Possible examples of such a model are provided in Chapters 5 and 7 of this volume. A detailed examination of smooth transitions modelling is thus not warranted in the current chapter, although it is worth emphasizing that the model caters for discrete structural breaks as well as smooth transitions. It remains valid, therefore, even if a discrete structural break occurs. A number of additional comments can, however, be made. While smooth transitions analysis is certainly a promising development, it is no panacea to the difficulties associated with modelling the effects of liberalization. In particular, it is simply tells us whether a transition has occurred in the data and whether this occurrence is post-liberalization. As to whether it is due to liberalization remains a matter of speculation. To attribute a transition to a programme one has to rule out other possible causes. This is a problem that it shares with dummy variable analysis, especially if one allows for delayed impacts. Smooth transitions also shares the black box problem of these analyses, telling us nothing of how and why liberalization may or may not have seemingly had an impact and is subject to the same ambiguity over the size effect (or in the jargon of smooth transitions, the transition in the intercept term). It is also a relatively complex, and more difficult to apply than the other econometric approaches discussed above. Finally, the studies conducted to date have tested only for symmetric and not other equally plausible transitions, such as quadratic. The problem of specification bias therefore emerges.

## 2.4. DIRECTIONS FOR FUTURE EVALUATIONS

Let us consolidate the preceding material with the following question. Precisely what should an evaluation of the impact of liberalization tell us and what technique or techniques ought be used to provide this information? First, an evaluation ought tell us what has happened subsequent to the introduction of a programme. This is not alone an evaluation of a programme; it simply provides useful background information. Before and after comparison is suitable for this purpose, provided one tests for significant differences between the pre-liberalization and liberalization periods.[31]

Second, and more fundamentally, an evaluation must tell us whether a liberalization programme has caused a particular outcome rather than simply being associated with it. This, it has been argued, rules out before and after and with and without analysis in practice due to the related problems of controlling for the impact of extraneous influences and the counterfactual. Econometric analysis offers a solution to these problems. The parameters provided by such analysis can in principle tell us the extent and direction of liberalization's incremental influence on the indicator under consideration after controlling for the influence of extraneous factors. Yet econometric analysis will only partially answer this question if one only reports parameter estimates. As mentioned, a fully successful programme must not only achieve a better outcome than would otherwise be the case in the period after its introduction; it should also result in an improved situation relative to that which existed prior to its introduction. This information can be provided by econometric simulations, which facilitate comparison of pre-liberalization actual with simulated liberalization period scenarios. Of the econometric approaches outlined above, the smooth transitions modelling approach is arguably the most superior. Among its relative advantages is that it caters for both discrete structural changes and smooth transitions of various velocities, is based on time series rather than cross-section data and embodies both exogenous shocks and behavioural changes.

Third, an evaluation should also tell us how an impact of liberalization has emerged. That is, it must identify the precise processes or channels through which liberalization affects the indicator under consideration. Unfortunately, none of the techniques outlined above can shed light on this. Indeed, despite its strengths, smooth transitions analysis does especially poorly on this score as it is entirely a black box approach. Information of how a particular outcome has emerged can be provided by a comprehensively specified econometric model containing both structural and reduced-form equations. However, such a model has rather demanding data requirements which will be beyond the scope of the majority of developing country data sets, at least for many years to come. Econometric analysis will, it would seem, not be able to comprehensively evaluate and understand the impact of liberalization in developing countries until these requirements are met.

Socioeconomic evaluations deserve special comment. It is no coincidence that these evaluations have almost exclusively on with and without and/or before and after comparison.[32] Evaluator preference will have played a part in this, but even those who may have intended to apply econometric techniques will have been prevented from doing so by the sparse availability and generally poor nature of developing country socioeconomic data. As these data essentially rule out any time series analysis, one can at best apply relatively simple socioeconometric models using cross section data or, less preferably, with and without analysis.[33] One ought therefore treat socioeconomic evaluations with even more caution than their economic counterparts due to this methodological constraint.

## 2.5. CONCLUSION

This chapter has reviewed different methods used to evaluate the economic and socioeconomic impacts of economic liberalization programmes. It was concerned exclusively with the two main types of techniques used in the literature: simple data description and econometric modelling. Two data description techniques were examined: before and after and with and without comparisons. It was argued that while these techniques offer very useful descriptive insights they suffer from extremely restrictive *ceteris paribus* assumptions and the related problem of the counterfactual. These techniques cannot consequently provide information essential to an evaluation: whether liberalization causes a particular outcome rather than merely being associated with it.

A number of different econometric approaches were then examined in this chapter. These approaches included those which look at the extent of reform, the underlying behavioural relationships on which a successful liberalization programme depends, discrete and sudden changes in economic performance due to the presence of a programme and a smooth transition from one state to another due to liberalization. It was pointed out that econometric analysis can in principle tell us whether liberalization has caused a particular outcome largely by controlling for the impact of extraneous factors. The relative merits of these approaches were considered. Smooth transitions analysis was thought to be a welcome development, although like other approaches it does have it weaknesses. One main weaknesses is that it is entirely a black box approach, telling us little of how liberalization may have caused a particular outcome. This information was considered to be vital in the assessment of a programme. Indeed, smooth transitions analysis shares this limitation with all the approaches surveyed. It was however emphasized that providing information on how particular outcomes emerge is an extremely demanding task: limitations of developing country data sets will invariably prevent estimation of the sorts of econometric models which can shed light on this. Moreover, these limitations place even greater constraints on evaluations of the socioeconomic impact of liberalization. Consequently, significant caveats need to be placed on the results of those evaluation techniques that can be applied to socioeconomic data. Removing these constraints will result in a significantly richer, more informative literature on the impact of economic liberalization.

## Notes

* This chapter is based partially on a paper presented at the Fourth Workshop of the ODA/CREDIT Structural Adjustment Forum at the University of Nottingham in January 1995. Comments from the workshop participants are gratefully acknowledged, especially those from Tony Addison, Joe Durkan, Diane Elson, David Greenaway, Scott McDonald, Andrew McKay, Oliver Morrissey and Jim Thomas. Any remaining errors or omissions are the sole responsibility of the author. Parts of the paper rely on McGillivray *et al.* (1995).

1. Nor does the paper attempt to look at evaluations specifically concerned with programme design and implementation, although these issues are obviously related to the impact of liberalization.
2. Throughout this chapter the terms 'adjustment' and 'liberalization' are taken as being synonymous.
3. Another approach is to compare actual adjustment experience to programme targets. See Mosley *et al.* (1991, pp. 183–4) for a discussion of this approach.
4. Zuckerman (1991) provides before and after comparisons of social indicators using times series data for individual countries. Cornia *et al.* (1987) provide a number of applications of these comparisons.
5. See Guillamont (1994) for a before and after analysis of agricultural production.
6. EIALs were defined as those which had received two or more structural adjustment loans (SALs) or three of more structural adjustment loans (SALs plus sectoral adjustment loans (SECALs)) starting in 1985 or earlier. OALs were defined as all other receipients of SALs and SECALs in 1985 or earlier (Corbo *et al.*, 1992, p. 12).
7. With respect to with and without comparisons, the *ceteris paribus* assumption perhaps best applies to the external or international environment faced by countries. In the case of before and after analysis, the basic economic structure of a country will be similar between the before and after scenarios.
8. See Goldstein and Monteil (1986) for further details of this argument with respect to IMF stabilization programmes. In short, they argue that countries adopting a stabilization programme are likely to exhibit poorer performance than those which do not adopt such a programme.
9. This comment also applies to with and without comparison of country pairs. See Mosley *et al.* (1991) for such comparisons.
10. Killick (1995) considers this issue with respect to the impact of liberalization on poverty.
11. Note that Goldstein's comments were made with respect to before and after analysis.
12. Note, however, the sample sizes on which these tests are based are in some instances uncomfortably low.
13. For Table 2.11, the EIAL group average for educational expenditure is significantly different to that for the NAL group, as was the difference between the two averages and the EIAL average for 'Other' expenditure for 1985–87 was significantly different to that of the NAL group. For Table

2.12, the EIAL and OAL male-female difference averages for 1995 are significantly different to that of the OAL group. This was also the case for the EIAL low-income group average female/male ratio for 1995 relative to that of the NAL low-income group and the EIAL full and low-income sample ratios relative to that of the corresponding OAL samples.

14. Also see Mosley and Harrigan (1991), Mosley (1991) and Iqbal (1993).
15. It follows that Mosley *et al.* use the first and second of the above mentioned indicators of the extent of reform. The third has been used by Conway (1994a), who was concerned with the extent of participation in an IMF lending programme.
16. Specifically, Mosley *et al.* acknowledge that there were 'many other independent variables which could have been included as explanatory variables However, since it is specifically the impact of Bank finance and policy conditions which we wish to quantify, we have refrained from more complex specification of the equations' (p. 210).
17. See Mosley *et al.* (1987) for a model which captures this process.
18. Ikhide also looked at countries which had achieved positive real rates of interest through reducing inflation. For another study of this type see Khalid and Ling (1997).
19. This assumes that both parameters are significantly different from zero. If either or both are not, then this test is superfluous.
20. Also see Faini *et al.* (1991b), Bleaney and Fielding (1995), Rashid (1995) and Doroodian (1993).
21. Growth rates in this case refer to the difference between pre-adjustment and adjustment period values.
22. It takes into account changes in real interest rates, real GDP, export and import prices, real export and real import values and gross outstanding debt. See Faini *et al.* (1991, pp. 960–961).
23. Doroodian (1993) also uses an intercept dummy to model the impact of IMF-supported adjustment policies. As in Faini *et al.*, cross section data are employed.
24. Conway (1994a, 1994b) and Fielding (1997) also consider this issue.
25. This argument assumes that decision-makers do not have perfect foresight and that variables change over time.
26. Greenaway and Sapsford (1994b) test for these effects using cross country data. Ikhide tested for a sensitivity, but not size, effect.
27. In most applications of error correction models, including that of McGillivray *et al.*, $x$ is a vector of variables and $\beta$ and $\delta$ vectors of coefficients.
28. Note that Greenaway and Sapsford (1994a) were concerned with the effects of trade liberalizations.
29. Greenaway and Sapsford found little evidence of a positive impact of liberalization. In only four cases (Turkey, Colombia, Spain and New Zealand) did there appear to be a significant size effect. This effect was negative in New Zealand's case. The sensitivity effect was significant in two of the twelve cases only: Greece and Spain. It was negative in Spain's case.
30. Note, however, that it could be argued that the effect of the devaluation on inflation would be picked-up through the operation of the size effect dummy.

31. With and without analysis can also be applied, but it is arguably of limited use as a precursor to econometric analysis which focuses only on the experience of programme countries.
32. The author is unaware at the time of writing this chapter of any published econometric analyses of the social impact of liberalization.
33. While it is possible to locate time series for these data (see, for example, Zuckerman, 1991), they are rather too short and, one suspects, contain many extrapolated observations.

## References

Ahmed, S. (1991), 'Indonesia: Stabilization and Structural Change', in Thomas *et al.* (1991), pp. 361–381.

Bleaney, M. and D. Fielding (1995), 'Investment, Trade Liberalization and Structural Adjustment', *Journal of Development Studies*, Vol. 32, pp. 175–194.

Commonwealth Secretariat (1989), *Engendering Adjustment for the 1990s*, Report on the Commonwealth Expert Group on Women and Structural Adjustment, Commonwealth Secretariat, London.

Conway, P. (1994a), 'IMF Lending Programmes: Participation and Impact', *Journal of Development Economics*, Vol. 45, pp. 365–391.

Conway, P. (1994b), 'An Atheoretic Evaluation of Success in Structural Adjustment', *Economic Development and Cultural Change*, pp. 267–292.

Corbo, V., S. Fischer and S.B. Webb (eds) (1992), *Adjustment Lending Revisited: Policies to Restore Growth*, World Bank, Washington, DC.

Corbo, V. and P. Rojas (1992), 'World Bank-Supported Adjustment Programs: Country Performance and Effectiveness', in Corbo *et al.* (1992).

Cornia, G.A., R. Jolly and F. Stewart (eds) (1987), *Adjustment with a Human Face: Protecting the Vulnerable and Promoting Growth*, Vol 1 and 2, Oxford: Clarendon Press.

Dailami, M. (1991), 'Korea: Successful Adjustment', in Thomas *et al.* (1991), pp. 386–404.

Doroodian, K. (1993), 'Macroeconomic Performance and Adjustment Policies Commonly Supported by the International Monetary Fund', *Economic Development and Cultural Change*, pp. 847–864.

Faini, R., J. De Melo, A. Senhadji and J. Stanton (1991a), 'Growth-oriented Adjustment Programs: A Statistical Analysis', *World Development*, Vol. 19, No. 8, pp. 957–967.

Faini, R., J. De Melo, A. Senhadji-Semlali and J. Stanton (1991b), 'Macro Performance under Adjustment Lending', in Thomas *et al.* (1991), pp. 222–242.

Fielding, D. (1997), 'Adjustment, Trade Policy and Investment Slumps: Evidence from Africa', *Journal of Development Economics*, Vol. 52, pp. 121–137.

Goldstein, M. (1986), *The Global Effects of Fund-supported Adjustment Programmes*, Occasional Paper No. 42, International Monetary Fund, Washington, DC.

Goldstein, M. and P. Montiel (1986), 'Evaluating Fund Stabilization Programs with Multicountry Data: Some Methodological Pitfalls', *IMF Staff Papers* 42, pp. 304–344.

Greenaway, D. and D. Sapsford (1994a), 'What does Liberalization do for Exports and Growth?', *Weltwirtschaftliches Archiv*, Vol. 130, No. 1, pp. 152–174.

Greenaway, D. and D. Sapsford (1994b), 'Exports, Growth and Liberalization: An Evaluation', *Journal of Policy Modelling*, Vol. 16, No. 2, pp. 165–186.

Greenaway, D., S. Leybourne and D. Sapsford (1997), 'Modelling Growth (and Liberalization) using Smooth Transitions Analysis', *Economic Inquiry*, October.

Greenaway, D., S. Leybourne and D. Sapsford (1999), 'Evaluation of Trade Liberalization using Smooth Transitions Analysis', Chapter 6 in this volume.

Guillamont, P. (1994), 'Adjustment Policy and Agricultural Development', *Journal of International Development*, Vol. 6, No. 2, pp. 141–155.

Ikhide, S.I. (1993) 'Positive Interest Rates: Financial Deepening and the Mobilization of Savings in Africa', *Development Policy Review*, Vol 11, No. 2, pp. 307–32.

Iqbal, Z. (1993), 'Macroeconomic Effects of Adjustment Lending in Pakistan', mimeo, Tilburg University.

Khalid, A.M. and T.M. Ling (1997), 'Macroeconomic Effects of Financial Liberalization: Evidence from Selected Asian Economies', mimeo, Department of Economics and Statistics, National University of Singapore.

Khan, S.R. and S. Aftab, (1994), 'Assessing the Impact of Financial Reforms on Pakistan's Economy', *Pakistan Journal of Applied Economics*, Vol. 10, pp. 99–116.

Killick, T. (1995), 'Structural Adjustment and Poverty Alleviation: An Interpretative Survey', *Development and Change*, Vol. 26, No. 2, pp. 305–331.

Maasland, A. and J. van de Gaag (1992), ' World Bank-supported Adjustment Programs and Living Conditions', in Corbo *et al.* (1992).

McGillivray, M., H. White and A. Ahmad (1995), 'Evaluating the Effectiveness of Structural Adjustment Policies on Macroeconomic Performance: A Review of the Evidence with Special Reference to Pakistan', *Pakistan Journal of Applied Economics*, Vol. 11, Nos 1 & 2, pp. 57–75.

Mosley, P., J. Hudson and S. Horrell (1987), 'Aid, the Public Sector and the Market in Less Developed Countries', *Economic Journal*, Vol. 97, pp. 616–641.

Mosley, P., J. Harrigan and J. Toye (1991), *Aid and Power: The World Bank and Policy-based Lending*, Vol. 1, London: Routledge.

Mosley, P. and J. Harrigan (1991), 'Evaluating the Effects of World Bank Structural Adjustment Lending, 1980–88', *Journal of Development Studies*, Vol. 27, No. 3, pp. 63–94.

Mosley, P. (1991), 'Structural Adjustment: A General Overview, 1980–89', in V. N. Balasubramanyam and S. Lall (ed), *Current Issues in Development Economics*, London: Macmillan.

Rashid, A.I. (1995), 'Trade, Growth and Liberalistion: The Indian Experience, 1977–89', *Journal of Developing Areas*, Vol. 29, pp. 355–370.

Rose, P. (1995), 'Female Education and Adjustment Programs: A Crosscountry

Statistical Analysis', *World Development*, Vol. 23, No. 11, pp. 1931–1949.
Singer, H.W. (1994), 'Structural Adjustment Programmes: Evaluating Success', in J.W. Gunning, H. Kox, W. Tims and Y. de Wit (ed), *Trade, Aid and Development*, London: Macmillan.
Thomas, V., A. Chhibber, M. Dailami and J. De Melo (eds) (1991), *Restructuring Economies in Distress: Policy Reform and the World Bank*, Oxford, OUP.
Thomas, V, (1991), 'Trade Policy Reform', in Thomas *et al.* (1991), pp. 47–71.
World Bank (1988), *Adjustment Lending: An Evaluation of Ten Years of Experience*, Country Economics Department, The World Bank, Washington, DC.
World Bank (1990), *Adjustment Lending Policies for Sustainable Growth*, Country Economics Department, The Word Bank, Washington, DC.
Zuckerman, E. (1991), 'The Social Costs of Adjustment', in Thomas *et al.* (1991), pp. 247–271.

# 3 Measuring Trade Liberalization in Africa

Chris Milner and Oliver Morrissey*

## 3.1 INTRODUCTION

Central to any approach to evaluating the impact of economic policy reforms is the chosen measure of the implementation of reform. Adjustment has often been described as 'getting prices right' and, without implying that this means completely free markets, we accept this succinct definition: the broad purpose of adjustment, and more generally liberalization, is to remove price distortions so that agents (public and private) can perceive and react to the correct relative incentives, i.e. to ensure that prices convey correct signals regarding relative (social) opportunity costs. It follows that a true measure of implementation should capture the price effect of reform, and the impact is how the economy responds to the relative price changes (as these alter incentives). In some cases the price effect of liberalization is easy to measure, notably where the reform is to a price (e.g. the exchange rate or decontrol of regulated prices). In other cases, such as tax reform, a summary measure of the price effect should be calculated; and in yet others, such as initiating reform of parastatals or reducing public spending, there may be no immediate price effect (but the reforms will affect the future functioning of the price mechanism). In this chapter we take the case of trade liberalization to detail the problems inherent in attempts to measure the implementation of reforms; for convenience, we limit attention to sub-Saharan Africa (SSA), but the arguments can be generalized to other LEs.

We do not wish to define trade liberalization as establishing a free trade regime, but are satisfied with a definition where liberalization removes price distortions favouring relatively inefficient import-substituting (IS) activities and encourages the reallocation of resources to relatively efficient export-oriented activities (EO). This benefits the economy as the reforms reduce anti-export bias, export growth facilitates economic growth and fewer price distortions facilitate improved resource allocation and greater economic efficiency (for a general discussion of the benefits from trade liberalization see Greenaway and Morrissey, 1994; Morrissey, 1995a). For benefits to ensue the trade reforms must be implemented and must reduce anti-export bias; Greenaway *et al.* (Chapter 6 below) find no consistent relationship between liberalization and subsequent economic growth, but this may simply be because effective reform was not implemented. To resolve this issue, a reliable (and understood) measure of implementation is required.

We will argue that many commonly used measures of reform are deficient because they fail to identify which relative prices are affected and how. In rare cases such as devaluation the reform relates to a single price, is readily quantified and implementation can easily be verified. More often, the target is some type of price index, as when trade policy reforms are set in terms of reducing the average nominal rate of protection. In such cases problems relate to calculating the index and assessing its reliability as a summary indicator of reform. For example, changes in nominal protection could be calculated from alterations to the published tariff schedule but this would give a misleading impression of trade policy reforms if many scheduled tariffs are redundant and/or there are numerous exemptions and exceptions. A more reliable summary measure is required; this chapter addresses the difficulties in constructing such a measure and highlights the errors of inference on policy reform that can result from using unreliable measures.

Many of the reforms required in adjustment programmes do not relate directly to a price, single or aggregate, but to regulations and institutions. Again, trade policy provides immediate examples, such as the removal of quantitative restrictions (QRs) or support for establishing an export promotion agency. Reforms of this nature are particularly difficult to quantify in a comprehensive way, but this in no way implies that their implementation is any less important than more easily quantifiable reforms. For example, QRs are a very distortionary impediment to trade but partial removal could as easily increase as reduce distortions. Assume initially that 40 per cent of imports by value are covered by QRs and that after reform this is reduced to 20 per cent; while overall distortions have probably been reduced, it would be wrong to suggest they have been halved and one would need to analyse which products were affected before evaluating the potential effect of removal of QRs. In other words, to get a more meaningful evaluation of the impact of regulatory reforms we need a measure that attaches a price effect to the quantitative reforms. This is feasible for some regulatory reforms, for others it is not. Institutional reforms such as a requirement to 'set up a Commission to review the tax system' can be said to be implemented or not, but cannot be quantified in their impact; nevertheless, such reforms may be essential bases for future reform.

In this chapter we will review the ways in which the implementation of trade reforms, whether price, regulatory or institutional, have been measured, beginning with the most simple (and misleading) measures and progressing through more sophisticated approaches. In doing so it will be apparent that, regrettably, much of the evaluation literature uses unsuitable measures. Section 3.2 reviews the most simple measure, compliance indices, which do little more than ask if a reform was attempted or not. Section 3.3 considers the range of summary measures of trade reform through nominal and effective protection. Although the data requirements can be great, these measures are useful and if not entirely reliable are in general strongly indicative of the relative price effects of trade reform. Section 3.4 addresses general equilibrium issues more explicitly and considers how relative prices might be measured directly with the aid of true protection concepts and real exchange rates. Section 3.5 briefly outlines a number of other factors, such as infrastructural and institutional constraints, relevant to trade reform before Section 3.6 concludes.

## 3.2 COMPLIANCE INDEX MEASURES

Much of the literature critically reviewed in the previous chapter, uses very simple proxies for implementation, either a dummy for reform periods (e.g. Corbo and Rojas, 1992) or a compliance index (Mosley *et al.* 1991; Mosley and Hudson, 1995). A dummy variable can at best only indicate if there was a structural change in the dependent variable during the period of (purported) reform (see Chapter 2 above). A compliance index appears more informative as it reports the percentage of reforms implemented such that a number closer to 100 is interpreted as better performance:

> Of the conditions in the legal agreements for the adjustment programs in the sample, which covered the entire decade of the 1980s, the overwhelming majority – 84 per cent – were implemented at least substantially by the time the final tranche was released, and 66 per cent were implemented fully or more than fully. (Webb and Shariff, 1992: 71)

This has an authoritative sound and, as Webb and Shariff (1992) is a comprehensive discussion of implementation in a World Bank volume on evaluating adjustment, it warrants closer examination. The authors accept that statistical analysis is unable to 'capture all the nuances' of implementation and caution for care in interpreting the results. Their concern is that as economic and political circumstances change the reforms needed may alter and hence non-implementation would be sanctioned (Webb and Shariff, 1992: 91, note 5). This is one reservation about the compliance index: it does not distinguish between reforms that should be implemented (a 'good' thing) from implementation of reforms that should not be implemented (a 'bad' thing), either because events have rendered them unnecessary or because the reforms were inappropriate in the first place. The indiscriminate nature of compliance indices is evident in other criticisms:

1 All reforms are weighted in exactly the same way. In effect, a devaluation of 50 per cent is treated identically to establishing a Tax Commission. This extreme contrast serves to make the important point that the types of reforms listed in an agreement vary from some that are easily quantifiable and have an immediate (and often quite dramatic) effect, to others whose impact, if any, is long term. Webb and Shariff (1992) do distinguish 'critical' actions, although these are not clearly defined: at best this means that devaluations would be grouped with tax and price reforms, but even this does not justify equal weights.

2 Any judgements on the degree of implementation of a reform are arbitrary and subjective. Webb and Shariff (1992) distinguish 'substantial' and 'full' implementation, the residual category by implication being non-implementation. But this does not help us much: full implementation of a 50 per cent devaluation is easily verified, but at what point is less than 50 per cent still substantial? The problem is even greater if the reform is less precisely defined: we will see in the next section the difficulties of measuring the implementation of tariff reforms, such as to reduce by half the average nominal tariff. The problem is most severe if the reform is of a form such as 'initiate a study of parastatals as a prelude to privatisation' (Turkey): these reforms may be fully implemented, but may have no ultimate effect (for many possible reasons). Furthermore, the subjective judgement of substantial implementation is made by Bank staff who will be sensitive to the fact that

successive tranches can only be realized if current implementation is deemed satisfactory (referring to the quote above, release of the final tranche would be conditional on a high level of implementation). Thus, judgements on implementation may vary from country to country depending on their relationship with the Bank (Morrissey, 1995c, argues that Turkey was deemed to have high compliance as it had a close relationship with the Bank, but that actual compliance was highly selective and almost zero on parastatal reform).

3 A measure of the implementation of reform should capture the effect of the reform on relative prices; compliance does not do this in general (unless the reform being complied with itself directly affects a price, such as devaluation). To say that a specific number from a long list of policy reform actions were in fact acted on tells us very little about what changes in relative incentives were effected. Given the long and varied list of reforms in a typical structural adjustment programme, one could easily imagine a country in which 50 per cent 'compliance' represented a dramatic change in relative prices, whereas 80 per cent compliance in another country may represent only minimal actual relative price changes. Put simply, a compliance index in itself cannot be interpreted as a measure of the reforms implemented: only reforms that have effect are important, and their importance is in terms of their effect (on relative prices). This is the most important reason why the use of compliance as a comparative measure of reform in cross-country regressions is inappropriate.

4 Compliance indices implicitly assume that all reforms listed in the legal agreement are fully desirable; this may not always be the case. An example from Tanzania will serve to illustrate the point (Morrissey, 1995b). Following an IMF recommendation the introduction of VAT became a component of tax reform, although local economists, policy advisors and tax officials argued that VAT would be too sophisticated and a simple sales tax would be a more efficient means to raise revenue. If Tanzania did not introduce VAT it would be deemed as non-compliance, which may affect the flow of Bank funds; if it did comply, a relatively inappropriate tax would be introduced (as it happens, VAT was not introduced and, for separate reasons, the donors' agreement with Tanzania broke down).

It is not possible to adjust compliance index measures to meet these criticisms. One could in principle attach weights to the different reforms, but these would be arbitrary and points 3–4 would remain. A more fruitful response would be to address point 3 and identify measures of implementation which capture the effect of policy; in doing so one may also be able to address the other criticisms, but all remain potentially relevant. Any index which weights components is subject to 1, while any judgement is subject to 2 and it is always possible that the reforms are inappropriate (4).

Monitoring of compliance has an operational purpose, being required to trigger release of tranches. The operations section of the Bank will wish to know whether reforms were implemented as requested, in which case further funds can be released, or not, in which case funds will be held back and the agreement stalled. Policy analysts are not actually concerned with compliance in this sense; their concern is with identifying the effects of the policy reforms that are implemented (if reforms are not implemented, the analyst may ask why, the subject of Chapter 4 below). To identify the effects of reform, one needs reliable measures of policy implementation.

## 3.3 NOMINAL AND EFFECTIVE PROTECTION

Trade policy has been one of the single most important areas for reform under adjustment programmes. Some 58 per cent of all loan agreements in the 1980s included trade policy measures, and 16 per cent of all conditions were specifically related to trade, although only 62 per cent of these were deemed to have been fully implemented (Webb and Shariff, 1992: 70–72). Trade policy is a suitable focus for our purposes as it relates directly to relative prices (importables versus exportables; tradables versus non-tradables; domestic versus world) and includes reforms which impact directly on prices (e.g. tariffs), on quantities (e.g. QRs) and on institutions (such as export promotion agencies). From an initial situation of anti-export bias (arising principally from protection), two types of liberalization can be posited. Import liberalization refers to reducing the price of importables and increasing the ease of importing (by removing QRs and reducing transaction costs). On the other hand, direct export promotion increases the relative return to exports, perhaps through temporary export subsidies or through less direct measures of export support (with marketing or trade finance for instance). Exchange rate reforms are an element of trade liberalization:

devaluation increases returns to exports; liberalizing the foreign exchange regime reduces transactions costs and makes it easier to import, and encourages exports if exporters can retain foreign exchange earnings. Essentially, trade liberalization is intended to increase the price of exportables relative to importables, and to bring these domestic relative prices into line with world relative prices.

There is a large literature on theoretical representation and empirical measurement of trade policy stance; it is not our intention to review that literature comprehensively (see Greenaway and Milner, 1993), but to highlight the issues most relevant to the discussion of trade reforms under liberalization. Before doing this it is important to point out that there are a range of informational and data quality barriers to any investigator seeking to measure trade policy stance in a low-income developing country. This issue is examined more fully in Milner (1996), but it should be taken for granted in all the ensuing discussion that the use of any particular measurement tool may be data-constrained.

The most simple measure of trade policy is some average of the scheduled tariffs, a measure of nominal protection, or some proxy for trade policy, such as the real effective exchange rate. More sophisticated measures will incorporate the combined effects of varying tariff rates, in measures of effective protection, and try to allow for non-tariff barriers. Even more sophisticated measures will try to allow for effects on factor prices, such as in domestic resource cost, or incidence of protection. The nominal rate of protection (*NRP*) might be a simple average measure of tariffs (the average based on summation over all *i* products):

$$NRP = (\Sigma_i w_i t_i)/N \tag{3.1}$$

where

- $t_i$ is the tariff rate on product *i*
- $w_i$ is the weight attached to product *i* (usually its import share)
- $N$ total number of products with scheduled tariffs

There are numerous deficiencies in this measure, exacerbated frequently when no weights are used. There is often a very large number of scheduled tariffs but many of these are redundant (i.e. apply to products which are not actually imported). Secondary tariffs (taxes on imports that are not called tariffs) are excluded, and many imports will not attract the scheduled rate, either because the importer is entitled to exemptions or relief (widespread in African countries) or the source country is in a preferential trading arrangement. A more reliable measure is provided by the implicit nominal tariff (*INT*):

$$INT = \Sigma_i(T_i/M_i) \tag{3.2}$$

where

| | |
|---|---|
| $T_i$ | total customs revenue on product $i$ |
| $M_i$ | total value of imports of product $i$ |

If available, *INT* would be an indicative (trade-weighted) measure of average nominal protection. However, this is only an average measure of gross protection on output, which fails to account for the effect of trade taxes on intermediate inputs. Consequently, the effective rate of protection (*ERP*) is advocated as a measure of net protection to the production process: by accounting for taxes on inputs and outputs, *ERP* measures the protection afforded to value added. We can note that as nominal protection is generally greater for importables than for exportables (which often have zero protection or are taxed), effective protection of exports is frequently negative and invariably less than that for import-competing goods. A standard definition of *ERP* is:

$$ERP_j = (t_j - \Sigma_i a_{ij} t_i)/(1 - \Sigma_i a_{ij}) \tag{3.3}$$

where

| | |
|---|---|
| $t_j$ | is the tariff on final good $j$ |
| $t_i$ | is the tariff on intermediate goods $i$ |
| $a_{ij}$ | the physical input coefficient representing the share of $i$ in the unit cost of producing $j$ (in the absence of trade distortions). |

The formula in (3.3) is a representation of the ratio of domestic to world value added which can be extended, data permitting, to incorporate non-tradables and the 'taxing' and subsidy effects of non-tariff barriers (Greenaway and Milner, 1993). We do not consider those issues here, but will consider related matters and effects on exchange rates in later sections. Although *ERP* data have been compiled for many countries, such data have not been brought together for evaluations of trade policy reform; rather, evaluations have been based on *NRP* measures (Dean *et al.*, 1994) or tariff equivalents (Foroutan, 1993; Nash, 1993).

To measure tariff equivalents one begins by estimating the import demand function given by (expressed in natural logs):

$$M = a + bY + c[Pe(1+t)] \tag{3.4}$$

where $P$ is import price in \$, $e$ is the real effective exchange rate, $Y$ is income and $t$ is the (average) tariff rate; $a$, $b$, and $c$ are coefficients to be estimated. This can be rearranged in terms of percentage changes (denoted $\Delta$) as:

$$\Delta(1+t) = [\Delta M - b\Delta Y - c(\Delta P + \Delta e)]/c \tag{3.5}$$

Using $b = 1.25$ and $c = -1.0$ (as consistent with various estimates), $d(1+t)$ can be estimated as 'the residual change in imports that cannot be explained by changes in income or the major variables that affect domestic prices (international price and exchange rate fluctuations)' referred to as the *change in tariff equivalent* or *TE* (Nash, 1993: 36). For SSA overall the mean tariff equivalent for non-food consumer imports fell 50 per cent while for non-fuel imports it fell 40 per cent (based on comparing the average for three years before adjustment to the average for the three most recent years since adjustment). This implies fairly significant levels of import liberalization.

Noting that $\Delta(P_D/P_M) = \Delta e + \Delta(1 + t)$ represents the change in incentives for importables, where $P_D$ is the domestic price and $P_M$ the import border price, one can derive a measure of the change in the incentive to produce import substitutes (Nash, 1993: 38). For non-CFA countries in the before-recent comparison, this incentive rose for non-fuel imports (1.4 per cent) but fell for non-food consumer imports (−15 per cent); for CFA countries it fell in both cases (−18 per cent and −5 per cent). There are a number of implications. The first is that devaluation (not available to the fixed exchange rate countries of CFA) tended to partially offset the reductions in protection (which may help to explain the lack of import response). Second, non-CFA countries reduced protection on consumer imports by more than on imports overall (but the reverse for CFA). Third, the failure of CFA countries to devalue probably meant that their reductions in protection were effectively greater than for non-CFA countries. This latter is the only measure on which CFA liberalization seems to have performed better. We can note finally that as devaluation is implemented more rapidly than import liberalization, reductions in $(P_D/P_M)$ take time to occur.

Table 3.1 provides some evidence on trade liberalization during the 1980s for seven SSA countries covered by both the Dean *et al.* (1994) and Foroutan (1993) studies. The tariff ratio is the ratio of the post-reform average nominal tariff to its pre-reform level, and provides a summary measure of liberalization: a ratio above unity implies an increase in average nominal tariffs while a ratio below unity indicates the

*Table* 3.1 Measures of Trade Liberalizations in Africa

| Country | Average Nominal Tariff[1] Initial | Current | Ratio | Tariff Equivalents (Δ)[2] ER[3] | After | Recent |
|---|---|---|---|---|---|---|
| Côte d'Ivoire (1981, 1989) | 26 | 33 | 1.27 | CFA | –15.6 | –15.9 |
| Ghana (1983, 1991) | 30 | 17 | 0.57 | –11.1 | –236.5 | –298.2 |
| Kenya (1980, 1992) | 40 | 34 | 0.85 | –5.4 | 34.1 | 67.6 |
| Madagascar (1985, 1990) | 46 | 36 | 0.78 | –11.2 | –46.8 | –73.5 |
| Nigeria (1983, 1990) | 35 | 33 | 0.93 | –71.2 | –92.3 | –107.1 |
| Senegal (1982, 1991) | 98 | 90 | 0.92 | CFA | 20.2 | 1.0 |
| Tanzania (1986, 1992) | 30 | 33 | 1.10 | –145.2 | –114.9 | –114.9 |

*Notes:* Years given in parenthesis are pre-reform and current.
1. Unweighted average nominal tariff, rounded; Ratio is Current/Pre-Reform.
2. Percentage change in tariff equivalent of all restrictions on (non-fuel) imports relative to the three years before programme; 'After' refers to the three years after initiation of programme, 'Recent' to the most recent three years.
3. Percentage real exchange rate depreciation between the first year of reform and 1992.

*Source:* Derived from tables in Morrissey (1995a)

proportional reduction. As mentioned above, there are serious weaknesses with this measure. First, the unweighted *NRP* attaches heavy weight to the highest tariff rates, which cover very few goods and are often redundant, hence tends to be biased upwards. Second, as there is no distinction between input and output tariffs, the ratio may not even be positively correlated with changes in effective protection. Third, it does not account for quantitative restrictions which are often significantly reduced under trade liberalization. However, it is one of the easiest measures to obtain which is perhaps why it has been employed in international negotiations (such as in GATT) and by the World Bank.

The final two columns of Table 3.1 give measures of the change in tariff equivalents (*TE*s) as defined above. These, albeit only estimated approximately, do account for changes in QRs in addition to (average) tariffs and as such should be superior to *NRP* measures (as defined above). It can be seen from Table 3.1 that in only three of the seven countries do the two measures yield the same implication for the direction of trade reform. On both criteria, Ghana, Madagascar and Nigeria did reduce trade restrictions (we can also note that they also devalued their currencies). Côte d'Ivoire and Tanzania would appear to have increased *NRP* but reduced *TE*s, consistent with the view that failing to allow for reductions in QRs could lead one not to recognize the true trade liberalization that occurred. This is certainly the case for Tanzania, which significantly liberalized its import regime and devalued (Morrissey, 1995b). The opposite applies for Kenya and Senegal; the former gained a reputation for lack of commitment and consistency in reform, while it seems that Senegal achieved little in either direction.[1]

A failure to devalue significantly suggests import liberalization without general export promotion, and is likely to have been revenue-depleting as lower tariffs applied to a relatively unchanged domestic currency price. Muñoz (1994) provides support for this reasoning, arguing that revenue loss is one explanation for the failure of so many Latin American countries to sustain reforms. Nash (1993: 31–39) uses a number of indicators, variables which should affect or reflect trade reform, to evaluate the implementation and impact of trade reforms. Of relevance here, he found that Ghana and Tanzania were among those with the largest real effective exchange rate devaluation and the largest reduction in the black market premium, indicating substantial liberalization of the foreign exchange system.

Nash (1993) makes the important observation that the major (binding) instruments of protection in most SSA countries were quantitative – exchange controls, import licences and restrictions. Consequently, tariff reductions and other tax/subsidy liberalizations may often have had little impact on true effective protection if the binding constraints remained in place. For SSA, more so than elsewhere, removal of quantitative controls is essential to eliminate the anti-export bias, but SSA actually had a poorer record on implementing 'critical' trade policy reforms than had other regions both in terms of speed and extent (Nash, 1993: 27). This poor record, the frequency of 'backsliding' on exchange rate liberalization and the tendency for tariff reforms to precede removal of restrictions, given the redundancy of tariffs, helps to explain the weak export response to adjustment in SSA. This reinforces the point that changes in nominal tariffs will not proxy changes in effective protection very well, but changes in tariff equivalents may.

## 3.4 TRUE PROTECTION AND IMPLICIT TAXATION OF EXPORTS

It is evident from the discussion so far that protection is a relative concept, and that by implication trade liberalization strictly requires a general rather than partial equilibrium framework within which to measure changes in relative prices. Of course one can infer something about changes in relative prices from a comparison of the average rate of (nominal or effective) protection in the import substitution sector with that in the export sector over time. But this is an indirect approach and one that may be data intensive, especially if measured at several points in time. A direct approach to measuring summary changes in relative prices, and one that has been used by a number of researchers, involves the measurement of changes in the relative price of tradables in terms of non-tradables. Such an approach yields a true protection measure (Greenaway and Milner, 1987). Alternatively, the change in the relative price of tradables can be expressed in terms of the real exchange rate (Milner and McKay, 1996). Both approaches take the price of non-tradables as the reference point, i.e. there is 'true' protection if trade policy interventions actually raise the price of tradables relative to the price of non-tradables. Thus a positive true tariff (actual depreciation of the real exchange rate for importables, *M*) or positive true subsidy (actual depreciation of the real exchange rate for exportables, *X*) requires that the nominal increase in the price of the tradable good following policy intervention exceeds any increase in the price of non-tradables (*N*) that is induced by substitution or complementarity effects between tradables and non-tradables. Thus the true rate of protection (*TRP*) is:

$$TRP_i = \Delta\left({}^{P_i}\!\big/_{P_N}\right) \tag{3.6}$$

where $P_N$ = price of non-tradeables
$P_i$ = price of tradeable good $i$ [$i = M$ or $X$]

For convenience, and setting initial relative prices to unity, the true rate of protection can be written as.

$$TRP_i = \frac{NRP_i \hat{P}_N}{1 + \hat{P}_N} \tag{3.7}$$

where $\hat{P}_N$ = endogenous and proportionate adjustment of $P_N$ following trade policy intervention.

Given substitutability in production and/or consumption between tradables and non-tradables and homogeneity properties for the general equilibrium model of the determination of non-tradables prices, then increases in nominal protection of tradables will tend to drive up the price of non-tradables (i.e. $\hat{P}_N > 0$). Further, $\hat{P}_N$ will be a weighted average of the increase in the price of each tradable:

$$\hat{P}_N = wNRP_M + (1 - w)NRP_X \tag{3.8}$$

where $w$ = an index of substitutability between $M$ and $N$.

In this case of substitutability and a positive relationship between the prices of tradables and non-tradables ($0 < w < 1$), true protection rates are always lower than nominal protection rates (i.e., $TRP_I < NRP_I$). Further $TRP_I \gtrless 0$ according to the pattern of trade policy intervention. If there is only protection of importables through import barriers ($NRP_M > 0$ and $NRP_X = 0$), then true protection of importables will be positive (albeit less than nominal protection) but true protection of exportables must be negative; the price of non-tradables rising in response to the rise in price of importables.[2] This relative disprotection of exportables might be offset by protecting exportables (e.g. through export subsidization), but the effect of this will be to raise the price of non-tradables further. True protection of importables will fall further, therefore, as true protection of exportables rises (becomes less negative) in response to greater nominal protection of exportables. As examination of (3.8) shows, however, the logic of this is that once the nominal rates of protection of both tradable goods is equalized, the true rate of protection of both tradables will have converged on zero. Uniform nominal promotion of both tradables is like free trade in the sense that the structure of relative prices is identical once the price of non-tradables has endogenously adjusted.

In order to measure true protection, we can see from (3.7) and (3.8) that we need information on nominal protection ($NRP_i$) and on substitution relationships between tradables and non-tradables. The measurement of $NRP_i$ is discussed in earlier sections. We concentrate here on the index of substitutability ($w$). All of the existing work, rather than trying to estimate the individual demand and supply elasticities which determine the overall index of substitutability, has sought to infer the overall index from time series regression analysis of movements in relative prices of tradables/non-tradables. An equation of the following general form has typically been estimated:

$$\ln\left(P_N / P_x\right) = a + b \ln\left(P_M / P_x\right) + u \tag{3.9}$$

where $u$ is the error term and $b$ provides an estimate of the index of substitution ($w$). Issues relating to the selection of time periods, construction of the price indices ($P_i$), and to estimation procedures are discussed in Greenaway and Milner (1993).

Given that data for consumer or producer prices may be more readily available and reliable than many other economic series in the case of low income developing countries, there is now (although the methodology is of fairly recent vintage) a reasonable amount of evidence on the estimation of $w$ (and therefore true protection) in the case of Africa. Table 3.2 summarizes the results for a number of African economies. In all cases the estimated index of substitutability lies between zero and unity, in line with prior expectations. The range of values, from 0.52 to 0.81, indicates a fairly high degree of substitutability between importables and non-tradables for this set of African economies. This is consistent with economies with exportables sectors dominated by traditional and resource-intensive activities, which are not highly substitutable with non-tradables. Even in the case of non-traditional, manufacturing exportables there may be low substitutability with non-tradables if goods are predominantly aimed at export markets and use a technology associated with foreign investment. As a result, true protection of importables in such economics will tend to be significantly lower than nominal protection. Similarly with low or zero nominal protection of exportables, a high estimate for $w$ (i.e. greater

*Table 3.2* Estimates of Substitution Indices ($w$) for Africa

| | Dates | ($w$) | Source |
|---|---|---|---|
| Cameroon | 1976–87(Q) | 0.81 | Milner (1990) |
| Côte d'Ivoire | 1960–84 (A) | 0.55 | Greenaway (1989) |
| Mauritius | 1976–82 (M) | 0.71 | Greenaway and Milner (1986) |
| Madagascar | 1974–84 (M) | 0.69 | Milner (1992) |
| Nigeria | 1960–82 (A) | 0.55 | Oyejide (1986) |
| Uganda | 1989–90 (M) | 0.66 | Maxwell Stamp (1993) |
| Zaire | 1970–82 (A) | 0.52 | Tshibaka (1986) |

*Notes:* A = Annual; Q = Quarterly; M = Monthly.

responsiveness of non-tradables prices) implies greater true 'taxing' or more true disprotection of exportables.

In Table 3.3 we report some comparisons of nominal and true protection estimates for a sub-set of the economies listed in Table 3.1, for which estimates of the substitution index (or shift parameter as it is sometimes described in the literature) are available in Table 3.2. In

*Table* 3.3 Nominal and True Protection in African Economies[1]

| | Nominal Protection (%)[2] | | True Protection (%)[3] | |
|---|---|---|---|---|
| | Importables | Exportables[4] | Importables | Exportables |
| Côte d'Ivoire | | | | |
| (1981) | 26 | 0 | 10.2 | –12.5 |
| (1989) | 33 | 0 | 12.6 | –15.4 |
| Change in *TE*[5] | | | Change in True Protection | |
| After Reform | –15.6 | 0 | –7.7 | +9.4 |
| Madagascar | | | | |
| (1985) | 46 | 0 | 10.8 | –24.1 |
| (1990) | 36 | 0 | 8.9 | –19.9 |
| Change in *TE*[5] | | | Change in True Protection | |
| After Reform | –46.8 | 0 | –21.4 | +47.7 |
| Nigeria | | | | |
| (1983) | 35 | 0 | 13.2 | –16.1 |
| (1990) | 33 | 0 | 12.6 | –15.4 |
| Change in *TE*[5] | | | Change in True Protection | |
| After Reform | –92.3 | 0 | –84.4 | +103.1 |

*Notes:*

1. The overlapping set of countries from Table 3.1 and 3.2.
2. Values taken from Table 3.1.
3. Estimated from equations (3.6) and (3.7) using substitution indices reported in Table 3.2; estimates of true protection are based on the estimates of nominal protection and can be compared with those.
4. For simplicity we assume that there is zero nominal subsidization and taxation of non-traditional exports
5. Change in tariff equivalents (*TE*) associated with tariff and non-tariff reductions reported in Table 3.1 in 'After' column. Estimates of *change* in true protection are based on change in *TE* and can be compared with those, but are not related to the estimated level of true protection on importables and exportables.

order to illustrate the principles described above, we report both the changes in the level of nominal protection indicated by tariff levels and the change in the tariff-equivalent (*TE*) of tariff and non-tariff barriers associated with trade policy reform in Côte d'Ivoire, Madagascar and Nigeria. Note, and in line with expectations, that true protection (including of importables) is always lower than nominal protection. Trade policy interventions push up the price of tradables, which in turn pulls up the price of non-tradables and gives less relative or true protection than indicated by a nominal measure of trade policy. Indeed true (tariff) protection of importables is lower in Madagascar (at both the start and end dates) than in Nigeria, even though nominal protection is higher in Madagascar. This is the result of the higher substitution or shift index in Madagascar (Table 3.2).

This greater responsiveness of the price of non-tradables means that the 'taxing' effect of import protection on exportables is also greater in Madagascar than Nigeria, even though the nominal rate of protection for exportables is (or is assumed to be) zero for both countries. In 1990 the true rate of protection of exportables is −15.4 per cent in Nigeria and −19.9 per cent in Madagascar; negative 'true' subsidization representing the implicit rate of taxation of exportables. Indeed the true protection rates for exportables are negative for all countries pre- and post-reform, as they must be if there is a positive substitution index and positive nominal subsidization of importables only. For constant substitution conditions, the implicit rate of export 'taxation' will only be lowered by lowering import barriers. As Table 3.3 shows the negative true subsidy (taxation of exportables) falls in Madagascar and Nigeria as nominal protection of importables falls, but it increases in the case of Côte d'Ivoire as average tariffs rose between 1981 and 1989.

The above discussion of Table 3.3 illustrates the principles and value of true protection measures of trade barriers or trade liberalization. But as mentioned earlier in this chapter, tariff barriers are a very inadequate measure of nominal protection where non-tariff barriers are pervasive. We report in Table 3.3 therefore on the 'true' effects of the lowering of tariff-equivalents of both tariff and non-tariff barriers for the same three countries. In all three cases the effects of trade liberalization are clear. The lowering of nominal protection of importables lowers true protection or subsidization of importables, albeit by less than the nominal reduction. The more marked effect, however, is on the exportables side. The fall in the price of non-tradables that will be induced in the long term by import liberalization raises the relative price of exportables dramatically. The rise in the true protection rate of exportables, ranging from +9.4 per cent in Côte d'Ivoire to +103.1 per cent in Nigeria, indicates the decline in the true or implicit taxation of exportables as trade regime or anti-export bias is reduced. It must be emphasized, however, that the increases in true protection of exportables reported here capture the effects of a decline in the rate of 'taxation', i.e. true disprotection of exportables is becoming less negative. The elimination of the 'tax' on exports or of anti-export bias requires full import liberalization, in the absence of explicit export subsidization.

## 3.5 INFRASTRUCTURE AND INSTITUTIONS

The design and implementation of trade reforms has typically not recognized the complementarities of policy, institutions and infrastructural barriers to exporting. Policy reform is often deemed to have taken place if a minimum compliance score is reached, without verifying that real incentives to exporters have been created. Investment often falls during adjustment, even though incentives require complementary investment. If sequenced at all, institutional reforms come late in the programme, but for lasting export response support institutions need to be in place. While little work has been done to identify the relative importance and complementary nature of different barriers, we can illustrate how these factors impact on the interpretation of measures of trade liberalization.

Clearly, the availability of institutional support, such as marketing and legal information or export insurance, and the transactions costs of obtaining support are important for encouraging a dynamic export sector. While reforms establishing institutions cannot be quantified, one can ascertain whether or not supports are in place. Similarly, the standard of infrastructure, including costs of services provided and costs attributable to poor provision, such as late delivery of inputs or interruption of electricity supply, is clearly important but not readily quantifiable. It is likely to be the case that such constraints have a more severe impact on exporters than import-competing firms, both because the latter are protected and because the former may be more likely to source raw materials from more remote parts of the country. Following the effective protection literature a summary measure of the importance of infrastructural barriers can be developed:

$$e_j = \frac{(-\hat{t}_j) - \sum_{i=1}^{n} a_{ij}\hat{t}_i}{1 - a_{ij}} \tag{3.10}$$

where

- $e_j$ effective disprotection equivalent of non-policy inefficiencies associated with exporting activity $j$ (assuming zero direct export taxes/subsidies).
- $a_{ij}$ share of input $i$ in production of $j$ (derived from technology information at enterprise level survey).
- $\hat{t}_j$ avoidable 'tax' associated with the inefficiencies in moving goods $j$ to export markets (derived from information from enterprises on actual costs less costs of comparator cases).
- $\hat{t}_i$ trade policy costs on inputs $i$ (e.g. tariffs) and avoidable costs in gaining delivery of inputs $i$ (trade policy distortions can be measured from official/customs sources, and from information reported by enterprises; non-tariff costs estimated by deviation of fob prices from world prices; excess costs due to non-policy barriers estimated from information provided by enterprises).

There may be interaction between trade taxes ($t$) and other export barrier costs ($c$) such that (as import taxes are imposed on cif value): $\hat{t}_i = t_i + (1 + t_i)c_i$. Hence the results of measuring disprotection due to barriers can be used to: i) identify the inputs to exporting activities where there is the greatest scope for reducing constraints; ii) identify which export activities would benefit most from improved infrastructure and institutional support; iii) provide a basis for identifying the types of first-best policies, such as expenditure priorities or administrative reforms, required to reduce non-policy barriers. The research would also permit some ranking of 'second best' policies; e.g. the allocations of expenditure that will reduce disprotection to exports by the most. Data on infrastructural constraints may be difficult to obtain, but a comprehensive measure of the impact of trade policy reforms on relative incentives and of the compatibility of non-trade policies with incentives to export, demands that attempts be made to allow for institutional and infrastructural constraints.

We can illustrate the importance of such information, by reporting on some preliminary work by Milner (1997) on the relative magnitude of policy and natural barriers to export in the case of Uganda, a land-locked country. The information on the nominal rates of 'taxation' associated with institutional/infrastructural barriers are taken from a study on foreign investment and trade in services in East Africa (World Bank, 1994). The study concludes that the inefficiencies in transit opportunities for Ugandan exports and imported inputs associated with inefficiencies in rail and road freight facilities and bureaucratic arrangements through Tanzania and Kenya are equivalent to an average seven per cent 'tax' on trade values.

Further, the study argues that the weakly capitalized and uncompetitive banking system in Uganda means that the costs of trade financing are on average twenty per cent higher as a result of this inefficiency. Applying information on trade barriers and technological coefficients used in conventional effective protection analysis, the level of effective protection or disprotection for exportables arising from policy-barriers can be estimated using a formula on the lines of (3.3). This can then be compared with an estimate of the level of effective disprotection associated with natural barriers, using (3.10) and the above estimates of the nominal costs caused by institutional/ infrastructural efficiencies.

Some estimates for Uganda applying this type of methodology are reported in Table 3.4. It is immediately evident that infrastructural barriers are a much more important source of effective disprotection or implicit taxation of exports than trade policy barriers. The average level of effective taxation (for the sample activities) arising from infrastructural barriers is −88.9 per cent compared with −15.6 per cent for trade policy barriers. Indeed infrastructural barriers are on average a more important source of effective disprotection across all activities. It should be noted also that the range of effective 'tax' rates is much higher in the case of infrastructural barriers than policy barriers and this, despite the fact that uniform rates of nominal taxation arising from infrastructural barriers are assumed across the sample. The non-uniformity of effective disprotection is explained by differences in technological characteristics, i.e. differences in dependence on traded inputs across activities. Clearly for some activities the lowering of policy-barriers to exports is unlikely to induce an export supply response, unless trade policy reform is accompanied by measures to lower infrastructural barriers.

## 3.6 CONCLUSIONS

In this chapter we have reviewed various ways in which the implementation of trade reforms (whether price, regulatory or institutional) have been measured, beginning with the most simple measures and progressing through to more sophisticated (and data-intensive) approaches. We have argued that much of the evaluation literature has used unsuitable measures. The most simple measure,

*Table* 3.4 Effective 'Taxation' of Exports in Uganda (1994)

| Activity* | Policy Barriers Only | Infrastructural Barriers Only |
|---|---|---|
| Assembly – electrical/electronic | –0.042 to –0.274 | –0.860 to –0.528 |
| Brewing | –0.243 | –0.796 |
| Clothing | –0.381 | –2.472 |
| Dairy products | –0.487 | –0.497 |
| Fish processing | –0.094 | –1.008 |
| Footwear | –0.015 | –0.124 |
| Grain milling | –0.258 | –2.999 |
| Horticulture | –0.211 | –0.212 |
| Leather | –0.022 | –0.399 |
| Light engineering | –0.091 | –1.063 |
| Misc. manufacture | –0.231 | –0.540 |
| Paints | –0.052 | –2.611 |
| Paper products | –0.265 | –0.704 |
| Plastic products | –0.024 | –0.127 |
| Soft drinks | –0.188 | –0.730 |
| Sugar | –0.174 | –0.524 |
| Timber processing | –0.009 | –0.793 |
| Tobacco products | –0.107 | –1.112 |
| Tyres | –0.103 | –0.570 |
| Average (unweighted) | –0.156 | –0.889 |

* These are estimates for a sample of enterprises or activities within each of the listed sectors.
*Source:* Milner (1997).

compliance indices, does little more than ask if a reform was attempted or not and is unsuitable for capturing the extent or potential effect of reform. Conventional summary measures of trade reform based on the concepts of nominal and effective protection are useful and in general strongly indicative of the relative price effects of trade reform, although the data requirements can be great and the measures may not be entirely reliable. General equilibrium issues can be incorporated explicitly to consider how relative prices might be affected by utilizing true protection concepts and real exchange rates. We also outlined how other factors, such as infrastructural and institutional constraints, relevant to trade reform can be incorporated into protection-based measures.

To evaluate the effect of policy reform it is necessary to have as accurate a measure as possible of the reform implemented, and the measure should be one that captures the impact of the reform (in particular, the effect on relative prices). Different measures can give very different results: we showed that in only three of seven countries did nominal protection and tariff equivalent measures yield the same implication for even the direction of trade reform, never mind attempting to evaluate the magnitude of trade liberalization. Consequently, one must try to use the measure that is most desirable on *a priori* grounds. In general, this will be the theoretically preferred measure, but one must restrict attention to concepts that can be measured (i.e. allowance must be made for data availability). A policy analyst should be aware of which measures are least reliable, usually the most simple to obtain, and if not eschewing their use should at least attach strong caveats. If evaluating reform, the first stage should be to identify the desired measure and then proceed to collect the data required to calculate it. We have argued for true protection concepts and have demonstrated that they can be calculated, and can be extended to incorporate infrastructural and institutional constraints (and thus, more importantly, to accommodate the impact of reforms which relax such constraints). We have used trade liberalization in African economies to illustrate our arguments, but they are more general: economic policy reforms affect relative prices, thus to evaluate reforms one must strive to measure the effect on relative prices.

There are a number of general implications. First, as the data requirements for a suitable measure of the impact of reforms on relative prices are quite demanding, we advocate detailed country case-studies. This is even more important if one wishes to incorporate the complementary effects of investment in infrastructure, institutions and non-trade barriers. Second, as simple measures are often misleading (and the more simple the more likely they are to be misleading), one should be very careful in interpreting the existing evidence on the extent of trade liberalization. It is quite probable that many studies over-estimate the amount of actual liberalization, in the sense of increasing the relative incentive to exporting, that has been achieved. Finally, we reiterate that the important issue is not what reforms have been attempted but what effects the reforms have actually had, and that is best measured in terms of changes in some relative prices.

## Notes

* The work on which this chapter is based, especially the final section, formed part of a CREDIT research project on 'Infrastructural and Institutional Constraints to Export Promotion for Private Enterprise', as part of the Trade and Enterprise Research Programme (DFID Research Grant CNTR 96 0494A). The authors are grateful to DFID for supporting the research.

1. Note that as *TE* refers to an unexplained residual that is approximated, a change in *TE* of above 100 per cent does not imply a reversal of trade policy stance. A technical problem with the measure is that the actual size of the residual may change for factors unrelated to trade policy. Nevertheless, the direction and size of *TE* is indicative of trade policy reform.
2. Of course there may be explicit taxation of some exports, for example traditional crops such as coffee or cocoa. The nominal tax rate will also in this case understate the true tax rate.

## References

Corbo, V., S. Fischer and S. Webb (eds) (1992), *Adjustment Lending Revisited: Policies to Restore Growth*, Washington, DC: The World Bank.

Corbo, V. and P. Rojas (1992), 'World Bank-Supported Adjustment Programs: Country Performance and Effectiveness', Chapter 3 in Corbo *et al.* (1992), pp. 23–39.

Dean, J., S. Desai and J. Riedel (1994), 'Trade Policy Reform in Developing Countries since 1985: A Review of the Evidence', *World Bank Discussion Papers 267*, Washington, DC: The World Bank.

Foroutan, F. (1993), 'Trade Reform in Ten Sub-Saharan African Countries: Achievements and Failures', *Policy Research WPS 1222*, Washington, DC: The World Bank.

Greenaway, D. (1989), 'Commercial Policy and Policy Conflict: An Evaluation of the Incidence of Protection in a Non-industrialized Economy', *Manchester School*, 57, 125-41.

Greenaway, D. and C.R. Milner (1986), 'Estimating the Shifting of Protection Across Sectors: An Application to Mauritius', *Industry and Development*, 16, pp. 1–23.

Greenaway, D. and C.R. Milner (1987), 'True Protection Concepts and Their Evaluation of Trade and Industrial Policies in Developing Countries', *Journal of Development Studies*, 23, pp. 200–219.

Greenaway, D. and C.R. Milner (1993), *Trade and Industrial Policy in Developing Countries*, London: Macmillan.

Greenaway, D. and O. Morrissey (1994), 'Trade Liberalization and Economic Growth in Developing Countries', in S.M. Murshed and K. Raffer (eds), *Trade Transfers and Development*, London: Edward Elgar, pp. 210–232.

Maxwell Stamp (1993), *Study of the Effectiveness of Policies, Facilities and Incentives for Investment Promotion in Uganda*, London: Maxwell Stamp.

Milner, C. (1990), 'Identifying and Quantifying Anti-Export Bias: The Case of Cameroon', *Weltwirtschaftliches Archiv*, 126, pp. 142–55.

Milner, C. (1992), 'Short and Long Run True Protection: The Case of Madagascar', *Applied Economics*, 24, 257–63.

Milner, C. (1996), 'Discovering the Truth about Protection Rackets', *The World Economy*, 19, 517–32.

Milner, C. (1997), 'On Natural and Policy-Induced Sources of Protection and Trade Regime Bias', *Weltwirtschaftliches Archiv*, 132, pp. 740–752.

Milner, C. and A. McKay (1996), 'Real Exchange Rate Measures of Trade Liberalization: Evidence for Mauritius', *Journal of African Economies*, 5, 69–91.

Morrissey, O. (1995a), 'Politics and Economic Policy Reform: Trade Liberalization in sub-Saharan Africa', *Journal of International Development*, 7:4, pp. 599–618.

Morrissey, O. (1995b), 'Political Commitment, Institutional Capacity and Tax Policy Reform in Tanzania', *World Development*, Vol. 23 (4), pp. 637–649.

Morrissey, O. (1995c), 'Compliance and Conditionality: The Sustainability of Adjustment in Turkey', in O. Stokke (ed.), *Aid and Political Conditionality*, London: Frank Cass for EADI, pp. 295–321.

Mosley, P., J. Harrigan and J. Toye (1991), *Aid and Power: The World Bank and Policy-Based Lending*, two vol, London: Routledge.

Mosley, P. and J. Hudson (1995), *Aid Effectiveness: A study of the effectiveness of overseas aid in the main countries receiving ODA assistance*, Draft Report to the Overseas Development Administration, London.

Muñoz, O. (1994), 'Toward Trade Opening: Legacies and Current Strategies', in Joan Nelson (ed), *Intricate Links: Democratization and Market Reforms in Latin America and Eastern Europe*, Washington, DC: Transactions Publishers and ODC, pp. 61–104.

Nash, J. (1993), 'Implementation of Trade Reform in Sub-Saharan Africa', *Policy Research Working Paper 1218*, Washington, DC: The World Bank.

Oyejide, T.A. (1986) *The Effects of Trade and Exchange Rate Policies on Agriculture in Nigeria*, Research Report 55, International Food Policy Research Institute, Washington, DC.

Tshibaka, T.B. (1986) *The Effects of Trade and Exchange Rate Policies on Agriculture in Zaire*, Research Report 56, International Food Policy Research Institute, Washington, DC.

Webb, S. and K. Shariff (1992), 'Designing and Implementing Adjustment Programs', in Corbo *et al.* (1992), pp. 69–91.

World Bank (1994), *Eastern Africa Survey of Foreign Investors*, Report prepared by Economisti Associati, World Bank Public Information Centre, Washington, DC.

# 4 Political Economy Dimensions of Economic Policy Reform

Oliver Morrissey*

## 4.1 INTRODUCTION

Assuming that the issues raised in the previous two chapters have been properly addressed and one has reliable measures and an accepted method of evaluating the impact of reforms, it remains difficult to establish why a set of reforms may appear to have failed. More generally, even if one has agreed criteria for establishing failure and success of reforms, there is still a problem in attributing causality. To allow us to focus on domestic politics, let us assume that external events have been controlled for, that the correct economic reforms were prescribed and that we can measure the degree of implementation. In such circumstances, observed failure of the reforms, in the sense that the expected improvements in economic outcomes have not occurred, can be attributed to incomplete implementation and/or inadequate responses (of agents to incentives, typically on the supply side). This chapter addresses the first of these, namely the reasons why implementation can be incomplete. We adopt a political economy approach, by which we mean we are concerned with the interface of politics and economics, rather than with politics and political systems *per se*. Political systems are clearly important, but attention here is confined to how economic considerations, especially the effect of reforms, influence politicians and their constituencies.

Implementation failure can arise for a number of reasons but there are three general possibilities. First, perhaps the government did not ever intend to implement reforms; this can be termed 'intentional slippage' and the specific purpose of conditionality is to avoid this possibility. Second, it is possible that the government was not politically strong enough to push through reforms in the face of opposition; such political constraints are widespread and not easily resolved (at least not by external agencies). Third, perhaps the government lacked the necessary administrative capability; donors can help relax administrative constraints by supporting institutional capacity-building. Which of these constraints is 'binding' will depend on the policy environment, the balance of political power in the country and the political (policy-making) and administrative (implementation) capacity available to the government. The aim of this chapter is to offer a means of classifying the policy environment, concentrating on political capacity (the second point above); White and Morrissey (1997) address failures of conditionality (the first point above), while Grindle and Thomas (1991) provide detail on administrative failures in implementation (the third point).

There is a large literature on the politics of economic policy reform, and this is not a review. Many writers consider the political constraints on a government's ability to implement reforms (e.g. Frey and Eichenberger, 1994; Haggard and Webb, 1993; Morrissey, 1995b; Nelson, 1994), while others focus more on the role of institutions and administrative capacity (e.g. Grindle and Thomas, 1991; Levy, 1993; Morrissey, 1995a, 1995b; Sandbrook, 1996). Originating from this literature, our thesis is that development economists should be aware of the political and institutional features (the policy environment) characterizing the liberalizing economy (LE) under study. Awareness of the policy environment permits an informed advisor to design reform programmes that are more likely to succeed. Often, this implies an argument for gradual, sequenced reform. More generally, the policy analyst should be familiar with the policy environment as it helps identify reasons why a reform programme failed or succeeded, facilitating better design of future reforms and a more informed evaluation of any particular liberalization episode.

While our arguments extend to economic reform in general, we will take most of our illustrative examples from trade and tax reforms (which are related as tariffs are an important source of tax revenue in most LEs). Trade reforms have the important feature of generating winners and losers quite quickly and transparently; the ability of these groups to convey their preferences (for or against reform) to the government will have an impact on political commitment to (sustaining) the reform process. Commitment depends on political capacity, the ability of the government to translate preferences into reform proposals, facilitated by its ability to mobilize support for reform (a coalition of winners) and to withstand, circumvent or compensate the opposition. Commitment, and the capacity to create it, is not enough: the policies must be implemented, turning commitment into reforms, which will depend on institutional, especially administrative, capacity.

Section 4.2 addresses political constraints, and considers how preferences combined with the political capacity of a government (to make and adopt policy) create a commitment to reform. Section 4.3 brings these issues together to offer classifications of alternative policy environments and the implications for the design of reform programmes. Section 4.4 concludes, and extends the discussion to consider broader dimensions of politics and institutions.

## 4.2 IDENTIFYING POLITICAL CONSTRAINTS

It will facilitate discussion if we restrict 'government' to refer to the set of ruling politicians who are policy-makers (and may or may not be democratically chosen), and 'administration' to the arms of government that implement policy. Thus, we will talk about government as making and adopting policy, but not implementing (as this requires the administration). Policy-making will depend on factors such as dialogue and balance of power within government, and the quality of technocrats involved in this process (as distinct from those involved in implementation – the distinction may encompass the same individuals, but refers to different functions). Adoption of policy is intended to refer to the political process in which a government reveals the policies it intends to implement. Examples of such processes would be parliamentary debates, ministerial proclamations, national committees (e.g. trade unions or employers groups may be consulted). It can be the case that structural adjustment programmes (SAPs) represent policies adopted but not made by a government, in the sense that the policy design was by the World Bank (or some other donor granting external funds conditional on adoption of the reforms); as we will show this may not be a constraint provided the government agrees with the policy programme.

A number of political considerations will influence governments in determining which policies to adopt (summarized in Table 4.1 below). Foremost of these, a government has to want to undertake the reform in question. It may reach this decision because it believes, on the basis of the arguments and evidence, that it is the best thing for the country. It may also be the case that a new government has a political commitment to reform. In either of these cases, the perceived need for reform may be a reaction to a crisis. External influences, especially the World Bank in respect of countries in need of external financing, can be persuasive in prompting a government to undertake reforms (and can be supportive where the government lacks the technical capacity for detailed policy-making). The central issue here, and the first question the analyst can ask of the politics, is what are the government's preferences (towards each specific element of a reform programme)?

In addressing preferences, one wants to gauge how the reforms will affect the (economic and political) interests of members of the government. For example, if members of the cabinet are large landowners one may question their desire for (uncompensated) land reform, or if they have interests in protected industries they will be reluctant to liberalize the import regime (or if they do, may retain sectoral protection). This lies at the root of observations that established regimes tend to be less likely to initiate major liberalization – they have vested interests they will want to protect. The attempt to gauge government preferences for reform is a useful exercise, if only as an indicator of which areas of reform are most feasible, and which are least likely to find favour. A number of scenarios are worth distinguishing. For illustrative purposes we will consider four regime forms: established political; established technocratic; new ideological; and new reformist.

The notion of an established political regime is intended for those governments that are in power to represent particular interests, be they political (such as particular tribes or classes) or economic (such as landowners); frequently the vested interests have combined the political and economic. African countries such as Kenya fall in this group, as do political regimes associated with a personality (Zambia under Kaunda and Tanzania under Nyerere; Marcos' Philippines may also fit); so too do many Central American regimes (El Salvador and pre-Sandinista Nicaragua). Such regimes are unlikely to embrace reforms that weaken their vested interests (power base), Kenya being a case in point. These countries provide a particular problem for SAPs: how does one impose conditions on a regime with a political interest in intentional slippage? We do not propose to resolve this dilemma, merely to observe that such regimes represent a set of preferences that are not conducive to liberalizing reforms; White and Morrissey (1997) demonstrate that conditionality will not be effective in promoting reform in such cases.

History shows that established regimes can reform, often quite dramatically, and our suggestion is that such regimes are technocratic in nature. Although vested interests exist, in a technocratic regime they are at least balanced by a desire to maximise the performance of the economy, and the latter is guided by technical arguments emphasizing management and economic efficiency. It follows that capacity building as a means to transform political into technocratic regimes is also a means of facilitating reform. Such regimes are more likely to embrace liberalization if they are convinced by the arguments that liberal policies will improve economic performance. South East Asian economies such as South Korea and Thailand seem to fit into this group, as do Mauritius and Costa Rica. In this type of regime, preferences are conducive to reform; given that technocratic regimes are likely to have good administrative capacity, successful reformers are often found in this group. We can also note that the economic policy technocrats, those in Finance and Planning Ministries and the Central Bank, are often found to have been US-trained and to have worked in Washington with either the Bank or Fund.

A special feature of the South East Asian economies is that they maintained strict and stable macroeconomic policies (the stabilization element of SAPs) but usually had many microeconomic distortions. Examples include widespread government intervention in the operation of markets, including protection and regulation (thus, these regimes did not fully adopt the liberalization element of SAPs). Rodrik (1996) suggests a number of reasons why South Korea and Taiwan were able to maintain microeconomic distortions without allowing rent-seeking to emerge and constrain economic performance (as appears to have happened in Latin American and African countries). The regimes had strong and technocratic governments and, perhaps more importantly, initially had relatively high levels of human capital and a relatively equitable distribution of income. Taken together, this permitted them to design, adopt and implement policies that focused on improving economic performance, and there was less pressure on governments to serve vested interests. Vartiainen (1996) points out that both countries faced real external military threats and argues convincingly that this reinforced the efficiency of State-led economic policy.

Just as one can try to distinguish types of established regime more likely to embrace liberalization so too will the preferences of new regimes differ. Some are new reformist almost by nature (such as the Central European states immediately following the collapse of communism), others are persuaded to adopt liberalization (such as Ghana by the mid-1980s and Uganda by the early 1990s). Others are new ideological, opposed to economic liberalization on principle (as would seem to apply to fundamentalist regimes such as Iran or Sudan). Much depends on how the new regime emerges. Some respond to the collapse of an autocracy such that the new regime has power before it has formed policies, and may be encouraged to adopt liberalization

(Uganda and Ethiopia in the 1990s). In others the new regime won an election on a reformist platform (such as Benazir Bhutto in Pakistan). There are no simple rules, but the policy analyst should be aware of the background of the government.

We do not claim that all regimes can be classified as one of the four types suggested, most countries probably fall or move between types, but suggest indicators of which governments are more likely to have preferences for reform than others.[1] This in itself is not a predictor of which governments will adopt liberalization, as government attempts to realize their preferences will depend on perceptions of the preferences, strengths and reactions of other groups that will be affected by the reforms. A particular problem is that the reforms associated with SAPs typically involve the removal of protection or rents from a clearly defined and often relatively small but powerful group, whereas the benefits of liberalization are likely to be spread (thinly) across many groups and may only accrue in the future contingent on successful reform. Put simply, losses are certain but benefits are often elusive, so it is difficult to build political support for reform to offset the opposition. This problem is often exacerbated by the tendency of stabilization measures to impose immediate losses on much of the population, with future benefits uncertain (for an informative analysis of this dilemma see Frey and Eichenberger, 1994).

A further problem of great relevance to government preferences is the likely fiscal impact of reforms. In the context of SAPs, it is often the case that governments are expected to reduce budget deficits, yet they have limited scope to cut expenditure or increase tax revenue (as mentioned in Chapter 1 above). Generally, social sector expenditures are to be maintained and the two major remaining areas of recurrent spending are interest payments (which governments may be required to meet) and the wage bill. In practice, the wage bill is cut both through unemployment and reduced real public sector wages; this generates resistance but the opposition is rarely effective (however, administrative capacity may be reduced). The scope to increase tax revenue is limited: in many cases the private sector is very small, so the base for income and profits tax is narrow; the sales tax base is narrow; and there is often heavy dependence on trade taxes, but trade liberalization demands tariff cuts. One implication is that trade and tax reforms should be sequenced so that they are not revenue-depleting (Morrissey, 1995b). Another implication is that countries with a narrow tax base, such as African economies, will be more concerned about the fiscal impact of reforms than, say, East Asian economies; this will also be an influence on government preferences.

It follows that even a government with a preference for reform will not automatically adopt (politically risky) liberal reformist policies. The willingness to attempt reform will be constrained by political and institutional capacity, the former reflecting its perceived ability to push through reforms, the latter being, in particular, the ability of the administration to implement the reforms required. A government with weak preferences needs to be encouraged and supported to adopt reformist policies (donors negotiating conditionality can help here). A government lacking evident preferences for reform is unlikely to comply with conditionality; SAPs are inappropriate under such circumstances, and if donors wish to grant aid it should be under some other criteria (e.g. humanitarian). Identifying the preferences is only the first element of the policy analysts 'political checklist' of questions: the full range of political dimensions to be addressed, and how they are linked, is outlined in Table 4.1.

*Table* 4.1 Political Dimensions of the Policy Reform Process

| Dimension | Principal Features |
|---|---|
| A. Preferences | Do individuals in the government benefit from reform?<br>Which groups benefit and lose from reform? |
| B. Political capacity | i) Ability to transform preferences into commitment<br>ii) Strength of opposition (attributability)<br>iii) Mobilization of support (appropriability) |
| C. Political commitment | Government support for and promotion of reform:<br>I No capacity or preference ⇒ weak/no commitment<br>II Capacity only ⇒ weak commitment (ownership?)<br>III Preference only ⇒ commitment (not open)<br>IV Capacity + preference ⇒ commitment + ownership |
| D. Administrative capacity | Determines effectiveness of implementation |
| E. Institutional capacity | Determines effectiveness of implementation |

Having identified preferences, one should consider political capacity, which depends on: i) the ability of the government to transform preferences into policy commitment, which reflects the nature of policy-making within government; ii) the strength of opposition to a particular reform and; iii) the ability of the government to mobilize support in favour of reform. These factors are related. If policy-making within government is relatively open, that is based on dialogue rather than dictat, there is scope for developing new policies and even for involving, or at least identifying, opposition and support in the policy-making process. This may be especially true if the policy-making dialogue includes technocrats. In deciding whether to support reforms the government will be concerned with relative opposition. This relates to what Frey and Eichenberger (1994) term 'attributability', to what extent is the government held responsible for effects of the reform (if the government can reduce attributability it can deflect opposition), and 'appropriability', the governments control over the allocation of resources (that can be used to mobilize support).

The government is less likely to be held responsible for the immediate costs of reform if it can blame a previous regime, one reason why new governments can have a honeymoon period (see Haggard and Webb, 1993). The same applies if it can blame exogenous shocks or external forces (sometimes it may be helpful for the IMF or World Bank to take the blame). Attributability is also lessened if public expectations are low, which may favour gradual reforms because 'big bang' reforms are often associated with high public expectations but adjustment costs can be pervasive. New regimes have a window of opportunity for reform when they can claim it is essential to undo the harm of a previous regime, whereas existing regimes may find it convenient to claim external forces compel them to undertake reforms. If adjustment costs persist or the benefits of reform are slow in materializing, attributability will begin to attach to the government. The continuity of reform then depends on the strength of the government (failed liberalization saw the restoration of communists to power in some Eastern European states, but Pinochet in Chile was able to oversee a long and often painful reform process).

Appropriability refers to the ability of the government to raise and distribute income, or allocate rents, to generate support. Governments are likely to have greater control over resources if the economy is relatively closed and highly regulated and/or there is a relatively developed tax system. Consequently, liberalization intended to deregulate and open the economy is likely to reduce appropriability, an obvious reason why government preferences may oppose reform (as it weakens their power; this combined with worry about the fiscal impact offers some insight into why so many African governments resist liberalization). Trade liberalization provides a good example. Reducing protection means reducing government control over the economy and reducing the rents available for allocation; a government attempting import liberalization constantly runs the risk of losing appropriability, hence being more vulnerable to opposition. This relates back to the types of regime we identified earlier: technocrats will be less concerned with appropriability than will 'political' regimes, while new regimes may see (successful) reform as their way of building support by having more resources to share.

The interactions of preferences and capacity permit us to try and identify the nature of political commitment – how openly and convincingly will the government adopt and promote reform? Political commitment is difficult to define as ideally one needs to know the true intentions of the government and its capacity to carry them through. Some observers (e.g. Levy, 1993) use 'announcement' as a proxy for commitment to a particular reform; however, one can imagine circumstances where a government is reluctant to declare its commitment (even if genuine), perhaps due to strong opposition or because it is unsure if the reforms will be successful. In such cases the government may not be willing to declare ownership; underlying commitment is not picked-up by a focus on publicly announced policies. One can also envisage situations where a government committed to reforms may allow external ownership so as to deflect attributability if worried about costs (for example, blaming the IMF); the government can benefit from success but minimize the political costs of failure.

Table 4.2 illustrates a number of possibilities. Terminology is difficult but we are seeking indicators of commitment. Announcement, which implies ownership, is sufficient but not necessary: willingness to declare intent will depend on political capacity.[2] If opposition is weak, and/or the government is relatively strong, the government would feel confident to declare ownership; the reverse also holds. Generally, if political capacity is high a government should be willing to declare ownership. This is especially true if preferences are high (favour reform), and may even be true if preferences are low (governments with weak commitment to reform may still make announcements because they want to receive conditional aid, and they have the capacity to renege on announcements and on conditionality). The latter is represented in cell II of Table 4.2. This 'cyclical' case refers to regimes,

*Table* 4.2 Identifying Political Commitment

| | | Political Capacity Low | High |
|---|---|---|---|
| Preferences | Weak | **I (inertia)**<br>weak commitment<br>no ownership<br>little potential<br>e.g. Bolivia, Malawi | **II (cyclical)**<br>weak commitment<br>possible ownership<br>need convincing<br>e.g. Kenya, Nigeria |
| | High | **III (conflict)**<br>commitment<br>external ownership<br>needs support<br>e.g. Ghana, Tanzania | **IV (effective)**<br>strong commitment<br>ownership<br>strong potential<br>e.g. Turkey, Mauritius |

such as Kenya in the 1980s and 1990s, that are politically strong but not committed to liberalization. Reforms are agreed as part of a SAP, the government gets external funding, it slips on conditionality, further funding is witheld, the agreement breaks down, then negotiations begin again, leading to a stop–go cycle of reforms that does the country no good (but the regime little harm). Regimes that are political rather than technocrat are likely to fall into this category, thus we could include Nigeria in the 1990s.

In this way we identify various levels of commitment (which in Table 4.1 correspond to the cells in Table 4.2). Cell IV is the preferred case conducive to 'effective' reform, where preferences are strong and the government has the capacity to propose reforms. Commitment will be strong and announced, as in these cases donors are often just supporting governments following their own reform programme (i.e. true ownership). Mauritius, South Korea, Thailand and Turkey are examples; all had relatively competent technocratic governments and were relatively successful cases of adjustment (although Turkey faces problems in the 1990s).[3] Cells II and IV both refer to regimes with political capacity; in such cases, reforms can be implemented if the government wants to.

Perhaps the most interesting cases are those where the government has limited or low capacity. Cell I represents a typical case of inertia: the regime has weak preferences and low capacity; under pressure from the Bank or Fund conditionality may be agreed but implementation will be limited and the SAP is likely to collapse. This would seem to apply to Bolivia, and perhaps Jamaica and Malawi (for discussions of these countries see Mosley *et al.*, 1991). Many countries may find themselves in the 'conflict' of cell III: the government has strong preferences but weak capacity, which may be due to a new inexperienced regime or a 'declining' established regime facing strong potential opposition. Cell III indicates the limitations that can face new regimes, for whom building capacity is the desired strategy (which implies a move from III to IV). Such regimes will have commitment but weak capacity may preclude a declaration of intent (or ownership, especially given that they will not have been able to fully design a reform programme of their own). Tanzania in the late 1980s and Pakistan in the 1990s are examples of governments that could fairly claim to have been constrained by limited political capacity. Ghana (when Rawlings took power) and Uganda (when Museveni won power) had limited capacity (and perhaps unformulated preferences) initially, but began to resolve conflicts and implement reforms, gradually moving towards cell IV.

There is a desired direction of progress through Table 4.2. Assuming the starting point is cell I, then the 'reform' path is I → III → IV, i.e. build preferences and then build capacity, so that effective reforms can be implemented.[4] This appears to have happened in Uganda as Museveni encouraged dialogue within the government and became convinced of the merits of liberalization (Harvey and Robinson, 1995). If governments are truly to own their reforms, in the sense of designing the reform programme themselves, then they must have preferences and require capacity, both to design the programme and commit themselves to it. Technical support can help in establishing the capacity to design and administer programmes. Once commitment exists, administrative and institutional capacity determine the ability to implement effective sustainable reforms.

We can illustrate the preceeding arguments in reference to trade reforms. A government is more likely to be committed to trade liberalization if opposition is weak, as this means attaching less weight to the preferences of anti-reformists. As trade liberalization tends to reduce appropriability, the government will wish to minimize any attributable losses at the early stages of reform. In cases where the public sector dominates the private sector, opposition to liberalization will tend to be strong and the potential loss of appropriability great, both of which undermine political capacity. Public sector employees, especially those in parastatals, and those gaining rents from government regulations are the first to lose from liberalization. To enhance its capacity, the government needs to build a consensus in favour of reform (and such attempts are a sign of commitment). Export promotion, for example, creates gainers in favour of liberalization. More generally, establishing a private sector is necessary to generate the political support for reform. Institution-building of this form poses a dilemma: on the one hand, a private sector will support reform and enhance political capacity; on the other, a private sector reduces appropriability, which weakens political capacity. This suggests that governments will benefit from complementary reforms, reducing public sector control in one area (e.g. import liberalization), while introducing new means of appropriability (e.g. increased tax collection efficiency) or, more generally, creating an environment in which the government facilitates the liberal economic regime which benefits the private sector.

An open reading of the literature suggests that radicalism and gradualism both have a place, and that much depends on the prevailing political situation. Following a new regime (whether a dictatorship or emergent democracy), attributability is muted and the public are willing to accept costs in the belief that they are temporary. Reforms in this period should be radical, as there is only a short 'window of opportunity' and it may be only ajar, but then an element of luck is needed. If stabilization is achieved quickly, the groundwork is laid for gradual and sustained liberalization and institution-building. If stabilization has not been achieved and/or major political dissatisfaction has been created, as in labour demands for wage increases, further reform may be impossible and reversals are likely. Insufficient is known about achieving effective radical reforms in honeymoon periods: Chile succeeded eventually; Brazil achieved much less (Muñoz, 1994). We do know that periods of normal politics are more likely to prevail, especially in the context of institutional change that takes a long period, and thus focus on policy reform when politics is operating.

## 4.3 THE POLICY ENVIRONMENT FOR REFORM

We have shown that many factors must be taken into consideration in trying to identify what commitment governments have to reform. However, even if governments adopt a reform to which they are openly committed there is no guarantee of successful implementation. As shown in Table 4.1, the implementation phase involves the administration (the officials who have to put the details of policy into effect) and institutions (the forms and norms of behaviour governing economic relationships) and may fail for many reasons. An obvious possibility is administrative constraints, which we consider in this section. Institutional constraints are also relevant: for example, privatization is constrained by the absence of a functioning financial sector; it takes time for private markets to develop and replace dismantled state marketing boards during agricultural sector liberalization. The basic point is that an economy which has been dominated (and distorted) by the public sector under a particular regime will have developed a set of institutions which are not conducive to establishing a more liberal economic regime. Liberalization also requires institutional change (see Section 4.4).

To identify the policy environment for reform, we can classify political commitment as either low, essentially where preferences are weak, or high, where preferences are strong (on the assumption that even if political capacity is weak, efforts are made to strengthen it). These are the political dimensions and categories 'high' and 'low' can also define the administrative dimensions. Both dimensions together define the policy environment. Note that this approach allows one to attempt to identify the prevailing policy environment in a country: what is the commitment for (particular policy) reforms and what is the ability to implement them? Some policies are politically and administratively easier to implement than others. Effective reform programmes are those which match reforms to the environment; if the environment is not appropriate to the specific reforms, one should aim to change the policy environment before trying to implement the reform. Specific reforms can be classified as either requiring greater or lesser capacity and commitment, and then one must study the country to identify the policy environment (which may differ according to the reform in question).

The framework linking political and administrative dimensions of the policy environment, applied to trade liberalization, is presented in Table 4.3 (following Morrissey, 1995a and 1995b). The four cells classify the policy environment according to political commitment and administrative capacity, the latter depending on the scope of reforms and the resources available to administrative units. Scope has two dimensions: the complexity or administrative difficulty of the reform, often associated with innovative reforms which require new skills; and the range or number of policy areas affected by the reform. Both are positively correlated with resource requirements, especially human capital. Wide-ranging complex reforms obviously require high capacity, and should not be attempted unless that capacity is in place. Narrow

*Table* 4.3 Policy Environment for Trade Liberalization

| | | Political Commitment | |
|---|---|---|---|
| | | Low (weak preference and capacity) | High (strong preference and capacity) |
| Administrative Capacity | Low (narrow, simple) | **I (minimal)**<br>Ease exchange restrictions<br>Export incentives | **II (innovative)**<br>Remove exemptions<br>Reduce tariffs<br>Devaluation |
| | High (wide, complex) | **III (incremental)**<br>Export incentives<br>Remove QRs | **IV (extensive)**<br>Rationalization<br>Full liberalization |

and simple reforms are feasible even if capacity is low. An appropriate objective of sequencing can be to keep the range of reforms narrow and increase complexity as capacity is expanded. Furthermore, the experience of implementing even simple narrow reforms can enhance the capacity for attempting more complex reforms, and helps to build political commitment (as success breeds success).

If a country has neither the desire nor capacity to commence reform (cell I) then any attempts will probably result in failure; the policy environment is conducive to minimal reforms only. The implication is that sustainable reform is not feasible and the policy environment must be changed before meaningful reform can be attempted. Some export incentives are relatively easy to provide, such as allowing retention of foreign exchange earnings or even tax rebates, and fit in this cell; they are easy to administer, do not require strong commitment and can help build support for reform. Similarly, easing exchange restrictions is easy to implement and can help build support for liberalization policies. A more general point is that if both commitment and capacity are low it is inadvisable to attempt wide-ranging complex reforms.

If commitment is high but capacity low (cell II), then feasible reforms are likely to be of the innovative (in the sense of altering the distribution of rents) or dismantling type, i.e. gradual reforms of limited scope which can have major implications, such as removal of regulations or reductions in taxes. Many import liberalization measures will fall under this cell as tariff cuts or eliminating the need for licences are relatively easy to administer provided the political will exists to over-ride opposition. Similarly, devaluation and the removal of tax exemptions are easy to administer but require very strong political commitment. If this is the policy environment, then administrative capacity is the constraint that must be relaxed if extensive reforms are to be implemented successfully.

If capacity is high but commitment low (cell III), there is potential for gradual incremental reforms, but the political system may not support innovative reforms (nor is it likely to support rapid dismantling because this is likely to create opposition from immediate losers). In such a situation the reforms attempted should be those which build commitment. This includes (administratively) sophisticated export incentives, such as providing market information, export credit insurance, legal and marketing advice, which helps establish an export lobby in favour of an outward-oriented trade policy stance. Another example would be removing QRs and replacing them with tariffs; this is welfare-improving in economic terms and revenue-enhancing, especially if the tariff structure is properly designed, and does not require strong commitment as protection is only partly dismantled.

Cell IV is the objective, where extensive reforms can be implemented successfully. Although none of the individual elements of trade liberalization require this environment for their implementation, it would be necessary to be in this cell if all reforms were to be implemented together. Similarly, if macroeconomic, sectoral, trade and fiscal reforms are all to be attempted (as in many SAPs), they are unlikely to all be effectively implemented unless there is strong commitment and capacity. Thus, our notion of the policy environment cautions for gradual sequenced reform and, especially, for building administrative capacity so the process can gather momentum and reforms be implemented in a sustainable manner. Furthermore, efforts to enhance administrative capacity should be interpreted as encouraging: a government willing to invest in administration and implementation capacity is more likely to be technocratic and reformist. Donors can do much to assist in capacity building.

Moving from left to right (cells I to II or III to IV) requires measures that will increase political commitment. This may arise through the normal policy-making process. If the government, or a group of influential policy-makers, accepts that reform is essential they will have a preference and may attempt to alter opinion and form coalitions in favour of reform (they could utilize control over appropriability to achieve this, effectively by creating new rents or redistributing existing ones). Generally, some prompting will be required to encourage consensus; this is most often provided through external pressure. Regimes not committed to reform are likely to be susceptible to external pressure, and such pressure can alleviate the problem of attributability (which is often asymmetric as governments attract more blame for a worsening of economic conditions than credit for an improvement). However, the likely result is external ownership and capable regimes that are not committed, hence it would be optimistic to predict success. Once commitment exists, institution-building, especially of administrative capacity, is required to facilitate moves downward in the figure, especially from II to IV. Institution-building itself requires political commitment but can be greatly furthered with technical assistance. If commitment is high then administrative capacity is the major constraint.

The essence of this approach is to identify the policy environment before recommending a reform programme. The types of reforms attempted first should be those compatible with the prevailing environment; more extensive reforms necessitate interventions to change the environment. The approach is not intended to cover the situation of rapid stabilization during periods of suspended politics. Rather, it is intended to outline an approach to determining the appropriate sequence, of reforms and associated technical assistance (to improve administrative capacity), for implementing a particular set of reforms. The approach is best applied in a relatively detailed case study, where the information necessary to assess political commitment and administrative capacity can be considered. The approach may not offer solutions, but we hope it directs attention to where technical assistance is most required to enhance the policy reform process. A policy advisor that is aware of the prevailing policy environment and the needs of the proposed reforms is better placed to turn the possible into the probable; an analyst should be aware of the context in which an economy embarks on liberalization. The same considerations apply if one is attempting to chronicle and evaluate a period of reform.

## 4.4 CONCLUSIONS

The discussion of policy reforms involves institutions in the narrow and broad senses, as organizations and as systems of rules and norms governing (expectations of) behaviour, especially but not uniquely in the economic sphere. We have only considered the former, in the even narrower sense of administration. Williamson (1994) identifies a central core of institutional economics as being credible investment and credible contracting; the institutions necessary to facilitate and guarantee investment and contracts in the market are essential for a private sector to emerge and prosper. The process of privatization requires financial institutions (to raise finance), management institutions (for new organizational structures) and legal and market institutions (so the private sector can develop). While these issues are of great relevance, hence we mention them, they are beyond our scope.

Policy advisors, who tend to be the major proponents of reform, should be aware that economic arguments are not sufficient even to encourage preferences in support of reform. It takes more than persuasive economic arguments to generate commitment to reform; while ultimately it is an internal political issue, if advisors are aware of the political dimensions of the process they should be better able to identify the optimal sequence and timing of reform. However, even this is not enough: administrative capacity-building is essential and, more generally, institution-building is a prerequisite to effective liberalization. Liberalization, however, should not be considered as moving (either adjustment or transition) to an actual 'free market' situation, but rather refers to removing the more distortionary and counter-productive government interventions. Reforms sequenced and timed to the policy environment are the most likely to succeed.

The experiences with economic policy reform over the last decade or so yield much that can be of benefit to economies attempting reforms in the future. No country would claim to have completed the reform process: some have gone quite far down that road (such as East Asian economies); others have made very little progress (especially African countries); and others have made halting or reversed progress (notably some in Latin America). There is now broad consensus on the types of economic reform needed, liberalization and the establishment of market institutions, although there remains considerable dispute regarding the appropriate role for government. There is also some consensus on the sequence; while appreciating that many reforms should be simultaneous, it is accepted that stabilization must, to some extent, be completed first (Latin American failures can often be traced to failing in this). There is less agreement about timing: it appears that stabilization is best attempted quickly when political circumstances are 'accommodating' of costs (such as honeymoon periods); it is acknowledged that institution-building takes time; but there is considerable dispute over liberalization. There is also general agreement that politics and institutions are important, and are amenable to analysis.

We have not aimed to provide a recipe for policy reform but have suggested a menu and identified the issues that advisors and policy-makers should address when designing (or evaluating fully) a reform programme. First, one should identify the preferences of those, winners and losers, affected. This will offer insights into the political capacity for reform, and will highlight particular reform measures that may mitigate opposition or generate support. Second, and following this, one should consider the degree of political commitment; in particular, if capacity exists, can the government be assured that its preferences should favour reform and is external support of the correct order (sometimes open, sometimes mute; in the form of financial assistance, or technical support).

Third, it is essential to offer administrative support – technical, resources, or both – or, at the least, to be aware of administrative constraints. Finally, sustained reform requires more general support for institution-building. With hindsight, it is often possible to claim that successful reforms have been those implemented by committed governments who declared ownership and had the administrative capacity. We cannot make committed governments. However, distilling the experiences of many countries, we can support administrative capacity, we can identify when a government may wish to declare ownership, and we can suggest steps to help build commitment. These are valuable lessons that can be applied in future.

## Notes

* Earlier versions of this chapter have been presented to various audiences. I am particularly grateful to Doug Nelson for comments and discussion, and to participants at the 7th SAF workshop (November 1996) and in seminars at Bradford, Glasgow, Lund and Stockholm. Much of the early research was part of a research project supported by the Ford Foundation (Grant No. 940–1427), to whom I am grateful.

1. In this regard we should note that some commentators appear to suggest that developing countries adopted liberalization almost *en masse* in the 1980s, with openers like 'an important question is why so many countries have caught the reform bug' (Rodrik, 1996: 11). Our point is that simply to observe attempts at liberalization does not imply the countries have caught the bug: some were inherently reformist anyway; some were convinced of

the desirability of reform; others remained unconvinced, but accepted the conditions because they needed external funding; while a few have clearly resisted.

2. There is an important issue of what is meant by ownership. Often, the approach taken is to look for evidence that the government associates itself with the reform, hence one looks for public announcements. However, ownership really requires that the government be involved in designing the reform programme, and that it be more than an equal partner. Donors should provide technical assistance and external financing if needed, but if they desire LEs to own their reform programmes then the governments must be able to design them.
3. Turkey is an interesting case (Morrissey, 1995c). Turgat Ozal was 'chief designer' of the reform programme and agreed it with the IMF and Bank, for which he had worked, in 1979. He remained Minister of Planning under the military government which implemented the severe stabilization policies in 1980–82, and was elected as Prime Minister in the 1982 elections, after which he continued liberalization with considerable Bank support. In essence, the problem of attributability was averted through use of the military in the severe stage, and through export promotion prior to import liberalization (creating winners from outward-orientation before creating losers by reducing protection). Appropriability remained something of an Achilles heel as State enterprises were not reformed and public subsidies were widespread throughout the 1980s; the resulting debt proved unsustainable in the 1990s.
4. Rodrik (1989) argues that aid may not be helpful for promoting reform because it is as likely to support continued inefficient policies as it is to encourage reformists. The essence of his argument, which incidentally assumes that the capacity to implement reforms is present, is that the aid cannot guarantee reform hence should only be granted if major reforms have already begun. Our argument can be interpreted as being that donors can help to persuade governments of the desirability of reforms and, once preferences are strong, aid can be used to help build capacity. Examples of such aid include compensating certain losers, avoiding a severe impact on the poor, and sustaining public spending on human capital during periods of fiscal rectitude.

## References

Frey, B. and R. Eichenberger (1994), 'The Political Economy of Stabilization Programmes in Developing Countries', *European Journal of Political Economy*, 10:1, pp. 169–190.

Grindle, M. and J. Thomas (1991), *Public Choices and Policy Change: The Political Economy of Reform in Developing Countries*, Baltimore: Johns Hopkins UP.

Haggard, S. and S. Webb (1993), 'What Do We Know about the Political Economy of Economic Policy Reform?', *The World Bank Research Observer*, 8:2, pp. 143–168.

Harvey, C. and M. Robinson (1995), 'Economic Reform and Political Liberalization in Uganda', *IDS Research Report 29*, IDS at University of Sussex.

Levy, B. (1993), 'An Institutional Analysis of the Design and Sequence of Trade and Investment Policy Reform', *The World Bank Economic Review*, 7:2, pp. 247–262.

Morrissey, O. (1995a), 'Political Commitment, Institutional Capacity and Tax Policy Reform in Tanzania', *World Development*, 23:4, pp. 637–649.

Morrissey, O. (1995b), 'Politics and Economic Policy Reform: Trade Liberalization in Sub-Saharan Africa', *Journal of International Development*, 7:4, pp. 599–618.

Morrissey, O. (1995c), 'Compliance and Conditionality: The Sustainability of Adjustment in Turkey', in O. Stokke (ed), *Aid and Conditionality*, London: Frank Cass for EADI, pp. 295–321.

Mosley, P., J. Harrigan and J. Toye (1991), *Aid and Power: The World Bank and Policy-Based Lending*, 2 vols, London: Routledge.

Muñoz, O. (1994), 'Toward Trade Opening: Legacies and Current Strategies', in J. Nelson (1994) (ed), pp. 61–104.

Nelson, J. (1994), (ed), *Intricate Links: Democratization and Market Reforms in Latin America and Eastern Europe*, Washington, DC: Transactions Publishers and Overseas Development Council.

Rodrik, D. (1989), 'Promises, Promises: Credible Policy Reform via Signalling', *Economic Journal*, 99, pp. 756–72.

Rodrik, D. (1996), 'Understanding Economic Policy Reform', *Journal of Economic Literature*, XXXIV (1), pp. 9–41.

Sandbrook, R. (1996), 'Democratization and the Implementation of Economic Reforms in Africa', *Journal of International Development*, 8:1, pp. 1–20.

Vartiainen, J. (1996), 'Understanding State-led Late Industrialization', mimeo, forthcoming in V. Bergström (ed), *Politics and Growth*, Oxford: OUP.

White, H. and O. Morrissey (1997), 'Conditionality when Donor and Recipient Preferences Vary', *Journal of International Development*, 9:4, pp. 497–505.

Williamson, O. (1994), 'The Institutions of Governance of Economic Development and Reform', *Proceedings of the World Bank Annual Conference on Development Economics 1994*, pp. 171–197.

# 5 Methodological Issues in Assessing the Impact of Economic Reform on Poverty

Andrew McKay*

## 5.1 INTRODUCTION

The 1980s in particular saw significant increases in levels of poverty in much of the developing world, notably in much of Africa and in many countries in the Latin America and Caribbean region, as well as in some Asian countries. Over the same decade, many developing countries began to undertake economic reform programmes (e.g. stabilization and/or structural adjustment programmes), often though not exclusively with the encouragement and financial support of the International Monetary Fund and/or the World Bank. These economic reforms were generally undertaken as a response to a present or impending economic crisis. However, the question of whether, and if so how, these reform programmes were related to the increase in poverty is a very pertinent one. This issue has been discussed extensively by academics, international agencies, practitioners and the general public, and there is a wide diversity of views on it. At one extreme is the commonly expressed view that the reform programmes impacted disproportionately on the poor, and so contributed to increased poverty. At the opposite extreme, it is argued that economic reform measures were a necessary response to the preceding economic crisis, and may have resulted in more favourable outcomes than would have happened in the absence of these reforms.

The question though is a very complex one. The 1980s were characterized by significantly increased indebtedness in many developing countries, adverse terms of trade shocks for many, increases in world interest rates, reduction in the availability of foreign credit from private sources, periods of recession in world trade, increased protection in some developed countries and other adverse economic conditions.

Many of these phenomena are also very good candidates for explaining some or all of the increases in poverty over this period. Moreover, an adequate answer to the question of the impact of economic reform on poverty needs to explain why many Asian countries, which also pursued apparently similar policies over the same period, did not experience significant increases in poverty, and some experienced significant reductions.

While the trends in poverty in the first half of the 1990s are apparently less remorselessly upward, the question of the link between economic reform and poverty remain a very important one, given the ongoing nature of economic reform. Our ability to address this question has been significantly enhanced over the last ten years or so by a large increase in the availability of data on poverty and social outcomes. It remains the case that the conceptual and methodological questions of how policy reforms at the macro and sectoral level impact on poverty at the micro level remain complex. But without being able to answer this question, it becomes difficult to identify policy improvements that we can confidently expect to bring about improved poverty outcomes.

This chapter surveys the general issues that arise in assessing the impact of economic reform on poverty. In discussing this, three major issues arise: the measurement of poverty; the channels by which macroeconomic reform can impact on poverty; and the methods by which this can be assessed empirically in any given country. These issues are discussed in turn. Section 5.2 discusses the measurement of poverty; section 5.3 then reviews some possible impacts of macroeconomic reform on poverty, stressing the complexity of this issue. Section 5.4 discusses general methodological approaches to assessing the impact of economic reform on poverty, while section 5.5 considers some recent empirical studies which have examined this issue. Section 5.6 concludes.

## 5.2 DATA NEEDS FOR MEASURING AND MONITORING POVERTY

A necessary starting point for considering the impact of economic reform on poverty is to know something about poverty in the country concerned. In particular, what is required is information which allows us (i) to characterize and understand the nature of poverty in a country; and (ii) to monitor changes in poverty over time, covering the period in which the economic reform took place. These issues are considered in turn.

**Characterizing and Understanding Poverty at a Point in Time**

For considering the impact of economic reform on poverty, the available information on poverty should possess two important characteristics. First, the data need to be available at a disaggregated level (ideally as disaggregated as possible); in thinking about poverty the interest is in extremes and in differences within the population, not in simple average or aggregate measures across the whole population. Second, as the question about economic reform and poverty is generally posed at the national level,[1] the available data should represent the whole country as well as possible. Where data are only available for a specific region, group, etc, then only a more limited question can be asked, i.e. the impact within that specific region, group, etc. This question is also an important one, but it is not the one to be addressed in this chapter.

In practice, what is really needed therefore are (nationwide) household survey data relating to the period of the reform. While not all developing countries have such data, many more countries do now than was the case at the beginning of the 1980s, especially in Africa and Latin America. This increased availability of household survey data is a consequence of a number of initiatives. Surveys have been conducted under the UN National Household Survey Capability Program (NHSCP; United Nations, 1984). Surveys have also been conducted under various World Bank initiatives, notably the Living Standards Measurement Study (LSMS; Grosh and Glewwe, 1995), and the Social Dimensions of Adjustment in Sub-Saharan Africa Programme (Delaine *et al.*, 1992; Grootaert and Marchant, 1991). Initiatives of this type in turn reflect a number of factors including an increased interest in poverty as a policy issue, and (partly as a result) an increased recognition of the importance of household level data. But there are still many countries for which such data are not available; the issue of what can be said about poverty in such instances will be considered shortly.

First, consider the case where household survey data are available and of reasonable quality. Given such data, the most common approach is to measure living standards, and thus poverty, based on consumption or income measured at the household level (Lipton and Ravallion, 1996). This reflects the widely held view that consumption or income, measured appropriately for the context (in particular allowing for consumption of own production and other types of non-market transactions),[2] are the most comprehensive measures of the standard of living. These however, are not the only alternatives, and in some circumstances they may fail to capture sufficiently important dimensions of living standards not easily expressed in monetary terms (e.g. health or nutritional status). Thus, direct measures of satisfaction of specified basic needs (or capabilities) in areas such as education, health and drinking water, which can also be measured in household surveys, may also be considered in parallel. Moreover, such measures offer alternatives where income or consumption cannot be measured or can only measured inaccurately. Another advantage of some 'basic needs' measures as collected in household surveys is that they may be able to provide some information on intra-household distribution, information that is not available in a measure of total household income or consumption.[3]

Note, however, that the concern is not just with measuring poverty but also with characterizing and understanding it. Most household surveys, by collecting different types of information about the household and its members, enable the construction of a detailed picture of poverty (e.g. looking at the relationships between poverty and economic activities, school enrolment, gender, household size/composition, etc).

But the question of the impact of economic reform on poverty is equally urgent in countries where household survey data are not available. Approaches based on measuring household income or consumption will then not be feasible, and measures of basic needs fulfillment may or may not be available. So what can be said about poverty in these circumstances? Clearly in such cases it will be necessary to make the best use of existing alternative sources of data. However, the importance of disaggregating remains; while trends in aggregate per capita GNP or private consumption are of some interest, they do not necessarily tell us anything about poverty without knowing how any increases or reductions are distributed. Moreover, the data used need to be relevant to the poor, and this requires judgement. For instance, trends in data on unemployment or in wage rates, often based on the formal sector, may be largely irrelevant to the poor in many low income countries in Africa, but may be much more relevant in some countries of Latin America.

In addition, it is important to recognize that household surveys need not be the only source of disaggregated, nationally representative information. Thus, for example, results of community level surveys (collecting data on, say, village characteristics, facilities and amenities) can be informative if they are reasonably representative; administrative data may be available at the local or regional level on, say health or education facilities; national accounts aggregates may be disaggregated in relevant ways (e.g. by sector). All of this can help in building up a more disaggregated picture of poverty, understanding the types of households most affected (e.g. according to geographic location), the types of economic activities in which they are engaged, and so on. With this type of information it becomes more feasible to map the impacts of macroeconomic policy at a more disaggregated level.

Finally, certain types of aggregate information may reveal some information on poverty if they can be used as the basis for comparison over time or across (similar) countries. This applies for example to information on net enrolment rates in primary school, on literacy rates, on infant or child mortality rates etc., even where these are only available at the national level. Thus if the aggregate infant mortality rate is higher in one country than in another similar one, this is suggestive of a higher level of poverty in the former than the latter. Alternatively, a decline in net enrolment in primary school over time can reasonably be expected to affect the poor disproportionately. But the point still stands that if this information on infant mortality or enrolment rates was available at a disaggregated level within the country, this would provide a lot more information about the nature and pattern of poverty.

## Monitoring Trends in Poverty Over Time

Ideally, the available data can also enable the monitoring of changes in the level and pattern of poverty, in its various dimensions, over time. As was the case in studying poverty at a point in time, these data will ideally be available at the household level. In practice this is most likely to mean that comparable houschold surveys are available over the period under study;[4] this would allow not just a detailed picture of poverty at a point in time, but also provides information on how the situation may have changed between the two surveys. However, in comparing two different household surveys, it is important to be sure that they are genuinely comparable. Thus, not only do the questionnaires need to be the same at the two points in time, it is also important that the data collection and sampling procedures have not changed significantly.[5] For example, in the case of Uganda, household surveys were conducted in 1989 and 1992, but based on very different questionnaires; this makes it very difficult to assess the evolution of poverty between these two surveys (Appleton, 1996). In the case of Ghana, though identical questionnaires were used for surveys conducted in 1987–88 and 1988–89, the extent to which these are comparable is still debatable because of doubts about the consistency of data collection procedures and of the sample (Coulombe and McKay, 1995).

Given two genuinely comparable household surveys overlapping with the period of the reform programme, it is then possible to examine changes in not only the level but also the pattern of poverty over time. However, many developing countries are not in the fortunate position of having household survey data available at two points in time overlapping with the reform programme, or other household level data on trends in poverty over time. In such instances there is obviously much less that can be achieved in deducing trends in poverty over time. Nevertheless, even where only a one-off household survey is available, the detailed picture of households it provides may still be useful in suggesting possible impacts of specific reform measures on particular groups of households. For example, if poor households consume certain commodities disproportionately relative to the general population, they will be hurt disproportionately by an increase in the price of this commodity. Or if the poor are disproportionately food crop cultivators, then policy measures directed at subsistence agriculture will hopefully lead to reduced poverty.

For countries where household survey data are not available at all, other disaggregated data may be available at more than one point in time, e.g. the sectoral composition of the national accounts may be available on an annual basis. Such information may provide some clues on likely changes in poverty over time, if the methods used to compute this disaggregated data are sufficiently accurate to be likely to pick up sectoral and other shifts. Disaggregated administrative data (e.g. on health facilities in different localities) may be another case in point. And as discussed above, the availability of even aggregate level information on variables such as net enrolment rates in primary school or infant mortality rates can give clues about likely directions of evolution of poverty.

In conclusion, all of this discussion relates to the issue of examining patterns of poverty at a point in time, and likely trends in this. Where the data that form the basis of this are of sufficiently good quality, it can tell us about how poverty has evolved over the period concerned, e.g. has poverty increased or decreased? In what ways has the pattern of poverty changed? But it does not tell us much at all about the likely explanations for the observed evolution in poverty; in particular, it does not tell us whether and to what extent the economic reforms put in place over the period account for the observed trends. Information on trends in poverty (however measured) over time is *necessary* for answering the question of how economic reform may have impacted on poverty *but by itself it does not answer this question*. This is the subject of the rest of this chapter.

## 5.3 THE IMPACT OF MACROECONOMIC REFORM ON LIVING STANDARDS

Unfortunately even more complex than the question of how to assess living standards and poverty, is the issue of how a given package of macroeconomic policy measures can be expected to impact on these. Here we are concerned with the impact at the micro level (households and their members) of a set of policy measures taken at the macro, aggregate or sectoral level. Complexities arise at a number of levels. First, in assessing economic reform, we are interested in assessing the impact of a *package* of policy measures; different components of this package can be expected to impact in different, and often conflicting, ways on living standards. Second, the contents of this package are not uniform from one country to another. While economic reform in the last decade and a half has generally meant a movement towards more market-oriented policies, the specific form this takes can vary significantly from one country to another, and this can matter for the impact on living standards. Moreover, different programmes differ also with regard to sequencing of reforms, credibility, extent of external financing, etc, and these factors may matter a lot in influencing outcomes.

Third, we are interested in the policy measures actually implemented by a country, not those the government said it would implement; the two are often different (Mosley, Harrigan and Toye, 1991, Chapter 5; Chapters 3 and 4 of this volume discuss this point in a more general context). Fourth, different countries undertaking reform programmes are different in nature; thus for example urban poverty may be a much more important issue in one country (say, in Latin America) than in another (say in Africa). Therefore, a policy measure which has an adverse effect in one country (such as measures which change the urban–rural terms of trade) may have a beneficial effect in another. Fifth, the extent of disequilibrium or instability from which countries start their reform programmes varies; this is likely to affect the severity of required stabilization measures and hence poverty impacts. Sixth, the critical question of counterfactual arises; how would the poverty situation have differed in the absence of the economic reform programme, or if a different programme had been adopted (in which case, which one)?

All of these issues inevitably arise in addressing the question of the impact of economic reform on living standards, and need to be addressed in any given case. However, probably the most fundamental problem of all is that of establishing the link between policy measures, almost always taken at the macroeconomic, aggregate and sectoral levels, and their micro-level impact on households and their members. This is an extremely complex question, on which existing theory offers only partial guidance.

The issues can be better illustrated by considering some specific instances of economic reform. As discussed elsewhere in this volume, economic reform commonly takes the form of economic stabilization and/or structural adjustment (although conceptually distinct, the two are often intertwined in practice). Stabilization packages are a response to a short-term though potentially serious problem, which often manifests itself as a significant balance of payments disequilibrium. Such a disequilibrium implies that the country's absorption level, plus payments made abroad (such as net interest payments, net factor income and transfers paid abroad), is in excess of its production. While it is possible to respond to this situation by taking measures either to restrict demand, or to stimulate supply, or both, measures to curb demand are generally used because these may be the only measures capable of controlling the disequilibrium sufficiently quickly. Common components of stabilization packages include measures to depreciate the real exchange rate (often through a nominal devaluation), and contractionary fiscal and monetary policies.

How can such measures be expected to impact on living standards?[6] The demand-reducing fiscal and monetary policy measures can be expected to reduce average living standards in the country relative to what existed before they were implemented, at least in the short term. However their precise impact will depend on the specific forms these measures take (e.g. how government spending is controlled, which taxes are increased, or how the monetary contraction is undertaken). The real exchange rate depreciation (if achieved) will increase the price of traded goods relative to non-traded goods; there will obviously be both gainers and losers in response to such a measure.[7] Other things being equal, the increase in the relative price of traded goods should benefit those involved in the production of such goods (whether through producing these goods themselves, or through being employed in these sectors), but hurt those who are net purchasers (e.g. if the tradable is a staple food crop). The devaluation obviously has a distributional effect, but the impact on poverty will depend on which groups are the main producers and consumers of traded goods. This can give a first order indication of which groups are likely to lose and gain from the devaluation.[8]

However, as argued elsewhere in this volume, the question of counterfactual is central. The question is not whether people become poorer during the period of the stabilization (given that stabilization is generally a process of curtailing demand, it is likely that on average they will have), but rather of what would have happened in its absence, or in the presence of a different stabilization package? Could a different package of measures (including no change) have had a more favourable poverty impact, as well as restoring basic macroeconomic stability?

Economic reform, though, is concerned about more than just stabilization; it is also concerned with establishing the conditions for long term growth. This is generally the stated aim of structural adjustment programmes, which are usually more complex and long term in their aims than stabilization programmes. In general they operate much more on the supply-side of the economy, seeking to increase efficiency and stimulate domestic production. Various policies have been undertaken to try to achieve this; in different instances these can include such measures as trade liberalization, financial liberalization, increasing producer prices in agriculture, removal of food subsidies, removal of minimum wage legislation, etc.

Before considering the poverty impact of these measures, the need to stimulate or re-establish economic growth should be stressed. In broad terms poverty can be reduced through increasing the average level of household incomes, or through redistribution, or both, but there are likely to be severe limits to what can be achieved by redistribution alone. Sustainable growth in average incomes then, is likely to be necessary for poverty reduction. But it is not necessarily sufficient, because the distributional pattern of growth matters. As appeared to occur in Brazil in the 1980s, it is possible for average incomes to grow, but for poverty also to increase, because the growth in average incomes is occurring only among the richer groups in society (Datt and Ravallion, 1992).

Seen from this perspective, two questions need to be asked about structural adjustment programmes: (i) do they succeed in stimulating economic growth in a country?; and (ii) if so, what is the distributional pattern of that growth? It is much beyond the scope of this chapter to treat these issues satisfactorily at a theoretical level, but a couple of examples may help to illustrate the issues. If the poor in a country are disproportionately rural and engaged in agriculture, measures designed to raise the producer price in agriculture may be thought to have a beneficial effect on poverty. This policy change, by increasing the rate of return, may stimulate agricultural production, and this may have various favourable impacts at the aggregate level (increased aggregate production, increased agricultural exports and/or reduced imports of food). But the question of the distributional impact arises; in particular, large farmers may be more able to respond to increased price incentives than small farmers, perhaps because the latter are more affected by market or infrastuctural failures (McKay, 1997). A further question that must be asked is how the increased producer price in agriculture is to be financed; does it for example imply a higher food price, or reduced revenue for the government? These in turn may have impacts on poverty (and perhaps on growth) elsewhere in the economy.

Taking another example, privatization of previously state-owned enterprises may increase the efficiency with which these enterprises operate, and as such stimulate growth, but it may also result in an increased concentration of wealth and so increased inequality. But then there is the issue of possible resultant reductions (or re-allocations) in government spending, and of who benefits from this. The overall poverty impact is unclear, and may differ from case to case.

Clearly not all types of growth are equally effective in reducing poverty. Moreover, the poverty impact of even individual measures is likely to be complex, and the poverty impact becomes even more ambiguous when a whole package is considered. But a general point that is important to make is that giving an increased role to market forces (as is implicit in many structural adjustment programmes) is not necessarily harmful to the poor. For example, policy measures which sustain an overvalued real exchange rate may well have an adverse effect on rural poverty; movement towards an equilibrium rate may then have a beneficial poverty impact.

None of the above is to argue that economic reform does or does not generally lead to increased poverty, but simply to illustrate the complexity of the situation. Stabilization and structural adjustment, anyway not fixed packages, are too complex in nature to look for straightforward or generalizable relations between economic reform and poverty. Indeed, the question at this level of generality is probably misconceived, in the sense of being impossible to answer satisfactorily. A given reform programme is likely to include measures which do hurt the poor, as well as others which may benefit the poor (relative to an appropriate counterfactual). It may be more profitable instead to focus on individual measures commonly included in economic reform programmes, and their impact on poverty. Finally, note that for certain types of measures (e.g. changing levels or patterns of public expenditure on education) this question may be more easily answered than for others (e.g. monetary contraction).

## 5.4 GENERAL APPROACHES TO ASSESSING THE IMPACT OF MACROECONOMIC REFORM ON POVERTY

There is no doubt that any economic policy reform will have distributional impacts; thus for any policy change it is not difficult to find groups who have been adversely affected, as well as groups who have benefited. The relevant issue in the present context is to know what the *net effect* on poverty of a given package of macroeconomic policy reforms is.[9]

The previous section has argued strongly against expecting to find a general relationship between economic reform and poverty. It may be possible to establish relationships between specific policy measures and poverty outcomes, which can be generalized; this is an open question. But it certainly does not apply to the package of economic reform as a whole. We should not look for generalizable relationships between economic reform as a whole and poverty, even though relationships between specific measures and poverty may be generalizable. The relationship between a whole economic reform package and poverty needs to be assessed empirically in any particular case. In any given country situation, the nature of the relationship between reform and poverty will depend, among other things, on the specific policy measures put in place, the extent to which they were implemented, their credibility, and on the counterfactual, i.e. what would have happened in the absence of the reforms.

As discussed elsewhere in this volume, a number of approaches can be adopted to evaluating the impact of an economic reform programme (see also Toye, 1995, Chapter 2). For the specific question of evaluating the impact on poverty, three broad approaches can be adopted, as follows:

(i) before-after comparisons: comparing the situation in a given country before and after the policy measure(s) have been implemented;

(ii) cross-country comparisons, comparing countries which did introduce a given reform or reform package with those which did not (i.e. a with-without comparison across countries);

(iii) with-without comparisons in a given country, evaluating how the outcomes in the absence of the policy would have been different from those occurring with the policy in place, i.e. a counterfactual analysis, as distinct from (i).

As in the use of these (and other) methods for assessing other impacts of economic reform, none of them is unproblematic. The first two of these methods have already been discussed above in Chapter 2; here we consider each in turn as they apply to the impact of policy reform on poverty.

**Before-After Comparisons**

These essentially involve assessing how the levels and pattern of poverty (measured as discussed in section 5.2 or otherwise) have changed since the economic reforms were put in place. This approach was used extensively in the first major study of the distributional impact of structural adjustment, that edited by Cornia, Jolly and Stewart (1987), and has also been widely used in many subsequent studies. What such studies reveal about trends in poverty over time is important and valuable information in its own right, *irrespective of what has caused the observed changes in poverty*. Moreover, this information about trends in poverty over time is important for the evaluation of the poverty impact of economic reform programmes, irrespective of which evaluation method(s) is (are) finally to be used. And in instances where poverty has been observed to increase over time, this clearly calls for policy measures that can help reduce and then reverse this increase in poverty (which might or might not involve modifying economic reform programmes).

While this information on trends in poverty is certainly of considerable value in its own right, as a means of assessing the impact of economic reform on poverty, this method suffers from two significant deficiencies. First, *from the point of view of this specific question of the poverty impact of economic reform*, it is not clear to what extent the comparison being made is valid. If the pre-reform situation was unsustainable (e.g. due to lack of foreign funding), and this is what precipitated the reform, then some policy response may have been inevitable; the *status quo ante* was not an option. The question is then whether the response adopted was the best one. Second, this method does not attribute causality. As discussed in section 5.1 above, many factors could account for this increase in poverty, and several probably do. And this is not just a technical or academic issue; the extent to which reform accounts for the increase in poverty is a critically important policy question. If most of the increase in poverty in fact occurs for other reasons, then reversing components of the reform package may not make the poverty outcomes any better, and could make them worse. On the other hand, if (specific elements of) the reform programme is (are) indeed responsible for the increase in poverty then reversing these policies may well be desirable. Thus identifying trends in poverty is not sufficient; it is also necessary to assess to what extent the economic reform measures implemented can account for the observed outcomes.

Both of these deficiencies reflect the general problem with this method used in isolation: the absence of a counterfactual. In advocating that existing policies should be changed, it is highly desirable to know what would have happened in the absence of the policies, or (which might be more relevant) in the presence of a different policy package. Without this, the evidence on which recommendations for changes to economic reform programmes are based may be fragile, and might not lead to improved policy outcomes.

**With-Without Comparisons across Countries**

This approach tries to introduce an element of counterfactual by comparing reforming countries with non-reforming countries. Such an approach has been widely used in assessing the impacts of economic reform programmes on poverty, notably a number of studies by the World Bank (e.g. World Bank, 1990, 1992, 1994) and a detailed study by Berg *et al.* (1994).

Rather than just distinguishing reforming countries and non-reforming countries, most studies rely on a more sophisticated classification, recognizing different levels of commitment to reform. Thus, for example, in the 1994 World Bank study of adjustment in Sub-Saharan Africa (World Bank, 1994), countries are classified into those with a 'large improvement', 'small improvement' or 'deterioration' in macroeconomic policy. Other classifications commonly used by the World Bank and others distinguish countries according to the length of time over which they have been undertaking economic reform, or their perceived commitment to reform. While such classifications recognize the reality of differing degrees of commitment to, or implementation of, reform measures, it is invariably difficult to classify countries in practice. It is also difficult to identify when reform episodes effectively began, a point which matters for the evaluation of these programmes.[10]

Apart from this issue of classifying countries, this method suffers from three additional problems. First, extreme care is needed in drawing conclusions from cross-country comparisons of this type, given that countries differ significantly in many other ways apart from the reform programme. Such differences may well be relevant to the comparison, e.g. institutional characteristics, policies other than those being evaluated, structure of their economies. Such factors must be taken into account in making cross-country comparisons, and may limit the domain over which comparisons should be made. Second, whether a country is reforming or not may be to some extent endogenous to the issue under discussion. Non-reforming countries may be so because their economies were historically well managed in any case (e.g. avoiding sustained fiscal deficits or debt build-up), or because they were fortunate (e.g. their terms of trade did not move adversely), while in many instances reforming countries undertake reforms in response to a crisis. Where this is the case, the comparison between reforming and non-reforming countries may not be providing the appropriate counterfactual, and may indeed be biased against reforming countries in the early stages of their reforms. Third, and operating in the opposite direction, reforming countries may enjoy larger foreign capital inflows (aid and loans) than non-reforming countries as a direct result of embracing reform. Again there is a question of whether the non-reforming country provides the appropriate counterfactual, given that there will be great difficulty in separating out the impacts of the reforms on poverty from the (presumably beneficial) impact of the foreign capital inflows.

### With-Without Comparisons within a Country

The third approach, the with-without comparison within a given country, seeks to tackle the issue of the counterfactual directly. The important question here is how the reforms put in place changed the outcomes relative to those which would have prevailed in their absence (or in the presence of different policy measures). The question now is not just whether poverty increased or fell (though this is important), but how to disentangle the effects of economic reform from the many other factors contributing to changes in poverty. Doing this enables us to answer the question about the impact of the reform on poverty, and can help in identifying modifications to the reforms which might have led to a smaller increase or larger reduction (as appropriate) in poverty.

The serious difficulty this method suffers from is the practical one, of specifying the counterfactual and knowing what its impacts would have been; by its very nature the counterfactual is not observed. Furthermore, the situation without the economic reform might not be the appropriate counterfactual, or at least might only be one of several possible counterfactuals. The issue is then that of the choice between the specific reforms put in place, and some alternative package(s) of reforms (which then needs to be specified).

The problem is predominantly technical: how to determine the poverty impacts under the counterfactual. In practice, as this is unobserved, it calls for modelling. But the models used need to be appropriate. In particular, they need to be able to capture the micro impact of policy measures taken at the macroeconomic or sectoral levels; they need to be disaggregated, capturing different type of agents (especially within the household sector) and different economic activities; they should ideally model the behavioural responses of agents to the changing economic environment.

The demands of such a modelling approach are great, even in countries where data availability is not a major issue. What is needed is a framework that allows us to examine the distributional consequences of macroeconomic and sectoral policies, consequences that are not necessarily considered in the design of such policies. In light of these considerations, conventional macroeconomic models, most of which anyway ignore the distributional issues of relevance here, are not appropriate. But recent developments in the use of Applied or Computable General Equilibrium (CGE) models perhaps offer most promise for assessing the impact of reform policies on the living standards of groups of households.[11] CGE models have been used to assess the poverty impact of economic reforms in a number of developing countries (e.g. Bourguignon, de Melo and Morrison, 1991; Bourguignon, de Melo and Suwa, 1991; Sahn, 1996).

However, it must be stressed that the CGE economic modelling approach, while better at addressing aspects of the impact of reform on poverty than many obvious alternatives, is not a panacea which can answer all questions of relevance, or provide answers which are beyond dispute. A number of difficult issues arise in their construction and application to this issue. First is the non-trivial issue of data availability, which means that it may not be feasible to construct such models for many countries.

A second big issue is the specification of the model. The models are based on behavioural assumptions, relating especially to consumers, producers, suppliers of factors of production and the functioning of markets, and the results can be quite sensitive to these assumptions. An important example relevant to the present issue is the characterization of the labour market; thus, for example, whether this is characterized by the presence of involuntary unemployment, or by a wage rate which adjusts to clear the market can have a significant impact on the results.[12] Moreover, information on key behavioural parameters required for the model, such as elasticities, may not be available.

A third issue is the types of questions CGE models are best designed for addressing. Their general equilibrium foundations make them better suited to modelling some types of policies than others. Thus, they can be applied relatively straightforwardly to issues such as taxation, trade policy, and relative price changes (e.g. following a real devaluation), but can only be applied with much more difficulty (and often more stylized assumptions), if at all, to questions involving nominal variables (e.g. nominal devaluations, monetary consequences of fiscal deficits, etc), or to issues where dynamics are very important (e.g. the important issues of growth or investment).

Fourthly, of direct relevance to this chapter, CGE models can only ever look at the impact of policy reforms on ('average' members of) broad groups of households, where these groups are defined according to appropriate criteria (e.g. location, main economic activity, initial income quintile, etc); they cannot say anything about what is happening within these groups. Thus if one of the groups of households is 'cash farmers', we can investigate how given policy reforms impact on the average cash farming household, but not how different types of cash farming households (e.g. according to crop, location or income level) are affected differentially. If this is a big issue, then it may be necessary to disaggregate the group of cash farmers further; data limitations, plus the need to keep the model manageable may limit the extent to which this can be done. Hence, use of CGE models to simulate impacts of policies is in no way a substitute for microeconomic analysis based on household-level and other data, aimed at answering the questions about why different households within a given group might be affected differentially by policy changes.

Finally, a fifth point is a straightforward practical one. Even where data availability is not a problem, construction of CGE models and their use for policy simulation is often a time consuming exercise. Yet in some countries the question of the poverty impact of economic reform may be an urgent one, to which preliminary answers are required before the results of the CGE based simulations are available. While this is not an argument against CGE models, which may be able to answer certain questions better than any alternatives, it does suggest the need to make use of other methods as well.

Overall, it should be clear that each of the three methods above suffers from significant limitations, and no one of the three methods is unambiguously superior to the others. In practice, it is highly desirable to be able to consider more than one of the above methods to reinforce or broaden the conclusions. Indeed this is what many of the more convincing studies of the impact of economic reform on poverty do. In the next section we discuss some of the conclusions that have been drawn from some recent empirical studies of this question.

## 5.5 EMPIRICAL EVIDENCE ON THE IMPACT OF MACROECONOMIC REFORM ON POVERTY

The complexity of the question of the impact of economic reform, or even of specific reform measures, on poverty should already be clear. Moreover, as theory only gives partial guidance, it is also clear that this question must be assessed empirically. Many empirical studies have been undertaken addressing this question. It is completely beyond the scope of this chapter to review such studies comprehensively; for illustrative purposes this chapter will focus only on a small number of more convincing (or influential) recent studies, trying to relate these to the general methodologies set out above.

Perhaps a useful starting point in this discussion is Berg *et al.* (1994), who compile and undertake a thorough study of the poverty related data available for most countries in the Sub-Saharan Africa (SSA) and Latin America and the Caribbean (LAC) regions, thus establishing facts about observed changes over time. Based on their data and countless other sources, there can be no doubt that in both regions, on average, the 1980s decade was characterized by declining per capita GDP (or consumption) and increases in absolute poverty as measured based on household income/consumption data. In Africa real per capita public expenditure in the social sectors of health and education fell, in line with falling public expenditure levels overall. In the LAC region the evidence on this point is more ambivalent: while overall public expenditure fell in real terms, the share devoted to health and education did not. But despite all this, in both regions they find improvements in most social indicators (e.g. relating to health, nutrition or education) over the decade, in direct contrast to the trends in incomes. These contrary trends in social indicators and monetary based measures of poverty are certainly possible; this suggests that any adverse effects of economic reform will be observed much more in monetary measures than in social indicators.

This compilation of data by itself provides a wealth of information about observed trends in various measures of poverty or social outcomes over the 1980s, but it does not yet tell us about the impact of economic reform on poverty. Berg *et al.* (1994) consider this question based on a combination of the first two methods set out above: making before-after comparisons, but comparing the changes across countries, especially comparing reforming and non-reforming countries. Based on comparisons across a large number of countries in these two regions, their overwhelming conclusion is the absence of a systematic relationship between economic reform and poverty. The poverty outcomes (however measured) of countries which did undertake economic reform were not generally worse than those which did not, and according to one or two criteria reforming countries may actually have performed better.

A similar combination of the before-after and cross-country comparison methods is used by Morley (1994) to consider the distributional effects of economic reforms across the countries of Latin America. Almost all countries in the region undertook economic reform programmes over the period, but as both the types of programmes followed and their outcomes varied significantly, careful cross-country comparisons can offer important lessons. The strongest lesson from this study is the importance of reductions in per capita income in accounting for worsening poverty outcomes (measured in monetary terms). Most countries in the region needed to undertake stabilization programmes over the 1980s. While these were generally associated with increased poverty initially, countries where the stabilization was relatively short-lived and followed quickly by a recovery (such as Chile in the early 1980s) experienced much more favourable poverty outcomes than countries where it was long and protracted (such as Mexico in the 1980s). The central importance of changes in per capita income is further reinforced by their tendency to be inversely correlated with changes in inequality; in other words, when per capita income increases inequality is observed to decrease in almost all countries, and conversely when income falls.

Moreover, the evidence suggests that social emergency programmes cannot offset the impact on the poor of declining per capita incomes, although they and social policies more generally can mitigate their effects. In terms of the relationship between economic reform and poverty, Morley (1994) argues that the increases in poverty are not due to the non-implementation of economic reform programmes; most were implemented. But economic reform is by no means the only cause of increased poverty.

However, despite the increases in poverty observed in countries pursuing orthodox reform programmes, at least in the stabilization phases, Morley (1994) finds that poverty (and other) outcomes were much worse in countries pursuing heterodox reform programmes, such as were pursued by Argentina, Brazil and Peru during this period. Among the countries that pursued orthodox programmes, in general those with small traded goods sectors or with inflexible production structures had more severe experiences of reform and worse poverty outcomes. Stimulating exports appears to have played a key role in generating growth, and hence reducing poverty; and indeed where the traded goods sector was an important employer of the poor (e.g. agriculture in Costa Rica) the poverty outcomes of reform were much more favourable.

These two studies are examples of cross-country comparisons across many countries. There is also value in studying the experiences of particular countries in depth. This can answer different questions and perhaps allow the mechanisms at work to be studied more carefully. Stewart (1995) includes some more detailed discussion of specific country experiences (in addition to a more general assessment).

She also argues that the experience of the 1980s (and indeed the beginning of the 1990s) was one of increasing poverty in many countries, notably in Sub-Saharan Africa and the Latin America and Caribbean regions; over the same time period the large majority of developing countries undertook reform programmes. Stewart, though, by comparing different countries' experiences, argues that the impact of these reform programmes on poverty was not uniform. Thus, in Chile, the early years of economic reform (early 1980s), involving mainly stabilization, did lead to rising poverty, but through the subsequent years of economic reform the country's record on poverty reduction has been good. This contrasts with Mexico over the 1980s, where economic reform was associated with increasing poverty, worsening social outcomes and increasing inequality. A significant point of difference between these two countries was the policies the governments adopted in relation to education, health and nutrition, with Chile protecting the poor by effective targeting of programmes in these areas, in contrast to Mexico. A similar comparison is made between Indonesia, where economic reform was associated with significant reduction in poverty, and the Philippines where the poverty record was ambivalent at best. In part this reflected Indonesia's ability to maintain some growth through economic reform, in contrast to the Philippines. In Africa, the poverty impact of Ghana's various reform programmes was more favourable than in the case of Tanzania, though as much of the poverty reduction in Ghana may be due to the rehabilitation of a stagnant, pre-reform economy, the sustainability of this poverty reduction is debatable.

Stewart (1995) uses this and other evidence to draw some general lessons about the types of reform programmes which can be expected to have less favourable poverty outcomes. In particular, she argues that programmes will have less adverse poverty impact where they involve less reliance on contractionary monetary and fiscal policies, and more reliance on expenditure switching via devaluation.[13] She also argues for the central importance of protecting the social sectors (education, health) during reform programmes.

This emphasis on the importance of the real exchange rate in determining the poverty impact is also made by Demery and Squire (1996), in their assessment of what survey data in Africa tell about changes in poverty over the 1980s and early 1990s, and the role of economic reform in this. Poverty has fallen in some African countries over the periods considered, and Demery and Squire (1995) identify an association between improved macroeconomic performance (measured following the methodology used in the World Bank's study of adjustment in Africa (World Bank, 1994)) and poverty reduction. Comparing the neighbouring West African countries, Côte d'Ivoire (1985–88) and Ghana (1988–92), over the periods studied poverty rose sharply in the former but fell in the latter. Over this period Côte d'Ivoire failed to adjust, while Ghana's record in economic reform was relatively good. In particular, the real exchange rate in Ghana underwent a devaluation, while it appreciated in Côte d'Ivoire, and this they consider to have played a major role in determining the different poverty outcomes.

However, one important lesson that Demery and Squire (1996) draw based on the countries they consider, is that in Africa there appears to be a tendency for increases in per capita income to be associated with increasing inequality, and conversely for reductions. This is in direct contrast to what Morley (1994) found for Latin America; it suggests that in Africa growth, while still necessary for sustained poverty reduction, is less effective in reducing poverty than it would otherwise be, because the benefits of growth accrue disproportionately to the non-poor. Thus, searching not just for growth in Africa, but for specifically broadly based growth, is clearly a priority.

Finally, we briefly consider some recent studies that have followed the third method discussed in section 5.4 above, tackling the question of counterfactual directly by modelling its impact on poverty, generally using Computable General Equilibrium models. Recent examples include studies by Sadoulet and de Janvry (1995) of Ecuador, and a series of studies of African countries undertaken by authors as part of a project conducted from Cornell University (Sahn, 1996).

Sadoulet and de Janvry (1995) use a sophisticated Computable General Equilibrium (CGE) model of Ecuador to compare growth and poverty outcomes under different stabilization and reform programmes. Their model has a number of interesting features; in particular, it is dynamic in nature and, in contrast to many other CGE models, it models the financial as well as the real side of the economy in some detail. This latter feature means that the model can be used to simulate monetary policy changes, and can also be used to model the financing of fiscal deficits; this obviously increases the range of policy issues that can be considered. They use the model to simulate responses to an adverse foreign shock experienced by the country, which they represent as a sharp fall in foreign borrowing accompanied by a significant fall in the price of oil (Ecuador's main export). They examine the growth and poverty outcomes of a representation of the actual policy response adopted (a combination of contractionary monetary policy, contractionary fiscal policy, and trade liberalization). This is compared to the outcomes achieved by applying each of these measures in isolation, and with a 'no adjustment' scenario that in practice means an exchange rate adjustment. Trade-offs inevitably exist, but the actual policy package adopted performs relatively well. A tighter fiscal policy would have enabled higher growth in the long term, but the authors judge that such a policy package would not have been politically feasible due to its adverse effects on medium and high education urban households. However, in terms of both growth and poverty outcomes, the no adjustment scenario performs badly relative to the alternatives considered.

Most of the studies collected together by Sahn (1996) examine specific, though central, aspects of economic reform programmes undertaken in various African countries. As argued above, this focus on specific policy measures may make the mechanisms generating poverty outcomes more transparent. The particular reforms considered are those relating to trade and exchange rate policy, fiscal policy and agricultural and food policy. The vast majority of these studies are again based on the third of the methods discussed in section 5.4 and most are based on CGE models, a technique well suited to the issues considered. As suggested above, a major advantage of these methods is their ability to separate out the effects of the initial crisis from the effects of the reform(s) designed to deal with it.

For the policy issues and the countries considered, the overall empirical results reject the view that the poor have borne a disproportionate share of the costs of reform. Sahn (1996) in fact argues the contrary, that policies such as real exchange rate devaluation and agricultural market liberalization, rather than hurting the poor, have if anything had a beneficial impact on their incomes, and that the costs are borne predominantly by the non-poor. Based on the case study evidence, Sahn (1996) argues that economic reform (at least the elements considered in this volume) is not inherently anti-poor, and so that concern with its possible adverse poverty impact is not a reason for avoiding economic reform. He argues that economic reforms of the sort considered in this study are generally consistent with concerns about poverty reduction, in contrast to what a number of commentators have suggested.

## 5.6 CONCLUSIONS

General arguments that economic reform exacerbates poverty, or the counter-argument that economic reform is beneficial for the poor, are completely unconvincing. For reasons set out above, there can be no clear-cut answers to the question of the impact of economic reform on poverty at this level of generality. Countries are diverse and heterogeneous; reform packages are diverse and heterogeneous; and both the circumstances in which they are undertaken and the degree of implementation are variable. The empirical evidence, reviewed in the previous section supports this view of the absence of a general relationship between economic reform and poverty.

It follows therefore that the poverty impact of economic reform needs to be assessed on a case by case basis. To the extent generalizations are possible, these can most profitably be made for individual measures commonly included in economic reform programmes. But even this is difficult; while we may know about trends in poverty in a country over a period of time, it is much more difficult to discern to what extent a given policy reform, as opposed to other factors, is responsible for this trend. This chapter has reviewed some ways which might help us to understand better links between policy measures taken at the macro level and outcomes at more disaggregated levels. Each of the three methods discussed is of value, and their value is enhanced where they can be used jointly. However, in addition to these methods, other issues can be addressed to some extent based on more disaggregated or micro data. Thus household survey data, community survey data, results from participatory poverty assessments etc. can all be of value, especially where they are nationally representative.

In conclusion, that poverty has increased in many developing countries is already grounds for serious concern, and calls for a policy response. Moreover, the need for this policy response is immediate; it cannot wait until we have a complete understanding of the precise factors responsible for the increase in poverty. But having said that, policy based on ignorance or an incorrect diagnosis of the problem may be bad policy, and could make matters worse rather than better. It is clearly crucial to develop our understanding of the factors behind adverse movements in poverty, including the role played by economic reform. One necessary first step is for more relevant macroeconomic analysis for developing countries which can consider the distributional consequences of policy actions; as long as macroeconomic policy discussion fails to consider this, it should not be surprising to find that some macroeconomic policy reforms in fact lead to increased poverty.

## Notes

* I am grateful to Tony Addison, John Mackinnon and Oliver Morrissey for very helpful comments and discussions based on an earlier draft. Of course, responsibility for opinions expressed and any errors present in this final version rests solely with me. This chapter was written in summer 1997 while I was visiting the Centre for the Study of African Economies (CSAE), University of Oxford. I am grateful to all at CSAE for providing a stimulating environment for working on this paper.

1. Moreover, many of the policy changes involved in economic reform are national level measures, e.g. devaluation, trade liberalization or monetary contraction.

2. In theory, it would be desirable to also include an imputation for leisure in the measure of the standard of living; in practice, though, this is very difficult to do because of identifying leisure, and valuing it. The reason for wanting to take account of leisure is that people, often but not always women, can suffer from 'time poverty' (lack of leisure) as well as, or instead of, money poverty.
3. Another approach to studying poverty is based on participatory poverty assessments, which are normally conducted at the community or village level, and in which respondents, normally as a group, are asked directly about living standards and poverty in their neighbourhoods. A good example of this approach is the study conducted by Norton *et al.* (1995) in Ghana. This approach is not considered in depth here because such studies tend (of necessity) to be conducted in specified localities rather than being nationally representative. More generally, though, there is probably a trade-off between more general studies at a countrywide level, which consider a wider range of policy impacts but which cannot hope to fully capture the heterogeneity and complexity of the country, and more specific local studies, whose conclusions are less generalizable, but which imply a more thorough understanding of poverty among the groups under study.
4. An alternative approach may be that data are directly collected at the household level on changes in their living conditions over an appropriate time period, collected based on retrospective questioning. Responses to such questions do not suffer from the comparability problem referred to above. The issue in this case, however, is how accurately interviewees can respond to such questions. In particular, such an approach cannot be expected to provide reliable estimates of magnitudes of changes in quantitative variables such as consumption or income, but the qualitative information it provides may be very useful.
5. Alternatively, where these conditions are not satisfied, it may be possible to make adjustments to allow over time comparisons to be made. Such adjustments were attempted in the case of Ghana, where the third of a series of three questionnaires was based on a different questionnaire, especially with regard to the collection of consumption data. Various attempts though have been made to try to make this third round comparable with earlier rounds (Coulombe and McKay, 1995; Jones and Ye, 1995; Demery and Mehra, 1997), though of course in these circumstances it is impossible to be sure how much of any observed change is genuine and how much reflects the change in the method of data collection.
6. Demery and Addison (1987) discuss the issue of the impact of stabilization on income distribution in more depth.
7. Other things being equal, producers of non-traded goods and services are likely to lose from the real exchange rate devaluation. In a number of countries these may disproportionately be women, a potentially important gender dimension to the poverty impact of stabilization.
8. This is only a first order indication, because the reality may be more complex than this. Thus, for example, producers may also purchase traded inputs; the benefits of increases in the price of traded outputs may not reach producers of these goods (e.g. small farmers) but rather accrue to

intermediaries; where tradable outputs are highly protected the devaluation may not make any difference to their producers.

9. Note that it can also be important to know which specific groups are likely to suffer increased poverty as a result of the reforms (even if poverty in aggregate falls).
10. See Berg *et al.* (1994), Chapter 8, for a more thorough discussion of these issues.
11 For more details on the nature and characteristics of CGE models, see, *inter alia*, Dervis, de Melo and Robinson (1982), Gunning and Keyzer (1996).
12. In addition the technical need to be able to 'solve' the model, and use it for policy simulations, necessarily restricts the type of behavioural specifications which can be used.
13. This emphasis on stabilization through expenditure switching rather than expenditure reduction cannot be a completely generalizable result; expenditure switching by means of a real devaluation is clearly desirable when the real exchange rate is overvalued, but it is highly unlikely that the real exchange rates of all developing countries are overvalued.

## References

Appleton, S. (1996), 'Problems of Measuring Changes in Poverty over Time: The Case of Uganda', *IDS Bulletin*, 27:1, pp. 43–55.

Berg, E., G. Hunter, T. Lenaghan and M. Riley (1994), 'Poverty and Structural Adjustment in the 1980s: Trends in Welfare Indicators in Latin America and Africa', Report prepared for USAID, September.

Bourguignon, F., J. de Melo and C. Morrison (1991), 'Poverty and Income Distribution During Adjustment: Issues and Evidence from the OECD Project', *World Development*, 19: 11, pp. 1485–1508.

Bourguignon, F., J. de Melo and A. Suwa (1991), 'Modelling the Effects of Adjustment Programmes on Income Distribution', *World Development*, 19:11, pp. 1527–1544.

Cornia, G.A., R. Jolly and F. Stewart (eds) (1987), *Adjustment with a Human Face*, 2 Vols, Oxford: Clarendon Press.

Coulombe, H. and A. McKay (1995), 'An Assessment of Trends in Poverty in Ghana 1988–92', *PSP Discussion Paper No 81*, Washington, DC: The World Bank.

Datt, G. and M. Ravallion (1992), 'Growth and Redistribution Components of Changes in Poverty Measures: A Decomposition with Application to Brazil and India in the 1980s', *Journal of Development Economics*, 38:2, pp. 275–295.

Delaine, G. and others (1992), 'The Social Dimensions of Adjustment Integrated Survey: A Survey to Measure Poverty and Understand the Effects of Policy Change on Households', *Social Dimensions of Adjustment Working Paper No. 14*, Washington, DC: The World Bank.

Demery, L. and T. Addison (1987), 'Stabilization Policy and Income Distribution in Developing Countries', *World Development*, 15:12, pp. 1483–1498.

Demery, L. and L. Squire (1996), 'Macroeconomic Adjustment and Poverty in Africa: An Emerging Picture', *World Bank Research Observer*, 11:1, pp. 39–59.

Demery, L. and K. Mehra (1997), 'Measuring Poverty over Time: Dealing with Uncooperative Data in Ghana', mimeo, Poverty, Gender and Public Management Department, Washington, DC: The World Bank.

Dervis, K., J. de Melo and S. Robinson (1982), *General Equilibrium Models for Development Policy*, Cambridge: Cambridge University Press.

Grootaert, C., T. Marchant and others (1991), 'The Social Dimensions of Adjustment Priority Survey: An Instrument for the Rapid Identification and Monitoring of Target Groups', *Social Dimensions of Adjustment Working Paper No. 12*, Washington, DC: The World Bank.

Grosh, M.E. and P. Glewwe (1995), 'A Guide to Living Standards Measurement Study Surveys and Their Data Sets', *LSMS Working Paper No. 120*, Washington DC.

Gunning, J.A. and M. Keyzer (1996), 'Applied General Equilibrium Models for Policy analysis', Chapter 35 of J. Behrman and T.N. Srinivasan (eds), *Handbook of Development Economics*, Vol IIIB, Amsterdam: Elsevier.

Jones, C. and X. Ye (1995), 'Accounting for the Reduction in Rural Poverty in Ghana 1988–1992', *PSP Discussion Paper No. 84*, Washington, DC: The World Bank.

Lipton, M. and M. Ravallion (1996), 'Poverty and Policy', Chapter 41 of J. Behrman and T.N. Srinivasan (eds), *Handbook of Development Economics*, Vol IIIB, Amsterdam: Elsevier.

McKay, A. (1997), 'Poverty Reduction through Economic Growth: Some Issues', *Journal of International Development*, 9:4, pp. 665–673.

Morley, S. (1994), *Poverty and Inequality in Latin America: Past Evidence, Future Prospects*, Washington, DC: Overseas Development Council.

Mosley, P., J. Harrigan and J. Toye (1991), *Aid and Power: The World Bank and Policy Based Lending*, 2 vols, London: Routledge.

Norton, A., E.B.-D. Aryeetey, D. Korboe and D.K.T. Dogbe (1995), 'Poverty Assessment in Ghana using Qualitative and Participatory Research Methods', *PSP Discussion Paper No. 83*, Washington, DC: The World Bank.

Sadoulet, E and A. de Janvry (1995), 'Poverty Alleviation, Income Distribution and Growth during Adjustment', Chapter 5 of N. Lustig (ed.), *Coping with Austerity: Poverty and Inequality in Latin America*, Washington, DC: The Brookings Institute.

Sahn, D.E. (ed) (1996), *Economic Reform and the Poor in Africa*, Oxford: Clarendon Press.

Stewart, F. (1995), *Adjustment and Poverty: Options and Choices*, London: Routledge.

Toye, J. (1995), *Structural Adjustment and Employment Policy: Issues and Experience*, Geneva: International Labour Office.

United Nations (1984), *Handbook of Household Surveys*, National Household Survey Capability Programme, Studies in Methods, Series F, No. 31.

World Bank, Country Economics Department (1990), 'Adjustment Lending Policies for Sustainable Growth', *Policy and Research Series No. 14*, Washington, DC: The World Bank.

World Bank, Country Economics Department (1992), 'Adjustment Lending and Mobilization of Private and Public Resources for Growth', *Policy and Research Series No. 22*, Washington, DC: The World Bank.
World Bank (1994), *Adjustment in Africa: Reforms, Results and the Road Ahead*, New York: Oxford University Press.

# 6 Evaluating Trade Liberalization Using Smooth Transitions Analysis

David Greenaway, Steve Leybourne
and David Sapsford

## 6.1 INTRODUCTION

This chapter is concerned with a new approach (known as smooth transitions analysis) to the analysis of trade liberalization. Although our exposition focuses exclusively upon the use of this new method in the analysis of trade liberalizations there is no reason, in principle, why the method might not be applied more generally in a variety of contexts involving the evaluation of policy reforms of various sorts. Previous studies of the influence of trade liberalizations upon economic growth performance have recognized the possibility that changes in the orientation of trade policies might influence growth via one or both of two channels. The first such channel views exports as one of the arguments of the growth equation and sees trade liberalizations as bringing about increased exports and therefore also increased real output. This is essentially the view adopted by Papageorgiou, Michaely and Choksi (1991) (PMC hereafter) in the large scale study of thirty-six liberalization episodes in nineteen countries that they undertook for the World Bank. The second channel sees trade liberalizations as having the potential to bring about a variety of dynamic changes which give rise to an alteration in the coefficient of the export variable in the growth equation, such that an increase in exports can have a greater growth promoting effect after liberalization.

In the analysis of the second of these two channels, most previous investigators have employed straightforward dummy variable techniques. As discussed in Chapter 2 above, such an approach is not without its limitations. A particular difficulty with the dummy variable approach is that it effectively assumes that any change that occurs in the relevant parameter takes place instantaneously. While it is conceivable that this may not be a totally unreasonable assumption under certain circumstances, it nevertheless seems, as will be argued below, unduly restrictive in the context of the influence of liberalization upon growth performance especially in developing economies. In this chapter we propose an alternative econometric procedure which, it will be argued, overcomes this (and other) limitations of the now conventional dummy variable approach.

The remainder of the chapter is organized as follows: section 6.2 provides a brief overview of the previous literature, while section 6.3 describes the smooth transitions model. Section 6.4 reports and discusses some results that were obtained when this new method was applied to growth behaviour in a number of countries. Section 6.5 summarizes the main findings and offers some concluding comments.

## 6.2 MODELLING TRADE LIBERALIZATION AND GROWTH: SOME ISSUES

Following Krueger (1978), it has become customary when evaluating the effects of trade liberalization upon the rate of economic growth to distinguish between two possible effects. The first of these (christened the *indirect* effect by Krueger) takes an export-led growth view of the world and sees liberalization as having the potential to increase the rate of growth of exports and thereby the rate of growth of real output. The second (or *direct*) effect views trade liberalization (seen by Krueger as a reduction in the degree of anti-export bias) as having the potential to exert a positive influence on aggregate real output growth irrespective of exports. According to this second line of reasoning, Krueger saw a more liberalized trade sector as having the potential to improve growth performance by offering a variety of dynamic advantages, including increased capacity utilization and the more efficient allocation of capital inputs. A number of subsequent investigators have accepted this broad distinction between the direct and indirect effects of trade liberalizations and employed straightforward dummy variable techniques in order to test for the presence of what Krueger termed direct effects.[1]

As was discussed in Chapter 2 above, the usual procedure in empirical studies has been to adopt what has been termed the production function approach to the determinants of the rate of real output growth. In essence, this approach involves the specification and estimation of a model that specifies the rate of real output growth as a function of the rates of growth of capital inputs (typically proxied by the share of investment in GDP), labour inputs and real exports (e.g. Salvatore and Hatcher, 1991; Greenaway and Sapsford, 1994; Balasubramanyam, Salisu and Sapsford, 1996). Within this framework, the usual approach is to see the direct effect of trade liberalization as having the potential to bring about a change in the coefficient of the export variable in this sort of growth equation. Stated differently, this approach allows for the possibility that via direct effects trade liberalization has the potential to increase the elasticity of output with respect to exports, the consequence of which is that a given increase in exports may exert a *greater* growth enhancing effect after liberalization than it did before liberalization. Econometrically this line of reasoning takes us into the realms of varying parameter models and as noted in Chapter 2, this existence of a direct effect has typically been tested for in previous work by the simple device of specifying an intercept dummy accompanied by a slope dummy variable on the export coefficient.

## 6.3 SMOOTH TRANSITIONS ANALYSIS

Smooth transitions analysis is an approach to modelling deterministic structural change in a time series regression originally proposed by Bacon and Watts (1971) and Maddala (1971, p. 396) and more recently considered by Lin and Terasvirta (1992) and Granger and Terasvirta (1993, Chapter 7). The basic idea is quite simple. Rather than attempt to identify any change as a single structural break, one identifies it as a smooth transition between regression regimes over time.

Where liberalization is concerned, this is intuitively appealing. Even where a liberalization is 'big bang' in its implementation, any subsequent effects on growth will typically be gradual rather than automatic, with the speed of adjustment being dependent on the efficiency of markets in the economy in question. In developing countries sequenced liberalizations are more common than big bang liberalizations. In these circumstances it can take time for the reforms to gain credibility and for agents to react. Either way, modelling the impact on growth as a discrete structural break is inappropriate.

More concretely, following Granger and Terasvirta (1993, Chapter 7) a simple logistic smooth transition regression (LSTR) model may be written, in the simple case of a trend only model, as:

$$y_t = (\alpha_1 + \beta_1 t) + (\alpha_2 + \beta_2 t)S(t) + \varepsilon_t, \qquad t = 1, ..., T \qquad (6.1)$$
$$S(t) = [1 + exp\{-\gamma(t - \tau)\}]^{-1}$$

where we assume $\varepsilon_t$ is a zero mean disturbance term and where $y$ refers to the natural logarithm of real output. Under this formulation, assuming $\gamma > 0$, the model transition occurs smoothly between the initial state

$$y_t = \alpha_1 + \beta_1 t + \varepsilon_t, \qquad t \to -\infty$$

and the final state

$$y_t = (\alpha_1 + \alpha_2) + (\beta_1 + \beta_2)t + \varepsilon_t, \qquad t \to \infty$$

corresponding to $S(-\infty) = 0$ and $S(\infty) = 1$, respectively. Hence, the growth rate of $y$, as indicated by the coefficient on the trend variable, changes from $\beta_1$ to $(\beta_1 + \beta_2)$ through time. Notice that the model simultaneously allows the intercept to change from $\alpha_1$ to $(\alpha_1 + \alpha_2)$. Here, $\tau$ is a location parameter that determines the timing of the transition. For $t = \tau$, we have

$$y_t = (\alpha_1 + 0.5\alpha_2) + (\beta_1 + 0.5\beta_2)t + \varepsilon_t,$$

such that $\tau$ identifies the transition midpoint. The velocity of transition is controlled by the parameter $\gamma$. If $\gamma$ takes a large value then the transition is completed in a short period of time and as $\gamma$ tends to infinity the model collapses to one with an instantaneous structural break in intercept and trend at time $t = \tau$. Thus (6.1) embeds the standard structural break model as a special case. The parameters $\alpha_2$ and $\beta_2$ determine the direction of transition in the intercept and trend, respectively. If $\gamma < 0$, the initial and final model states are reversed but the interpretation of the parameters remains unchanged.

The simple specification of $S(t)$ given above models the transition as being smooth and symmetric. This does not of course mean that the estimated transition will be an exact representation of that which occurred, nor that richer specifications are not possible. More flexible forms of the logistic trend model can obviously be adopted which, for example, can allow for a non-symmetric transition path (facilitated by including higher order polynomial terms in $t$ within $S(t)$). We also constrain the transitions in intercept and trend to occur once only, simultaneously, and with the same velocity. A model which does not impose these restrictions could be entertained. However, generalizations can rapidly increase the number of parameters which need to be estimated and as the number of observations available in studies of trade liberalization is sometimes relatively small, degrees of freedom problems can quickly arise.

Note that the methodology relies upon the data identifying the mid point of a transition, then fixing the start and end points. No prior information is used to fix the date of a transition. From the standpoint of modelling liberalization episodes, what this means is that the data determines when a transition in the real growth rate has occurred, its direction of change and its duration. If any such transition is found, and it need not be, one can then refer back to the dating of a liberalization episode, as established from policy accounts, to see whether or not there is any apparent coincidence of timing. In Greenaway, Leybourne and Sapsford (1997b) our central focus is the PMC study where a number of distinct episodes are identified by the authors. The specific questions we were interested in are as follows:

- Is there any evidence of a transition in the growth rate in the countries in question over the period to which the PMC study applies?
- Is there any connection in terms of timing between the transition and liberalization as identified by PMC?

## 6.4 MODEL ESTIMATION

The smooth transitions approach raises a number of statistical issues, relating to both estimation and inference. These issues are explored in depth in Greenaway, Leybourne and Sapsford (1997b) where the LSTR model is estimated using annual time series data for thirteen countries taken from the PMC sample. These consisted of Brazil, Colombia, Greece, Korea, Israel, New Zealand, Portugal, Spain, Sri Lanka, Argentina, Yugoslavia and Indonesia. The dependent variable $y_t$ was (log) real GDP per capita at 1980 purchasing power parity prices. In this section we seek to provide an accessible overview of the main results reported in that paper.

The Berndt-Hall-Hall-Hausman optimization algorithm in GAUSSX 3.2 was used to compute the non-linear least squares estimates of the unknown parameters in the model (6.1) for each country. For comparison, we also estimated the model (6.1) imposing the restriction $S(t) = 0$ such that the intercept and trend coefficients are constant over time (no transition between regimes occurs).[2]

The standard likelihood ratio test for the restriction $\gamma = 0$ does not provide us with a valid test of the null hypothesis of constancy of the intercept and trend against the smooth transition alternative. This is because under this null the parameters $\alpha_2$, $\beta_2$ and $\tau$ are no longer identified (i.e. they may assume any possible value). However, following a two-step approach originally suggested by Davies (1977) it is possible to construct a Lagrange Multiplier (LM) test of the null-hypothesis of constancy of the intercept and trend. Employing this procedure we found test results that indicated (at the 5 per cent level) the existence of a transition in intercept or trend (or both) in all 13 countries. Table 6.1 provides a summary. Inspection of the signs of the estimated values of $\beta_1$, $\beta_2$ and $\gamma$ reported in Table 6.1 indicates that the direction of transition of the growth rate of real GDP is *positive* for Colombia, Korea, Sri Lanka and Indonesia. For the remaining countries in the sample (namely, Greece, Israel, New Zealand, Portugal, Spain, Argentina and Yugoslavia) the transition is *negative*. In addition, the results indicate wide diversity in the transition speed. For example, Yugoslavia was found to have undergone a rather rapid transition between growth paths ($\gamma = 3.575$), whereas Korea's transition appeared to have occurred far more slowly ($\gamma = 0.230$ in absolute value).

To provide a flavour of the full array of results obtained in our study it is convenient to consider in a little more detail the evidence relating to the following three countries Colombia, Greece and Korea. In order to illustrate the differences in experience of these three countries estimated growth transitions are plotted in Figures 6.1 to 6.3. In these diagrams the quantity plotted against time is the estimated growth rate at each point of time.[3] As our main concern in the current discussion is whether the growth transitions, positive or negative, may have been triggered by a liberalization episode we have imposed the liberalization episodes identified by PMC as shaded areas over the estimated transition paths. The range of experience thus revealed is interesting.

In the case of Colombia, 'take off' appears to coincide with the first liberalization episode which the economy undergoes (as identified by PMC) and is sustained through the second phase of liberalization. The transition is relatively rapid. By contrast, where Korea is concerned the picture is altogether different. The model identifies a transition, however, it is so protracted that the start and end points are outside the sample period. It would be difficult to make any kind of case to the effect that liberalization and growth are causally related. When the model is estimated for Greece it identifies a negative and rapid transition. As with the Korean case it is not clear, however, that it has anything whatsoever to do with liberalization.

These examples are taken from the sample of countries investigated by Greenaway, Leybourne and Sapsford (1997b). They are included to

*Table* 6.1 Non-Linear Least Squares Estimates of Logistic Smooth Transitions in Trend Model

| | $\alpha_1$ | $\alpha_2$ | $\beta_1$ | $\beta_2$ | $\gamma$ | $\tau$ | $\phi$ | $R^2$ | LM |
|---|---|---|---|---|---|---|---|---|---|
| Brazil | 4.277 | –0.308 | 0.042 | | 0.889 | 19.11 | 0.389 | 0.997 | 16.2 |
| (1963–1985) | (5.53) | (–5.26) | (6.08) | | (3.77) | (48.1) | (3.52) | | |
| Colombia | 7.158 | | 0.026 | –0.017 | –0.495 | 15.72 | | 0.994 | 10.1 |
| (1955–1982) | (390.) | | (35.7) | (–6.48) | (–4.53) | (26.9) | | | |
| Greece | 3.249 | | 0.028 | –0.007 | 0.642 | 28.60 | 0.530 | 0.995 | 14.5 |
| (1952–1985) | (2.99) | | (2.93) | (–2.65) | (1.87) | (27.5) | (3.31) | | |
| Korea | 6.565 | | 0.055 | –0.072 | –0.230 | 12.56 | | 0.997 | 9.66 |
| (1955–1979) | (157.) | | (25.6) | (–4.09) | (–5.02) | (8.75) | | | |
| Israel | 5.170 | 0.660 | 0.031 | –0.028 | 1.121 | 18.45 | 0.321 | 0.997 | 9.92 |
| (1953–1985) | (4.31) | (3.90) | (3.66) | (–3.74) | (1.88) | (26.0) | (2.01) | | |
| New Zealand | 4.746 | | 0.014 | –0.003 | 1.784 | 26.08 | 0.431 | 0.989 | 7.85 |
| (1951–1984) | (3.47) | | (3.32) | (–2.99) | (1.06) | (42.5) | (2.61) | | |
| Portugal | 4.272 | 0.590 | 0.022 | –0.015 | 0.439 | 20.01 | 0.381 | 0.997 | 14.2 |
| (1950–1985) | (3.66) | (3.01) | (2.88) | (–2.57) | (2.88) | (18.6) | (2.22) | | |
| Spain | 7.480 | 0.953 | 0.031 | –0.022 | 0.267 | 19.97 | | 0.995 | 14.4 |
| (1950–1985) | (265.) | (3.30) | (3.20) | (–3.03) | (2.57) | (11.0) | | | |
| Sri Lanka | 6.699 | –0.945 | 0.012 | 0.031 | 0.857 | 24.23 | | 0.954 | 15.9 |
| (1950–1985) | (345.) | (–6.63) | (6.79) | (6.95) | (1.83) | (28.4) | | | |
| Argentina | 7.954 | | 0.026 | –0.020 | 0.478 | 22.27 | | 0.912 | 13.3 |
| (1959–1985) | (298.) | | (8.50) | (–415) | (2.45) | (25.4) | | | |
| Yugoslavia | 7.425 | 0.742 | 0.049 | –0.036 | 3.575 | 18.94 | | 0.996 | 11.7 |
| (1960–1985) | (519.) | (6.58) | (36.1) | (–7.13) | (4.20) | (40.0) | | | |
| Indonesia | 6.209 | | 0.041 | –0.077 | –0.351 | 7.519 | | 0.997 | 14.1 |
| (1962–1985) | (99.5) | | (16.5) | (–2.30) | (–4.65) | (4.38) | | | |

*Notes:*
(i) Figures in parenthesis are asymptotic t–ratios.
(ii) $\phi$ denotes the coefficient of the lagged dependent variable.
(iii) LM is the Lagrange multiplier statistic for the test of the null hypothesis of constancy of the intercept and trend, as described in the text. The 5% critical value is 7.82.

illustrate the application of the smooth transition model which provides a potentially fruitful framework for the analysis of growth and liberalization. Clearly there are obvious limitations with the model as specified, not the least of which being that it is not a fully specified growth model.

When moving from the simple trend formulation analyzed above to a smooth transitions model containing a fully specified vector of explanatory variables a number of challenging econometric issues arise. These issues have recently been tackled in a paper by Leybourne,

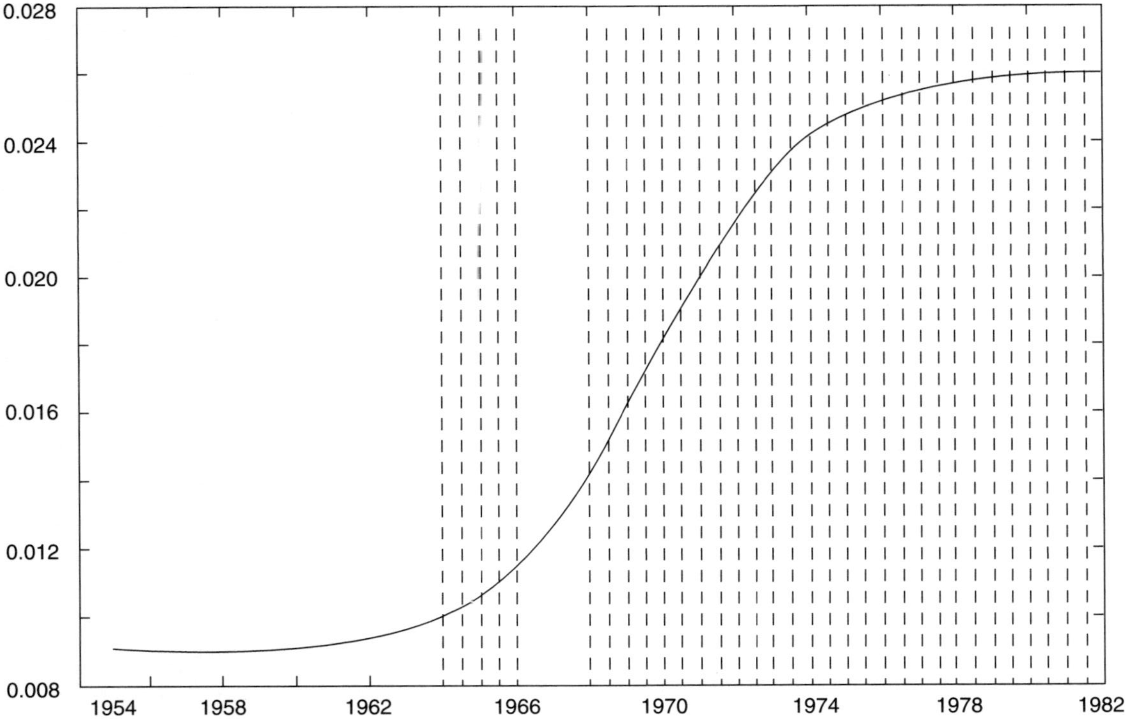


*Figure* 6.1 Estimated Growth: Colombia

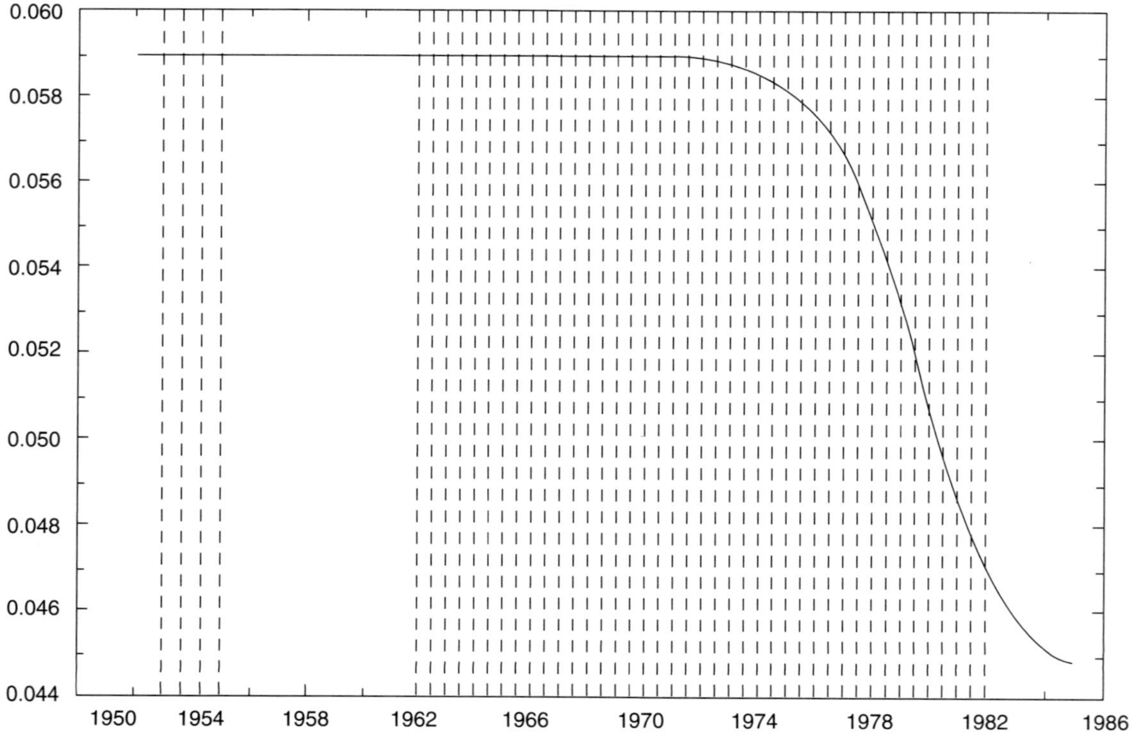


*Figure* 6.2 Estimated Growth: Greece

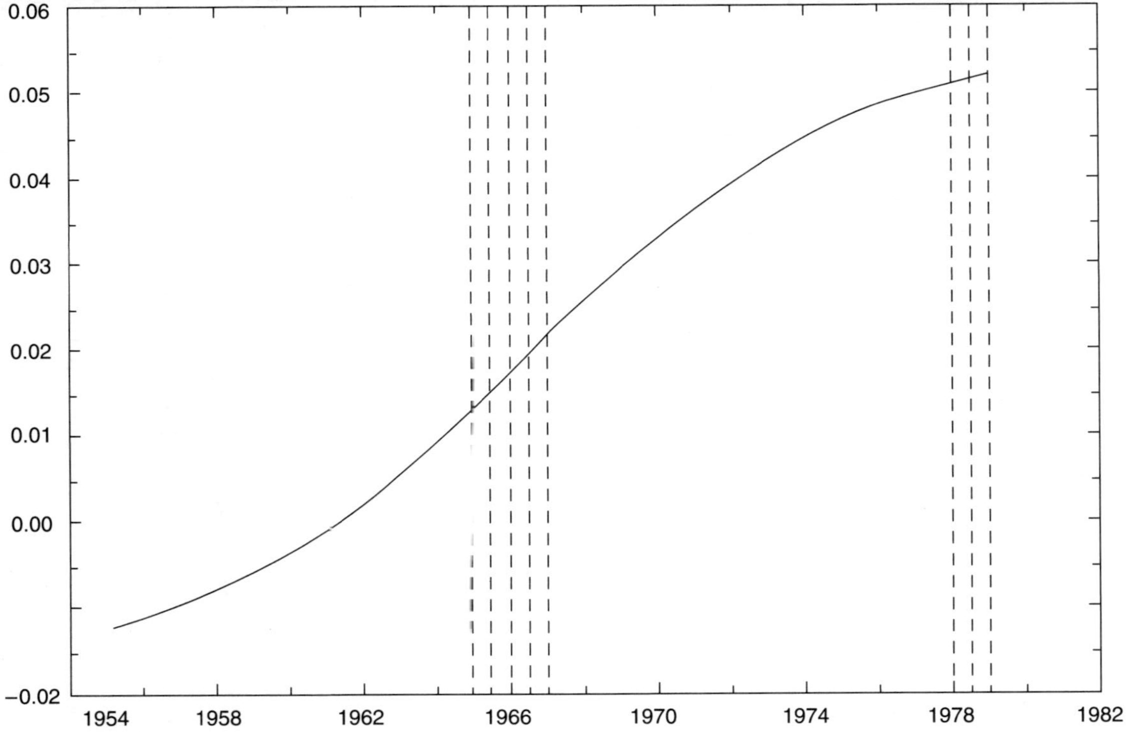


*Figure* 6.3 Estimated Growth: Korea

Newbold and Vougas (1998) (hereafter LNV) that successfully develops a suite of hypothesis tests allowing one, in principle, to distinguish between a range of possible alternative model specifications. The array of alternative possibilities considered includes, at the one extreme, the case of stationarity about a fixed deterministic trend and, at the other, the case where smooth transitions occur in both the intercept and trend term in a model containing a vector of explanatory variables. Space constraints prevent us from going into the full details of the LNV sequence of tests here (some are applied in Chapter 7 below). However, it is perhaps useful to notice that the procedures that they develop for testing whether a series is I(1) against the alternative of I(0) around a deterministic component which changes gradually and smoothly between two regimes are based on fitting a non-linear smooth transitions regression model to the series and performing augmented Dickey-Fuller (ADF) type unit root tests on the residuals from this fitted model. This testing procedure is then extended to smooth transitions models that contain additional I(1) regressors. In other words they develop cointegrating analogues to the tests described in the preceding sentence. In each case relevant critical values for the ADF type test statistics are derived by simulation methods.

The LNV approach is especially attractive in the context of the study of the influence of trade liberalization on real output in that it opens the way to structural modelling of GDP series where the possibility of smooth transition behaviour is catered for. In order to illustrate the application of the LNV procedure we may usefully consider the results that are obtained when their suggested approach is applied to the case of Turkey during the period 1950–1990. Although we omit the detailed results here, application of the LNV testing sequence (assuming logistic transition) to the Turkish case suggests the following as the appropriate model.

$$y_t = (\alpha_1 + \beta_1 t) + (\alpha_2 + \beta_2 t)S(t) + \delta_1 x_{1t} + \delta_2 x_{2t} + \varepsilon_t, \qquad (6.2)$$
$$S(t) = [1 + exp\{-\gamma(t - \tau)\}]^{-1}$$

In other words, the procedure leads us to conclude that (log) Turkish GDP is influenced by (log) capital stock ($x_1$) and (log) labour force ($x_2$) and that allowing for the effects of these explanatory variables, smooth transitions in *both* the intercept and trend are revealed. Table 6.2 summarizes our non-linear least squares estimates of the parameters of model (6.2) and the transition function *S*(*t*). The essential features of these results can be seen from the plots contained in Figure 6.4. The top panel plots the actual log GDP series overlaid with the fitted values

*Table* 6.2 Non-Linear Least Squares Estimates of Logistic Smooth Transitions Model of Turkish Economic Growth, 1950–90.

| $\alpha_1$ | $\alpha_2$ | $\beta_1$ | $\beta_2$ | $\delta_1$ | $\delta_2$ | $\gamma$ | $\tau$ | $R^2$ |
|---|---|---|---|---|---|---|---|---|
| –36.26 | 0.490 | –0.005 | –0.024 | 0.066 | 3.605 | 1.119 | 31.1 | 0.998 |
| (–1.72) | (1.44) | (–0.26) | (–2.17) | (2.46) | (2.83) | (3.09) | (59.3) | |

*Note:* Figures in parenthesis are asymptotic t ratios.

from (6.2) above. The middle and bottom panels of Figure 6.4 plot the estimated transition in the intercept and trend term respectively.

Following the approach discussed above it is instructive to compare the evidence regarding the timing of parameter transitions with the datings of liberalization episodes as given by PMC. PMC delineate two liberalizations in Turkey; 1970–73 and 1980–84. A number of conclusions may be drawn from our analysis. First, as can be seen from Figure 6.4 the parameter transitions that we have identified do not appear to be associated with the first of these two liberalizations. Second, it seems quite possible that the later liberalization exerted some influence on growth. Third, the effects of liberalization seem to have outlived the duration of the liberalization (as identified by PMC), continuing into the late 1980s. This particular finding is not entirely surprising given both the depth and breadth of the post-1980 Turkish trade reforms (Baysan and Blitzer, 1991; Olgun and Togan, 1991; Greenaway and Sapsford, 1995). Fourth, our evidence indicates that while the 1980–84 liberalization appears to have been associated with an upward intercept movement (representing an autonomous increase in Turkey's real GDP *level*), it also appears to have been associated with a downward transition in the trend rate of growth of Turkey's real GDP.

## Dummy Variables versus Smooth Transitions

In the preceding analysis it has been argued that the smooth transitions approach is superior to the conventional dummy variable approach in that it avoids imposing the arguably implausible restriction that the effects of liberalization occur in a discrete/instantaneous manner. Furthermore, we have seen that the instantaneous structural break model corresponding to the dummy variable approach is nested within

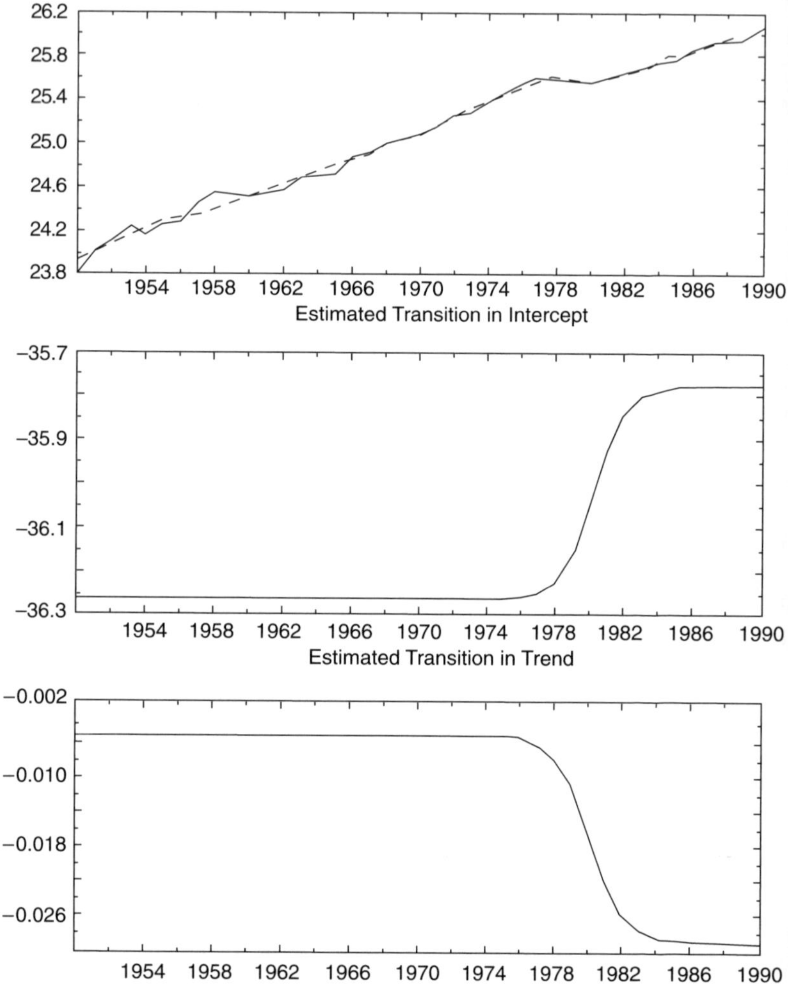


*Figure* 6.4 Log GDP for Turkey and Fitted Smooth Transition Model

the smooth transitions model, occurring when the speed of adjustment (*g*) becomes infinite. Indeed, given the size of the estimated *g* values reported in Tables 6.1 and 6.2 above, there would appear to be no evidence to suggest that the instantaneous break model (and therefore the dummy variable approach) represents, in any of the cases considered, anything approaching an adequate representation. This finding therefore raises some serious doubts about the adequacy of the specification of instantaneous break models of the sort widely found in previous studies of the effects of trade liberalization (and of adjustment more generally).

Some indication, albeit highly tentative, of the likely consequences of such mis-specification might be obtained by comparing the results obtained for the smooth transitions model of Turkey with those emerging from a dummy variable analysis of the conventional sort. The results of a conventional dummy variable analysis of growth and trade liberalization in Turkey within the framework of a production function type of model which is broadly comparable with formulation (6.2) above are reported in Greenaway and Sapsford (1994, p. 167). These results contrast sharply with those which emerge from the smooth transitions approach as discussed above, in that they reveal no evidence to indicate that the second Turkish liberalization (1980–84) exerted an influence on Turkish growth. However, in contrast again to the smooth transitions results, they did appear to provide some evidence to suggest that the first liberalization (1970–1973) exerted a significant positive influence upon the autonomous growth rate (as represented by an intercept shift in a *growth* equation). Clearly the two approaches to the analysis of the influence of changes in the orientation of trade policy upon Turkish economic growth lead to markedly different conclusions. However, if we accept the order of magnitude of the estimated value of the transition velocity parameter ($\gamma = 1.119$) reported in Table 6.2 then we would be led to reject the dummy variable model as badly mis-specified as a description of the Turkish experience and therefore to dismiss its results as erroneous.

## 6.5 CONCLUDING REMARKS

The proper evaluation of the effects of trade liberalizations upon the growth performance of liberalizing economies is an issue of some importance to both policy makers and development practitioners alike. The purpose of this chapter has been to introduce a new approach to the empirical analysis of this issue, an approach which we have argued overcomes some of the major limitations inherent in the hitherto most widely adopted method. In the chapter we have reported evidence of two main sorts. First, using a logistic smooth transitions trend model we revisited (a sub-set of) the countries analysed by PMC in their widely cited World Bank studies. The results thus obtained appear to raise some rather serious doubts about the validity of the conclusions drawn by PMC regarding the close positive relationship between trade liberalization on the one hand and growth performance on the other. Second, taking the Turkish experiences with trade liberalization as an example, we have reported results which were obtained from a structural model of the growth process of the conventional production function sort which allows for the possible existence of smooth transitions. The results that emerged from this model were contrasted with those from a conventional model of the dummy variable/ instantaneous change sort and it was argued, given the estimated velocity of transition, that the dummy variable approach leads to seriously misleading results.

The smooth transitions approach is in its infancy. However, despite this fact it is hoped that the evidence reported in this paper will lead subsequent researchers to treat the results which emerge from application of the dummy variable approach in this important area of research with an appropriate degree of caution, if not suspicion.

## Notes

1. On the basis of a two equation model, estimated with a selection of dummy variables included, Krueger was led to conclude that, in the sample of countries analyzed, trade liberalizations appear to have worked only through the first of the two channels described above. In essence, her conclusion was that 'the fact that the regime itself is liberalized (or restricted) does not seem to have any additional independent influence' (1978, p. 274) Krueger's analysis is not, however, without its limitations; Greenaway, Leybourne and Sapsford (1997a) provide a critique.
2. To account for the possibility of serial-correlation we included in the actual model estimated (equation (6.1) above) a term in the lagged dependent variable. Including at most a single lag in the dependent variable was found to be sufficient to yields serially-uncorrelated residuals for each country. Notice that imposition of the restriction $S(t) = 0$ reduces the estimated version of (6.1) to a Dickey-Fuller style regression.
3. Calculated as the estimated counterpart of $(\beta_1 + \beta_2 S(t))/(1 - \phi)$ where $\phi$ denotes the coefficient of the lagged dependent variable referred to in the preceding footnote.

## References

Bacon, D. and D. Watts (1971), 'Estimating the Transition Between Two Intersecting Straight Lines', *Biometrika*, 58, pp. 525–534.

Balasubramanyam, V. N., M. Salisu and D. Sapsford (1996), 'Foreign Direct Investment and Growth in EP and IS Countries', *Economic Journal*, 106, pp. 92–105.

Baysan, T. and C. Blitzer (1991), 'Turkey', in Papageorgiou, D., Michaely, M. and Choksi, A. (eds), *Liberalizing Foreign Trade, Volume 6*, Oxford: Basil Blackwell, pp. 263–405.

Davies, R. (1977), 'Hypothesis Testing when a Nuisance Parameter is Only Present Under the Alternative', *Biometrika*, 64, pp. 247–254.

Granger, C. and T. Terasvirta (1993), *Modelling Nonlinear Economic Relationships*, London and New York: Oxford University Press.

Greenaway, D., S. Leybourne and D. Sapsford (1997a), 'Trade Liberalization and Growth', in S. Gupta and N.K. Choudhry (ed.) *Growth, Equity and Sustainability: Studies in Globalization and Development* (Vol. 1), Dordrecht: Kluwer.

Greenaway, D., S. Leybourne and D. Sapsford (1997b), 'Modelling Growth (and Liberalization) Using Smooth Transitions Analysis' *Economic Inquiry*, 35:4, pp. 798–814.

Greenaway, D. and D. Sapsford (1994), 'What Does Liberalization Do for Exports and Growth?', *Weltwirtschaftliches Archiv*, 130:1, pp. 152–174.

Greenaway, D. and D. Sapsford (1995), 'Liberalization and the Terms of Trade in Turkey: A Causal Analysis', *Applied Economics*, 27:10, pp. 953–959.

Krueger, A. (1978), *Foreign Trade Regimes and Economic Development: Liberalization Attempts and Consequences*, Cambridge, MA: Ballinger for NBER.

Leybourne, S., P. Newbold and D. Vougas (1998), 'Unit Roots and Smooth Transitions', *Journal of Time Series Analysis*, 19(1), pp. 83–97.

Lin, C. and T. Terasvirta (1992), 'Testing the Constancy of Regression Parameters Against Continuous Structural Change', (mimeo) Department of Economics, University of California, San Diego.

Maddala, G.S. (1977), *Econometrics*, London and New York: McGraw-Hill.

Olgun, H. and S. Togan (1991), 'Trade Liberalization and the Structure of Protection in Turkey in the 1980s: A Quantitative Analysis', *Weltwirtschaftliches Archiv*, 127, pp. 152–170.

Papageorgiou, D., M. Michaely and A. Choksi (1991), *Liberalizing Foreign Trade* (7 vols), London and New York: Oxford University Press

Salvatore, D. and T. Hatcher (1991), 'Inward Oriented and Outward Oriented Trade Strategies', *Journal of Development Studies*, 27: 3, pp. 7–25.

# 7 Structural Adjustment and Economic Growth in Pakistan: A Smooth Transitions Analysis*

Mark McGillivray

## 7.1 INTRODUCTION

Policy-based lending, as we have come to know it, is a well established practice in Pakistan. This country was among the first to accept such lending, having received its first World Bank Sectoral Adjustment Loan of $50 million in 1980. It subsequently accepted its first World Bank Structural Adjustment Loan of $140 in 1982 and its first IMF Structural Adjustment Facility loan of $515 million in 1988. These lending agencies have advanced more than $4 billion in adjustment lending to Pakistan since the early 1980s (Iqbal, 1993; and Zaman, 1995). This is in addition to roughly the same amount of funds provided by the IMF through its Standby and Extended Fund Facility arrangements (Zaman, 1995). Based on the number of adjustment loans it has received, Pakistan has been classified by the World Bank as an 'intensive adjuster' (World Bank, 1992). In return for these loans Pakistan has committed itself to a fairly common package of reforms aimed at stabilizing and structurally adjusting its economy. These reforms include reducing the overall budget deficit, curtailing the rate of inflation, reducing the balance of payments deficit, decreasing the level of private external debt service ratio, increasing gross official foreign exchange reserves, containing the growth of domestic credit, liberalizing foreign trade, reforming financial markets, and deregulating prices and investment in the agricultural and industrial sectors. The main aims of these reforms were to contain inflation and restore growth (Zaidi, 1994).

Pakistan's adjustment experience is an especially interesting case study. Pakistan's economy had been performing poorly in the years leading up to the acceptance of its first adjustment loan. CPI inflation had been high (approaching 30 per cent in the mid-1970s), GDP growth had fallen and the current account had deteriorated. Yet, as is shown below, Pakistan's macroeconomic performance has improved appreciably following the introduction of its structural adjustment programme. This turnaround has caused a huge debate, both within Pakistan and internationally. Proponents of adjustment lending argue that the turnaround is at least in part due to the economic reforms to which this lending has been tied. Others argue that the improved performance is not related to these reforms. Empirical evaluations of Pakistan's post-1980 adjustment experience have done little, if anything, to resolve this debate. In some instances it has been concluded that adjustment has had a negative impact on Pakistan's macroeconomic performance, in others it has been judged to have had a positive impact and in others no significant impact at all.

The purpose of this chapter is twofold. First, it provides a brief overview of Pakistan's macroeconomic experience under its adjustment programme and debates over the efficacy of this programme.[1] This is accompanied by an overview of the approaches used and findings of empirical evaluations of the programme. Second, building on Chapters 2 and 6, it applies a smooth transitions model to Pakistani real GDP data for the period 1960–94. The central question under consideration is whether the adjustment programme been the prime source of Pakistan's improved performance with respect to GDP. Has the programme turned around Pakistan's GDP performance? Results of this analysis suggest that the answer to this question is no, and that the origins of Pakistan's growth performance well pre-date the adjustment programme. The chapter concludes that this is not inconsistent with, *inter alia*, the non- or partial attainment of the majority programme objectives during 1980–93.

## 7.2 PAKISTAN'S ADJUSTMENT EXPERIENCE: AN OVERVIEW

Comparisons of Pakistan's macroeconomic performance prior to and after the introduction of its adjustment programme are shown in Table 7.1. On face value these data are reasonably striking.[2] Each of the seven indicators, commonly used in assessing the efficacy of adjustment policies, show improvements in Pakistan's macroeconomic performance during the adjustment period. The biggest percentage improvements are in GDP growth and inflation, but perhaps the most striking outcome concerns investment. The general consensus is that based on the experience of other countries adjustment has had a negative impact on investment.[3] Although the difference between Pakistan's average 1970–79 and 1980–92 investment ratios is not statistically significant, the former is nonetheless higher than the latter. This certainly sets Pakistan apart from other adjustment programme countries.

The basis of many claims of the success of Pakistan's structural adjustment programme is the sort of comparisons shown in Table 7.1. McCleary (1991), writing from the World Bank, argues that this performance has at least in part been determined by those policies to which World Bank and IMF adjustment loans have been tied. He does, however, assert that Pakistan's strong economic performance has also meant that the programme has been able to be sustained by obviating the need for policy reversals. Yet within official circles there remain a number of reservations over the adjustment programme. Khan (1991, cited in Zaidi, 1994), writing from the IMF, while acknowledging that Pakistan's 1980s macroeconomic performance has been credible compared to that of many other developing countries that there have been some attempts to liberalize Pakistan's economy, it is tenuous to argue that its economy has become more open and outward in the 1980s compared with the previous decade.

The structural adjustment programme has support within Pakistan. Riazuddin (1994), for example, asserts that while the trade liberalization components of the programme will have some displacement costs, such costs will be significantly outweighed by greater industrial efficiency and better resource allocation. Critics within Pakistan have been candid in their assessments. Zaidi (1993, 1994) asserts that the

*Table* 7.1 Selected Macroeconomic Indicators, Pakistan

| Indicator | 1970–79 | 1980–92 | % Change |
|---|---|---|---|
| Real GDP Growth (%) | 4.1 | 6.2 | 50 |
| Investment (% GDP) | 16.0 | 18.9 | 18 |
| Current Account (% GDP) | –5.8 | –3.8 | 34 |
| CPI Inflation (%) | 12.5 | 7.3 | –41 |
| Exports (% GDP) | 10.1 | 13.6 | 34 |
| Govt. Budget Bal. (% GDP) | –8.2 | –6.7 | –19 |
| Gross Domestic Saving (% GDP) | 8.0 | 10.3 | 29 |

All percentages refer to yearly averages for each period.
*Source:* World Bank (1994).

adjustment programme has had little to do with Pakistan's improved macroeconomic performance, that the country does not need such a programme and ought therefore to be left to its own devices. Zaidi's position is based on two central premises (although he does not provide empirical support for the second): that the Pakistani economy was in much better shape in the early 1980s than was widely perceived, and that its performance since the introduction of the adjustment programme has simply been a continuation of a trend which commenced in the 1970s.[4] Zaman (1995) posits that Pakistan's reforms are folly, asserting that the root cause of Pakistan's economic problems has been a lack of 'fiscal discipline' which has led to 'unsustainably high budget deficits' (Zaman, 1995, p. 86).[5] Zaman further contends that Pakistan ought legislate to ensure such discipline, place on hold initiatives to liberalize trade and exchange, institute measures to increase investment (including if necessary tariff protection) and introduce government interventions to promote exports.

Khan's above-mentioned comments are not without supporting evidence, as Tables 7.2 and 7.3 make clear. Taken from McGillivray and White (1994), these tables provide details of Pakistan's adjustment policies during 1980–93, together with World Bank assessments of their outcomes. The adjustment programme is divided into two discrete phases on the grounds of an identifiable lull in the reform process in the mid-1980s. Intensive adjuster or not, a feature of Pakistan's adjustment programme is its inability to achieve objectives. Tables 7.2 and 7.3 list a total of 19 specific objectives. Nine of these objectives have unambiguously not been achieved. In particular, efforts to reduce the fiscal deficit to five per cent of GDP (see Table 7.3) seem to have fallen well short of the mark. So too have those aimed at reducing inflation to the target of six per cent. Of the remaining ten objectives, one can conclude partial success with seven and success with three (rationalization of public investment programme, increased gas price and financial sector reforms).

That the structural adjustment programme has achieved less than half of its objectives certainly casts a shadow over its contribution to Pakistan's improved macroeconomic performance. Yet as was argued in Chapter 2, questions about the direction (and extent) of influence can only be answered by more sophisticated empirical approaches than merely looking at before and after comparisons, as so often has been applied in evaluating the impact of adjustment.[6] Such studies of the Pakistani experience fall into one of the three categories mentioned in Chapter 2: those which assess the impact of the loans and/or the extent

*Table* 7.2 Structural Adjustment Programme, Pakistan, 1980–85

| Policy Areas | Objectives | Achievements |
|---|---|---|
| Agriculture | 1. Increased public expenditure on agriculture and water. | Not achieved. |
| | 2. Elimination of fertilizer subsidy. | Reduced, but not eliminated. |
| | 3. 'Proper relation' between input and output prices. | Prices of wheat, rice and cotton altered toward world prices, sugar price substantially higher. |
| | 4. Raise water charges to cover O&M expenditures. | Not done. |
| Energy | 1. Rise gas price | Target for 1988 reached by 1985. |
| Industrial and Trade Policy | 1. Industrial public enterprises to make profits. | Not achieved. |
| | 2. Relax controls and streamline procedures for investment. | Partially achieved. |
| | 3. Reduce import controls. | Estimated that the share of domestic industry protected by import bans fell from 65 to 45%. |
| | 4. Tariff reductions | Limited. |
| Development Planning | 1. Rationalization of public investment program | Achieved. |

*Source:* World Bank (1986).

of reform, those which investigate the behavioural assumptions on which a programme is premised and those which assess the impact of the presence of a programme itself. Unfortunately, the conclusions emerging from these studies are about as diverse as the methodologies they apply. Notwithstanding, it is instructive to briefly consider the results of these studies, keeping in mind the methodological caveats of Chapter 2 in mind.

Iqbal (1993), whose study falls into the first of these categories, estimated six multivariate regression equations using time series data. The dependent variables were real GDP growth, investment, exports, import demand, government current consumption and domestic inflation. The level of adjustment lending appeared as an explanatory variable in each equation, along with a range of common macroeconomic

*Table* 7.3 Structural Adjustment Programme, Pakistan, 1988–93

| Policy Areas | Objectives | Achievements |
|---|---|---|
| Public Finance | 1. Reduction of fiscal deficit to 5% of GDP through increased government revenue (achieved via improved tax administration) and expanding the tax base. | Target not achieved. Fiscal deficit was 6.5% of GDP in 1989, 8.7% in 1991 and 7.5% in 1992. No significant achievement in either tax administration or expansion of the tax base (tax rate stagnant throughout period). |
| | 2. Reduction in government expenditure to approximately 25 to 26% of GDP. | Not achieved. |
| Balance of Payments | 1. Reduction in current account deficit to 2.6% of GDP. | Despite strong export growth, deficit is 3.1% of GDP in 1992. Import growth remains high and private remittance have fallen. |
| | 2. Increase reserves from 3 to 6 weeks of imports. | No progress until 1991, but estimated at 5.6 weeks for 1992. |
| | 3. Correction of price distortions and tariff reforms. | Tariff reduced from 225% in 1987/88 to 95% in 1992/93. |
| Financial Sector | 1. Control of domestic credit expansion. | Not realized due to excessive government borrowing. |
| | 2. Rationalization of interest rate structure. | Partially implemented through auction of Treasury Bills and increased rates for concessionary lending schemes (which still remain negative in real terms). |
| | 3. Reform of financial sector. | Management of two nationalized banks transferred to private sector and 10 new commercial banks established. Liberalisation of rules enabling ongoing expansion of stock market. |
| Price Stability | 1. Inflation to be reduced to 6% over the programme period. | Not achieved. Inflation target averaged 10% per annum during adjustment period. |

*Source:* World Bank (1993).

variables. Adjustment loans were found to be significantly correlated with each dependent variable except exports. The direction of causation was not uniform, however. Adjustment lending was negatively associated with GDP growth and imports and positively associated with investment, government consumption and inflation.[7]

The research of Khan and Aftab (1994) falls into the second category. Recall that their objective was to test a series of neo-liberal hypotheses about the likely benefits of Pakistan's financial sector reforms. They questioned the likely benefits of these reforms on the basis of negligible or modest statistical relationships between the real interest rate and real saving, money demand and financial deepening and a significant negative relationship between the real interest rate and investment efficiency and output growth.

Studies falling under the third of the above-mentioned category include those by Balassa (1989), Mosley *et al.* (1991) and McGillivray *et al.* (1995). Balassa and Mosley *et al.* use comparator country analysis.[8] That is, they compare the experience of countries which have embarked on a adjustment programme with those which have not. In Balassa's study the latter was a group of countries while in Mosley *et al.* it was a single country, Egypt. Balassa found that Pakistan outperformed the control group with respect to output growth, exports, the balance of payments and inflation. Mosley *et al.* report somewhat mixed results, with Pakistan doing better in some indicators than Egypt and worse in others. The study of McGillivray *et al.* (mentioned above in Chapter 2) tested for discrete structural breaks within error correction models of Pakistani investment ratios and inflation rates for the period 1960–90. They concluded that on the basis of model simulations adjustment had either a minuscule impact on investment or none at all. Inflation, and the other hand, was thought to have been in the vicinity 1.2 to 2.6 percentage points higher than would have been the case without the adjustment programme.

## 7.3 A SMOOTH TRANSITIONS ANALYSIS

Against the preceding background our attention now turns to this chapter's evaluation of the impact of Pakistan's adjustment programme on that country's real GDP growth rate. Has the programme achieved one of its two main objectives, that being to transform Pakistan from a low to high growth economy? Recognizing the limitations of empirical evaluations discussed in the preceding section and reviewed in Chapter 2, smooth transitions analysis is employed in an attempt to answer this question. Such an analysis has many advantages, although far from perfect itself. The model is similar but not identical to the LSTR model used in the bulk of Chapter 6. The differences are in the specification of the smooth transitions term and the use of a vector of exogenous regressors. The model is:

$$y_t = \alpha_1 + \beta_1 t + (\alpha_2 + \beta_2 t)S_t + \lambda x_t + \varepsilon_t \qquad t = 1, ..., T \tag{7.1}$$

where $y_t$ is the chosen performance indicator (in this case real GDP) in year $t$, $\alpha_1$ and $\alpha_2$ are intercept terms, $\beta_1$ and $\beta_2$ are slope coefficients, $t$ is a time trend, $S_t$ is the transition term and $\epsilon_t$ is a residual. $S_t$ is defined as:

$$S_t = \left[1 + \exp(-\gamma[t - \tau T])\right]^{-1} \tag{7.2}$$

where $\gamma$ is a coefficient determining the speed (velocity) of transition and $\tau$ is a location parameter which determines the timing of the transition. More specifically, $\tau$ ranges between zero and one and shows the proportion of $y_t$ before the transition mid-point. The actual mid-point, therefore, is where $t = \tau T$ (in Chapter 6 it was where $\tau = t$).

As in Chapter 6, with $\gamma > 0$ transition under an adjustment programme occurs smoothly between the initial state of no transition

$$y_t = \alpha_1 + \beta_1 t + \lambda x_t + \varepsilon_t \qquad t \to -\infty \tag{7.1a}$$

and the final state of complete transition

$$y_t = (\alpha_1 + \alpha_2) + (\beta_1 + \beta_2)t + \lambda x_t + \varepsilon_t \qquad t \to \infty \tag{7.1b}$$

corresponding to $S(-\infty) = 0$ and $S(\infty) = 1$, respectively.

A number of points follow from the preceding equations. The level of $y_t$ smoothly changes (autonomously) from $\alpha_1$ to $\alpha_1 + \alpha_2$ over time while is rate of growth changes from $\beta_1$ to $\beta_1 + \beta_2$. It also follows that the model embodies two transitions: one in the intercept term and the other in the growth rate. These transitions are represented by $\alpha_1 + \alpha_2 S_t$ and $\beta_1 + \beta_2 S_t$, respectively, with $\alpha_2$ and $\beta_2$ therefore determining the direction of the transitions. For large values of $\gamma$, the transition is completed in a short period of time and as $\gamma$ tends to infinity the model collapses to one with an instantaneous transition as in the structural break (dummy variable-augmented) regression models mentioned above. In the event of $\gamma < 0$, the initial and final states are reversed but interpretation of all parameters remains the same. Finally, the intercept and growth transitions are similar to the size and sensitivity effects outlined in Chapter 2. This is to the extent that both the intercept transition and the size effect involve intercept shifts and the growth transition and sensitivity effect involves changes in slope coefficients. This means, however, that ambiguity associated with size effect's interpretation, as highlighted in Chapter 2, also applies to the intercept transition. In what follows our main focus is, therefore, on the growth transition.

## 7.4 DATA AND ESTIMATION PROCEDURE

The above model was applied to 1960–94 GDP data for Pakistan. The GDP data are measured in billions of rupees at constant 1981 prices. After surveying the extensive literature on growth in developing countries and taking into account the constraints imposed by data availability, four variables were chosen for the vector $x_t$: the gross domestic investment to GDP ratio expressed as a percentage; the labour force expressed in thousands of people, and two human capital variables; years of life expectancy and the total gross school enrolment ratio expressed as a percentage. All data were obtained from World Bank (1995).

Estimation was conducted in four discrete stages in accordance with the procedure suggested by Leybourne *et al.* (1998). In the first, the standard augmented Dickey-Fuller (ADF) test was used to determine whether $y_t$ is I(1) against the alternative of I(0) around a linear trend. The second stage involved application of the Leybourne-Newbold-Vougas (LNV) $s_{\alpha\beta}$ test to ascertain whether $y_t$ is I(1) against the alternative of I(0) around a smooth transition in a linear trend as defined above. Both the intercept and trend vary in this test.

The LNV $s_{\alpha\beta}$ test was conducted in two steps. In the first we estimated the smooth transitions alternative and computed the following residuals:

$$\hat{\varepsilon}_t = y_t - \hat{\alpha}_1 - \hat{\beta}_1 t - \hat{\alpha}_2 \hat{S}_t - \hat{\beta}_2 t \hat{S}_t \tag{7.3}$$

In the second step of the test an ADF test was conducted on these residuals by estimating

$$\Delta\hat{\varepsilon}_t = \varrho\Delta\hat{\varepsilon}_{t-1} + \sum_{j=1}^{\eta-1} \delta_j \Delta\hat{\varepsilon}_{t-j} + \eta_t \tag{7.4}$$

and comparing the resulting $t$ ratio for to $\hat{p}$ simulated critical values provided in Leybourne *et al.* (1998) to evaluate the null that the residual series is I(1).

The third stage of the estimation procedure considered the role of the vector of exogenous regressors, $x_t$. Essentially, this is to augment the basic smooth transitions model

$$y_t = \alpha_1 + \beta_1 t + (\alpha_2 + \beta_2 t)S_t + \varepsilon_t \tag{7.5}$$

when the null hypothesis of stage two above is not rejected. The objective is to ascertain whether the vector adds sufficient explanatory power to reject the I(1) null. Each element of the vector must be I(1) and was therefore be submitted to an ADF (with trend) test to determine whether this is the case.

The fourth and final stage of the estimation procedure computed the non-linear least squares estimates of the unknown parameters of the appropriate model – either equation (7.1) or (7.5) – using the Berndt-Hall-Hall-Hausman optimization algorithm (in this case, found in GAUSSX 3.2). The model incorporated an autoregressive error structure of order $n$ (found by downward testing in stage 2 above) defined as:

$$\varepsilon_t = \sum_{k=1}^{n} \varphi_k \varepsilon_{t-k} + v_t \tag{7.6}$$

A potential problem with this final stage of the estimation procedure is that the $t$-ratio for $\gamma$ is invalid owing to the model being unidentified (with $\tau$, $\alpha_2$ and $\beta_2$ taking any value) when the null is not rejected. An explanation can be found in Leybourne *et al.* (1998). This problem was overcome using the two step procedure originally proposed in Davies (1977) and used in Greenaway *et al.* (1997). According to this procedure the null is evaluated using the following Lagrange multiplier test:

$$LM = \frac{T(SSR_0 - SSR)}{SSR} \tag{7.7}$$

where $SSR_0$ and $SSR$ are the sum of squared residuals from, respectively, linear regression of $y_t$ on $t$ and $x_t$ (or $t$ alone if $x_t$ is ruled out in the third stage of estimation) and a regression of $\hat{\varepsilon}_t$ on a polynomial approximation of the smooth transition function.[9] $LM$ is asymptotically distributed as $\chi^2_m$ under $H_0$ assuming that $S_t$ adequately approximated by an $(m = 1)$th order polynomial (we take $m = 3$ here).

## 7.5 RESULTS

Application of the previously mentioned ADF test in stage one of the estimation procedure yielded a test statistic of –0.137. With a critical value of –3.18, which corresponds to the 10 per cent level of significance, one cannot reject the null hypothesis that $y_t$ is an I(1) series. Downward testing at the 10 per cent level could not find any significant difference lags (hence, $\rho - 1 = 0$). The LNV $S_{\alpha\beta}$ test of stage two produced an interesting result. Downward testing revealed that the fifth difference lag was significant at the 10 level of significance (hence, $\rho - 1 = 5$). This resulted in a $S_{\alpha\beta}$ test statistic of –4.311. The critical value required to reject the null (that $y_t$ is I(1) against the alternative of I(0) around a smooth transition in a linear trend) at the 10 per cent level is –4.26 (see Leybourne *et al.*, 1998). The null is not therefore rejected. This in turn dictates that we do not require the vector $x_t$ in final estimation.[10] Given this and the results of the downward testing in stage two our estimating equation is:

$$y_t = \alpha_1 + \beta_1 t + (\alpha_2 + \beta_2 t)S_t + \varepsilon_t \qquad \text{where}$$
$$\varepsilon_t = \phi_1\varepsilon_{t-1} + \phi_2\varepsilon_{t-2} + \phi_3\varepsilon_{t-3} + \phi_4\varepsilon_{t-4} + \phi_5\varepsilon_{t-5} + \phi_6\varepsilon_{t-6} + \nu_t$$

Results are shown in Table 7.4 and Figures 7.1, 7.2 and 7.3. The model has good explanatory power. The parameters $\alpha_1$, $\beta_1$, $\alpha_2$ and $\beta_2$ are all found to be significantly different from zero at the 95 per cent confidence level, and the fitted series closely resembles the actual series (see Table 7.4 and Figure 7.1, respectively). The key parameters, for our

*Table* 7.4 Econometric Estimates of Smooth Transitions Model of Pakistani GDP, 1960–94

| | Estimate | Test Statistic |
|---|---|---|
| $\alpha_1$ | 6.84* | 41.55 |
| $\beta_1$ | 0.87* | 12.63 |
| $\alpha_2$ | –2.88* | –10.00 |
| $\beta_2$ | 1.41* | 50.37 |
| $\varphi_1$ | 0.03 | 0.17 |
| $\varphi_2$ | –0.41* | –2.50 |
| $\varphi_3$ | –0.08 | –0.39 |
| $\varphi_4$ | –0.18 | –0.90 |
| $\varphi_5$ | –0.12 | –0.63 |
| $\varphi_6$ | –0.60* | –3.06 |
| $\lambda$ | 0.27 | |
| $\tau$ | 0.58 | |
| *LM* | 34.33* | |

*: null rejected at the 95% confidence level.

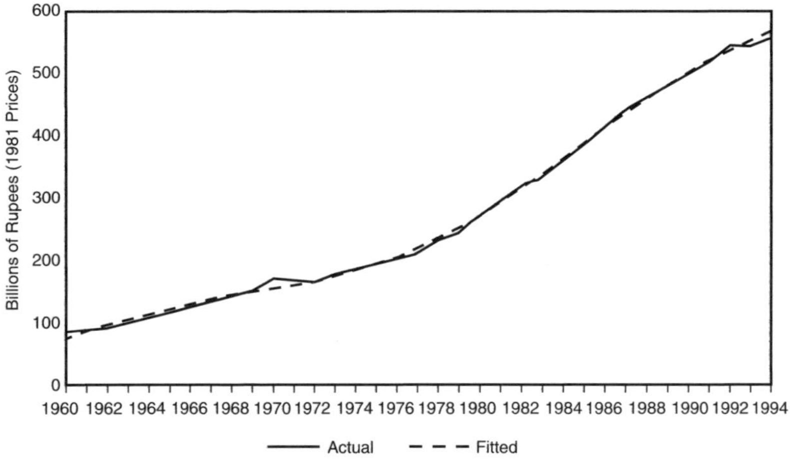


*Figure* 7.1 Fitted and Actual GDP – Pakistan, 1960–94

current purposes, are $\gamma$ and $\tau$. The estimated values of these parameters are 0.27 and 0.58, respectively, and the null hypothesis of the constancy and the intercept and trend against the smooth transition alternative is rejected at the 95 per cent confidence level. A transition is therefore evident in the data.[11] The growth component of this transition is positive given the signs of $\gamma$ and $\beta_2$ (see Figure 7.2) and the level of Pakistan's real GDP is much higher than would have otherwise been the case (see Figure 7.3).[12] It is though a very slow transition with the data being in transition for most of the period under consideration. A transition mid-point falling during 1980 certainly is consistent with this.

That the transition is slow and has a mid-point during 1980 has important implications for the role that adjustment has played in Pakistan's improved performance with respect to GDP. The origins of this improvement clearly well pre-date the adjustment programme, which has been implemented from late 1980 onward. This finding is consistent with the sort of speculation expressed by Zaidi (1993, 1994), as outlined above. It is of course possible that the adjustment programme has prolonged and therefore heightened what appears to be a pre-existing transition. Such an interpretation is in a sense consistent with the stance, alluded to above, of McCleary (1991). Yet if one is to solely attribute this transition and, therefore, the turnaround in Pakistan's GDP performance to the adjustment programme, one would have to observe it happening during the adjustment period. Except in

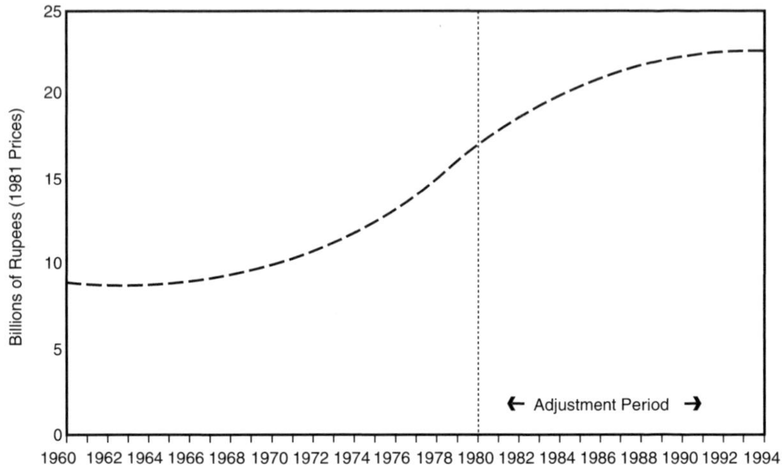


*Figure* 7.2 Estimated Growth Transition – Pakistan, 1960–94

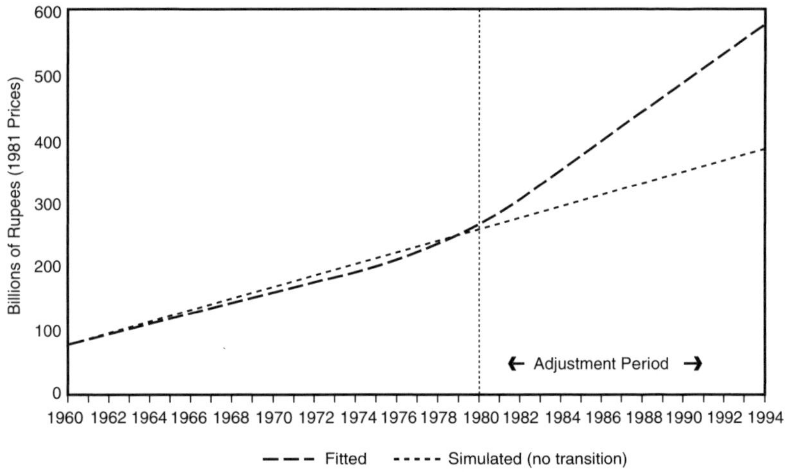


*Figure* 7.3 Fitted versus Simulated GDP Series – Pakistan, 1960–94

the case of an immediate and instantaneous transition (and there is no evidence of this), the mid-point clearly cannot occur in 1980.

Why, then, is it that the programme has not turned around Pakistan's growth performance, or at best prolonging a pre-existing transformation? Three possible, non-mutually exclusive interpretations emerge, building on the research discussed above. The first is the sort of view expressed by Zaman (1995): that the focus of the policy reforms is inappropriate to the Pakistani economy and what is required instead is a combination of fiscal discipline and strategic interventions including tariff protection and government intervention in export promotion. The second is that the underlying behavioural relationships, on which liberal economic reforms depend, do not exist, as Khan and Aftab (1994) purport demonstrate with respect to Pakistan's financial liberalization. The third is the partial implementation of the programme, as McGillivray and White (1994) argue. The results of this chapter's analysis are not inconsistent with any of these possibilities.

## 7.6. CONCLUSION

The main purpose of this chapter was to evaluate the impact of Pakistan's structural adjustment programme, introduced in 1980 with the assistance of the World Bank and (subsequently) the IMF, on that economy's real GDP growth. It attempted to model the impact of this programme as a smooth transition over time from one growth path to another, rather than as a discrete structural break fully observed at a single point in time. Evidence of a positive transition in Pakistan's real GDP series was found. Yet the origins of this transition well pre-date the adjustment programme. Pertinently, its mid-point is during 1980 and this must eliminate the adjustment programme as the determinant of the transition. At best, this programme may have prolonged the transition, but this remains a matter of speculation. That the programme has seemingly failed to transform Pakistan's GDP growth performance is consistent with the findings of some previous research. It is not consistent with some assertions based simple descriptive statistics relating to Pakistan's macroeconomic performance before and after the introduction of the adjustment programme. Insofar as GDP growth is concerned, this performance would seem to be a continuation of a prior phenomenon.

## Notes

* The author thanks David Harvey for invaluable research assistance, Steve Leybourne and Oliver Morrissey for useful comments and background discussions and Deakin University for financial assistance. The usual disclaimer applies.

1. Pakistan experienced a number of (seemingly weak) liberalization episodes during the 1959–65 and 1972–78 (see Papageorgiou *et al.*, 1991). It ought therefore be emphasized that the focus of this chapter is the reforms initiated from 1980 onward.
2. Each of the differences shown, except that relating to investment, are significant according to the tests described in Chapter 2.
3. See, for example, Mosley *et al.* (1991), World Bank (1988, 1990 and 1992), Corbo *et al.* (1992) and Reed (1992).
4. To this extent, Zaidi's position is not dissimilar to McCleary's. That is, McCleary (1991) does acknowledge that growth had begun to increase prior to the introduction of the programme, although unlike Zaidi he asserts that the adjustment programme has 'reconfirmed the process' (p. 421).
5. Zaman's comments were directly specifically at IMF adjustment lending.
6. McGillivray *et al.* (1995) argue that this and similar techniques are based on extremely restrictive *ceteris paribus* assumptions.
7. McGillivray *et al.* (1995) provide additional comments on Iqbal's analysis.
8. There was also an element of the before and after analysis in the approaches used by these studies, to the extent that comparisons were made of pre- and post-adjustment experiences.
9. The actual regression is:

$$\hat{\nu}_t = \alpha_1 + \beta_1 t + \delta_1 t^2 + \delta_2 t^3 + \delta_3 t^4 + \varepsilon_t$$

10. The inclusion of the vector was also considered using an alternative test to that described above. Rather than augmenting a smooth transitions model with exogenous I(1) regressors (as in third stage of estimation), we considered whether adding a smooth transition to cointegrating model (with $y_t$ as the regressand and the elements of $x_t$ as the regressors) led to rejection of the null that $y_t$ is I(1) against the alternative of I(0) around a smooth transition in a linear trend. It did not.
11. Tests were also conducted for a smooth transition in the log of real GDP. In this case a simple fixed linear trend model provided the best characterization of GDP series. As such, there appears to be neither a structural break or smooth transition in the logarithmic data. While it remains a matter of speculation whether one ought be modelling the raw or logarithmic GDP series, using either does not alter the main conclusion drawn in this paper.
12. The 'No Transition' series in Figure 7.3 has been simulated with $S_t$ set to zero. It is, therefore, the fitted values of $y_t$ without the transition.

## References

Balassa, B. (1989), 'A Quantitative Appraisal of Adjustment Lending', *Pakistan Development Review,* 28, pp. 73–94.

Corbo, V., S. Fischer and S.B. Webb (1992), *Adjustment Lending Revisited: Policies to Restore Growth*, Washington, DC: The World Bank.

Greenaway, D., S. Leybourne and D. Sapsford (1997), 'Modelling Growth (and Liberalization) Using Smooth Transitions Analysis', *Economic Inquiry*, October.

Iqbal, Z. (1993), 'Macroeconomic Effects of Adjustment Lending in Pakistan', mimeo, Tilburg University.

Khan, M.S. (1991) 'Comments', in Thomas *et al.* (eds), *Restructuring Economies in Distress*, New York: Oxford University Press.

Khan, S.R. and S. Aftab (1994), 'Assessing the Impact of Financial Reforms on Pakistan's Economy', *Pakistan Journal of Applied Economics*, 10, pp. 99–116.

Leybourne, S., P. Newbold and D. Vougas (1998), 'Unit Roots and Smooth Transitions', *Journal of Times Series Analysis*, 19, 1, pp. 83–97.

McCleary, W.A. (1991), 'Pakistan: Structural Adjustment and Economic Growth', in Thomas *et al.* (eds), *Restructuring Economies in Distress*, New York: Oxford University Press.

McGillivray, M. and H. White (1994), 'Structural Adjustment and Macroeconomic Performance in Pakistan', paper presented at the Economic Liberalization in South Asia Conference, Australian South Asian Research Centre, The Australian National University, Canberra, November 30 to December 2.

McGillivray, M., H. White and A. Ahmad (1995), 'Evaluating the Effectiveness of Structural Adjustment Policies on Macroeconomic Performance: A Review of the Evidence with Special Reference to Pakistan', *Pakistan Journal of Applied Economics*, 11, pp. 57–75.

Mosley, P., J. Harrigan and J. Toye (1991), *Aid and Power: The World Bank and Policy-Based Lending*, Vol 1, London: Routledge.

Papageorgiou, D., M. Michaely and A. Choksi (1991), *Liberalizing Foreign Trade*, Vols 1 to 7, Basil Blackwell.

Reed, D. (1992), *Structural Adjustment and the Environment*, Boulder, CO: Westview Press.

Riuzuddin, R. (1994) 'An Evaluation of Trade Policy', *Pakistan Journal of Applied Economics*, Vol. No, Nos 1 and 2, pp. 117–26.

World Bank (1994), *World Tables 1994*, New York: Oxford University Press.

World Bank (1995), *World Data 1995*, New York: Oxford University Press.

World Bank, 1986, *Project Performance Audit Report: Pakistan – First Structural Adjustment Loan/Credit*, World Bank Report No. 6308, Washington, DC.

World Bank (1988), *Adjustment Lending: An Evaluation of Ten Years' Experience*, Country Economics Department, Washington, DC: The World Bank.

World Bank (1990), Adjustment Lending Policies for Sustainable Growth, Country Economics Department, Washington, DC: The World Bank.

World Bank (1992), *Adjustment Lending and Mobilization of Private and Public Resources for Growth*, Washington, DC: The World Bank.

World Bank (1993), *Pakistan: Country Economic Memorandum FY93: Progress Under the Adjustment Programme*, World Bank Report No. 11590–PAK, Washington, DC.

Zaidi, S.A. (1993), 'Structural Adjustment Programme', *Journal of Islamic Banking and Finance*, 11, pp. 21–41.

Zaidi, S.A. (1994), 'The Structural Adjustment Programme and Pakistan: External Influence or Internal Acquiescence?', *Pakistan Journal of Applied Economics*, 10, pp. 21–46.

Zaman, A. (1995), 'The Government's present Agreement with the IMF: Misgovernment or Folly?', *Pakistan Journal of Applied Economics*, 11, pp. 77–94.

# 8 Mozambique: Economic Reform and Reconstruction

Tony Addison and Clara de Sousa[1]

## 8.1 INTRODUCTION

Mozambique today faces the enormous task of rebuilding its economy and society after a sixteen-year war which killed or maimed over one million people and destroyed much of the rural economy's infrastructure. Since the end of the war in 1992, some four million refugees have returned home to reconstruct their lives in a country which has seen its schools and clinics destroyed and its fields sown with land mines. To cope with the many demands of reconstruction the Government has at its disposal only limited public revenues and an overstretched administration.

Economic reform began over a decade ago, a process that has involved dismantling the system of state intervention and planning introduced soon after independence. While many African countries have introduced reform programmes over the last decade, few have had to do so in circumstances as difficult as those of Mozambique.[2] The many constraints on growth in Africa, such as weak supply responses, are in Mozambique's case compounded by the destruction of social and economic infrastructure and the loss of human capital.

This chapter discusses economic reform in a country now undergoing reconstruction. The quality of economic data for Mozambique is poor, and liberalization is a slow on-going process. Econometric evaluation of liberalization is not feasible, and even a 'before-after' analysis is of limited value as the initial situation was one of war. Nevertheless, we can gain much from considering what has happened. We highlight some important issues, in particular in fiscal policy, that has seen major disagreements between the IMF and other donors, and in agricultural policy, that is especially important for rural poverty reduction. Countries such as Angola now emerging from war can, together with donors, learn much from Mozambique's experience.

*Table* 8.1 Economic Reform and Reconstruction in Mozambique: Chronology of Events

| | |
|---|---|
| 1975 | Independence from Portugal |
| 1976 | Nationalizations and launch of communal agricultural production |
| 1977 | Marxism-Leninism officially adopted by FRELIMO |
| 1980 | Political campaigns against corruption and bureaucratization |
| 1982 | Priorities shift from state farms to smallholders and co-operatives |
| 1983 | Failings of the planning system discussed at FRELIMO's 4th Congress |
| 1984 | Mozambique joins the IMF and World Bank |
| 1985 | War with South African backed RENAMO intensifies |
| 1986 | Major drought, President Samora Machel killed in air crash |
| 1987 | Economic Rehabilitation Programme launched with IMF SAF support |
| 1988 | Prices of rationed goods increase |
| 1989 | FRELIMO drops reference to Marxist–Leninist ideology |
| 1990 | Economic and Social Rehabilitation Programme launched with IMF ESAF |
| 1991 | Financial reform begins. Major drought |
| 1992 | Rome Peace Accords, Foreign exchange market liberalized |
| 1993 | UN peace-keeping troops arrive to assist demobilization |
| 1994 | First multi-party elections held. New FRELIMO Government |
| 1995 | IMF criticism of policy sparks disagreement among donors |
| 1996 | New ESAF agreed. Privatization accelerates |
| 1997 | Government appeals for accelerated debt relief under HIPC initiative |

## 8.2 WAR AND PEACE

### The Colonial Legacy

Agriculture in colonial Mozambique was based on the export of cash crops including sugar, copra, sisal and tea, grown on plantations run by European companies or, in the case of cotton and rice, forced cultivation by smallholders.[3] Smallholder agriculture was left to stagnate thereby ensuring a supply of cheap labour to the colonial economy. To encourage industrialization at home and in the colonies, Portugal imposed high levels of tariff and quota protection on imports from outside its empire. In Mozambique, manufacturing consisted of textiles, basic consumer goods and processed agricultural produce. Mozambique's railways and ports handled goods in transit to and from South Africa and Central Africa. These earnings, together with the substantial sums paid to Portugal for supplying labour to the mines and farms of South Africa, covered much of the colony's trade deficit (Abrahamsson and Nilsson, 1995).

Resistance to colonial rule grew steadily, and the struggle for independence took off in the 1960s with the formation of FRELIMO (Frente de Libertação de Moçambique). By the 1970s, Portugal was heavily engaged in fighting independence movements across its African empire. The burden of these wars contributed to the Portuguese revolution of 1974–75, overthrowing a dictatorship in power since the 1930s. The ability of the Portuguese military to sustain its overseas operations rapidly collapsed, the new Government dissolved Portugal's empire, and Mozambique became independent in 1975. At independence 185,000 Portuguese settlers (92 per cent of the settler population) left, in some cases destroying capital equipment and infrastructure as they went (Hanlon, 1991).

FRELIMO opted for a socialist development strategy based on Marxist-Leninist principles. A comprehensive system of planning and regulation was implemented which involved output targets for key industries, and heavy industrialization, following the Soviet model, was emphasized in national plans, although it was never fully implemented (Tibana, 1994). The balance of payments was managed through barter trade with the Soviet bloc, which also provided technical and military assistance. By 1984, as a result of nationalization, the public sector contained over half of all Mozambique's registered firms. State farms were established upon abandoned Portuguese farms. Co-operatives and communal villages were formed in order to incorporate smallholder agriculture as part of the planning process and to facilitate the provision of social infrastructure and agricultural services which had previously been focused on the settler population (Srivastava and Livingstone, 1983; O'Laughlin, 1996). FRELIMO also launched ambitious literacy campaigns (80 per cent of the population was illiterate at independence), and developed an innovative primary health care system which reached into the rural areas.

## Impact of the War

Mozambique's balance of payments deteriorated after independence as a result of UN sanctions against Rhodesia, the diversion of South Africa's transit trade away from Mozambique's ports, and reductions in South Africa's use of migrant labour (both retaliatory measures for FRELIMO's support of the ANC). In the late 1970s Rhodesia and

South Africa began military destabilization using the opposition movement RENAMO (Resistência Nacional Moçambicano). By 1982, Mozambique had entered a period of bitter civil war, and by 1992 over one million people were dead or maimed (Finnegan, 1992). The Government lost control of large areas of the country, people fled to protected areas, and about one-third of the population became refugees abroad. Maputo became an enclave cut off from much of its hinterland (Hanlon, 1996; Kyle, 1991).

South Africa's democratic transition undermined RENAMO's political and military base, and the war ended with the signing of the Rome peace accords in October 1992. The United Nations Operation for Mozambique (UNOMOZ) assisted the demobilization over 1992–94. Donors provided considerable assistance for the resettlement of returning refugees and preparations for Mozambique's first multi-party elections which took place in October 1994 (UN, 1995). FRELIMO won the election, with about 55 per cent of the vote on a very high turn out, and formed a new Government with RENAMO as the main opposition party.

GNP per capita fell from \$170 in 1986 to \$80 in 1994 (World Bank, 1996). Recent estimates of GNP per capita vary from \$60 to \$100. The true level of GNP is uncertain, and the population figure is likely to be inaccurate as there is no recent census. The war, together with drought, hit the economy especially hard in 1985–86 (GDP fell by 2.3 per cent in 1986), and drought hit the economy again in 1992 when GDP fell by 0.8 per cent (Figure 8.1). By 1986 agricultural output was about 40 per cent of its 1980 level (Tschirley and Weber, 1994 World Bank, 1990). Food production

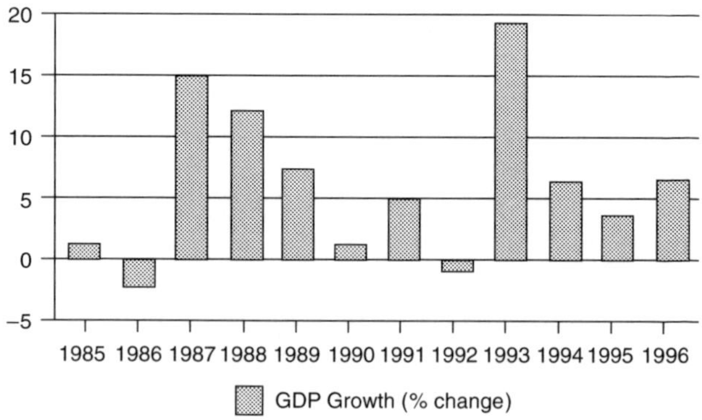


*Figure* 8.1 Real GDP Growth, Mozambique, 1985–96

*Table* 8.2 Basic Social Indicators for Mozambique

| | Mozambique | Sub-Saharan Africa | Low-income Economies |
|---|---|---|---|
| Life Expectancy at birth (years) | 46 | 52 | 63 |
| Infant Mortality Rate (per 1000 live births) | 146 | 92 | 58 |
| Adult Illiteracy (per cent) | 60 | 43 | 34 |
| Female Adult Illiteracy (per cent) | 77 | 54 | 45 |

*Source:* World Bank, *World Development Report 1996* (Oxford University Press).

began to improve in the late 1980s as a result of improved price incentives and the Priority Districts Programme that distributed seeds and inputs and started projects in areas safe from the war. A massive UN led food-aid operation prevented famine and by the late 1980s food aid accounted for up to 35 per cent of the national supply of cereals, and 60 per cent in the drought year of 1992 (Tschirley *et al.*, 1996). Nutrition programmes and a targeted cash transfer programme (GAPVU) reduced hunger in urban areas, but were under-funded.

The contraction in social services, together with the decline in household incomes and food-security, has left Mozambique with some of the worst social indicators in Africa (Table 8.2). Mozambique's human development index is 0.261, well below the average of 0.396 of UNDP's low human-development group of countries (UNDP, 1996). War reversed the early post-independence improvements in the provision of health care and education in rural areas. About one-third of all rural clinics were destroyed, and by 1994 only half the remaining clinics could provide primary health care (Addison and de Sousa, 1997).

As a result preventable diseases such as malaria and measles accounted for 50 per cent of all child deaths by 1994, and illnesses such as dysentery and cholera became widespread. The under-five mortality rate is 273 (per 1000 live births) well above the SSA average of 165 (UNICEF, 1993). The deterioration in health services contributed to an increase in the maternal mortality rate from 300 per 100,000 live births in the early 1980s to 1100 by 1994, nearly double the SSA average of 690 (GOM, 1995a). The war destroyed or closed 68 per cent of the primary school network, the quality of schooling fell drastically, and the gross enrolment rate in primary schools fell from 95 per cent in 1981 to 57 per cent in 1991 (GOM, 1995a). Female education has been hard hit; 77 per cent of adult females are illiterate, compared with 42 per cent of males.

## 8.3 ECONOMIC REFORM

By the start of the 1980s flaws in the planning system were increasingly evident and in 1980 political campaigns against corruption and bureaucratic inefficiency were launched. By this time it was also clear that state farms were failing to deliver higher agricultural growth, despite absorbing most of the agricultural budget, and the Government began to give more support to smallholder and co-operative production (Harris, 1980; Munslow, 1984). Policy failings were increasingly acknowledged by the FRELIMO leadership. Tentative liberalization occurred over 1985–86, including for example the removal of price controls on vegetables and fruits, which stimulated production in the 'green zones' around Maputo and other secure urban areas (Kyle, 1994).

In 1987 the government launched its Economic Rehabilitation Programme (after 1990 this became the Economic and Social Rehabilitation Programme). This has been supported by World Bank IDA rehabilitation credits and project lending, a SAF and ESAFs provided by the IMF (the current ESAF runs 1996–98), and project and programme aid from bilateral donors. Extensive liberalization and stabilization measures have been implemented since 1987, and these have reversed much of the state intervention introduced in the immediate post-independence years. These policy changes started amidst war, and are now continuing in a country that is rebuilding its economic and social fabric, and democratizing its political system.

### Public Finances

The main fiscal effects of the war were to raise military expenditures and to cut public revenues. Since the end of the war military personnel have been reduced from 100,000 to 11,000. Recurrent spending on the army was set to decline by 36.7 per cent in real terms between 1993 and 1995, and to fall from 5.1 per cent of GDP in 1993 to 1.6 per cent in 1995

(GOM, 1995b). However, the transition from war to peace has costs of its own which reduce the size of the initial peace dividend. The creation and equipment of a new national army, through the merger of FRELIMO and RENAMO forces, is expensive. Moreover, assistance programmes to help ex-combatants reintegrate into society have been necessary (Colletta *et al.*, 1996). Programmes for demobilization, the resettlement of refugees, and the 1994 elections, together amounted to 6 per cent of GDP in 1994.

Revenues from sales taxes, which provided half of all tax revenues in 1992, declined with the contraction of internal trade during the war. Internal trade, and therefore sales tax revenues, are now rising with the recovery in economic activity. However, as a percentage of GDP total public revenue was the same (20 per cent of GDP) in 1996 as it was in 1992. Growth in revenues from import duties (which provide about one-third of total tax revenues) has been slow, the result of inefficiency and corruption in the customs service (both exacerbated by the very low level of public-sector wages). In 1997, the Government took the radical step of handing over responsibility for the customs service to the British Company, Crown Agents, for three years. To reduce corruption Crown Agents will recruit new customs officers, and the pay of the customs service will be raised. The Government has set Crown Agents a revenue target of US$125 million in its first year, a 50 per cent increase on the 1996 level of customs revenue. Increases in petroleum prices, refinements to import duties, and the introduction of VAT (scheduled for 1998), will raise more revenue, but revenue growth will be slow until the administrative systems for tax collection are overhauled.

The government must set clear priorities if it is to use its scarce resources efficiently. Basic health services and primary education, especially in the rural areas, urgently need more resources if Mozambique's dismal human development indicators are to rapidly improve. In addition to the social sectors, infrastructure and services which improve the livelihoods of small-holders and micro-entrepreneurs, especially targeted help to women, are essential to reduce the incidence of poverty, particularly in the rural areas worst affected by the war, where poverty is deepest. This all adds up to a very large set of demands on the public purse.

At present public spending on the recurrent costs of health care is about US$1.5 per person, compared with US$4 in the early 1980s. Per capita spending on education is similarly low. The Government has found it difficult to increase social sector spending; in the early 1990s the share of education and health in the recurrent budget fell, but this decline

*Table* 8.3 Recurrent Government Expenditures for Health and Education

| | (billions of Meticals) | | | | |
|---|---|---|---|---|---|
| | 1991 | 1992 | 1993 | 1994 | 1995 |
| Education | 65.2 | 103.9 | 145.2 | 190.2 | 273.3 |
| Health | 31.4 | 56.5 | 75.8 | 94.5 | 133.5 |
| Total (current prices) | 96.6 | 160.4 | 221.0 | 284.7 | 406.8 |
| Total (constant prices) | 96.6 | 104.7 | 98.7 | 84.2 | 120.3 |
| % of recurrent expenditures | 21.1 | 19.9 | 18.8 | 19.2 | 22.9 |

*Source:* GOM (1995b).

appears to have been reversed over 1994–95 (Table 8.3). Donors and NGOs have funded not only the capital costs of the social sectors but also some of the recurrent costs as well. Much of this spending has been off-budget, making it difficult to determine what the respective contributions of government and donors have been, and complicating the process of budgeting and planning in the social sectors (similar problems prevail in the agriculture and infrastructure sectors). This problem is being resolved in the health sector by the adoption of an integrated programme approach which brings together donor and government projects into a common budgetary framework for the sector, therefore making it easier to prioritize and track resource allocations.

To fund reconstruction priorities savings must be found elsewhere. The IMF has been over-optimistic in its belief that substantial overall savings can be found in public administration. Inefficiency can be reduced, and some public-sector jobs lost. But civil service pay must increase to match levels in the private sector (and the local offices of aid donors). Moreover, strengthening the capacity of local administration, which is essential for reconstruction, places new demands on funding.

Since the start of privatization in the late 1980s, 740 state-owned enterprises (SOEs) have been sold off by the national privatization agency, UTRE. Most of these are small- and medium- sized businesses, taken over after their Portuguese owners fled in the 1970s, but more recently 40 large SOEs have been sold for US$100m. This has released resources and subsidies to loss-making SOEs fell from 1 per cent of GDP to 0.2 per cent over 1990–96. Privatization has stimulated foreign investment; foreigners have provided about half the privatization proceeds. UTRE is scheduled to complete the privatization programme by 1998, with the sale of large SOEs such as the national airline, which has debts of US$15m, together with sugar plantations, hotels and finance companies. Buyers for some of these large SOEs will be hard to find and they will sell at low prices, but at least the subsidy payments will cease, releasing resources for better uses in social and economic infrastructure.

## Controversy over the Fiscal Deficit

With many demands on public expenditures, and limited public revenues, the fiscal deficit remains a persistent problem. The fiscal deficit *before grants* was reduced from 29.2 per cent of GDP in 1990 to 22.2 per cent in 1993 (Figure 8.3). An increase in aid flows in the run up to the 1994 elections reduced the fiscal deficit *after grants* from 12.3 per cent of GDP in 1990 to 5.2 per cent in 1993. But the fiscal deficit before grants rose again to 29.7 per cent in 1994 (8.2 per cent after grants). Revenues stagnated while spending on resettlement programmes, elections, demobilization and public investment all rose. The level of the fiscal deficit and its relation to inflation has been particularly problematic. For much of the 1990s the IMF has maintained a resolutely orthodox view, namely that Mozambique's high fiscal deficit results in accelerating inflation which in turn undermines growth by appreciating the real exchange rate.

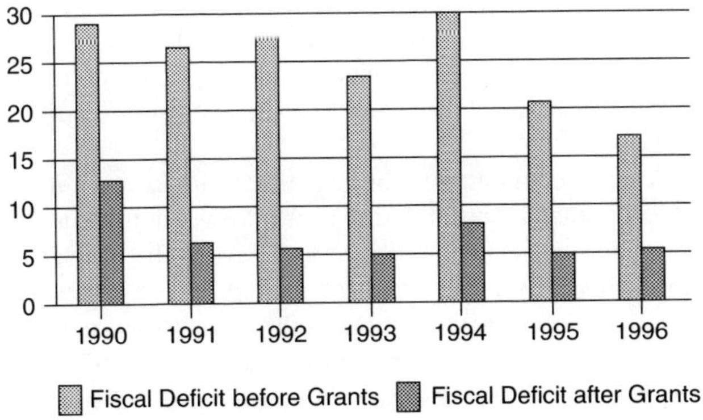


*Figure* 8.2 Fiscal Deficit, Mozambique (% of GDP)

While the orthodox view explains some of the fall in inflation from a high of 165 per cent in 1987 to 43 per cent in 1993 (as monetary financing of the deficit was reduced) the inflationary impact of very large aid inflows must also be taken into account. Inflation rose to 70 per cent in 1994, partly as the result of very large expenditures (at one point US$1 million per day) by UNOMOZ on the demobilization and election processes. This level of spending is a huge injection of demand into a supply-constrained economy.

Such aid-induced inflation is akin to the effect of a natural-resources boom in that the increase in demand leads to especially large increases in the prices of non-tradable goods and services, including the wages of skilled labour that is in very limited supply. Therefore, inflation is at least in part related to very large aid inflows combined with war-induced structural constraints (particularly in infrastructure and the supply of skilled labour) which limit the economy's overall supply response. Inflation fell to 17 per cent in 1996, due in part to the reduction of aid inflows, and the inflationary pressure associated with them, and is forecast to fall to below 10 per cent in 1997. The determinants of inflation in an economy rebuilding itself from war need closer investigation, not just for Mozambique but for other countries, such as Angola, in a similar position.

In 1995, the IMF, dissatisfied with the path of fiscal policy, threatened suspension of the ESAF programme. This proved too much for the bilateral donors who protested that the IMF's fiscal target was incompatible with investment for reconstruction. For example, a surge in public investment (to 4.3 per cent of GDP) contributed to the deficit's sharp rise over 1993–94, but infrastructure investment is crucial to recovery, and needs to rise further (see Hanlon, 1996, on the donor protest). Too tight a fiscal target also disrupts aid disbursement by the bilaterals and the World Bank, since it threatens the commitment of recurrent expenditures by Government to match donor capital funding (Wuyts, 1995).

The problem of reconciling fiscal targets with investment in economic reconstruction is eased by mobilizing more domestic revenue and grant aid (including debt relief). The former was part of the budget measures for 1996, that sought to reduce the fiscal deficit before grants to 16.5 per cent of GDP, a fall of four percentage points, consisting of a rise in total revenue by two percentage points and a fall in expenditures by two percentage points. If the revenue increases can be achieved then reconstruction spending can rise, while expenditures such as defence and SOE subsidies take the brunt of the cuts.

While the inflow of aid loans has provided much needed budgetary support, it has led to the accumulation of a large debt stock that is owed to the bilateral and multilateral donors (see further discussion below). This debt must be serviced from scarce public revenues. The ratio of total debt service to public revenues excluding grants is about 32 per cent; this is well above the 20 per cent level that is sometimes said to be reasonable for a poor aid-dependent economy. Rather than focusing on such 'rules of thumb', a better way of looking at the fiscal burden of debt is to identify the cost of meeting key targets for such human development indicators as infant mortality, and then meet that cost with debt relief (Addison, 1997). For example, health spending must at least double from the present US$1.50 per capita to US$3.00 if rural clinics are to be quickly rehabilitated; this costs US$25m, a small sum when compared with a debt stock over £5 billion.

While domestic revenues are at last starting to rise, these will not begin to cover essential expenditures until well into the next century. Debt relief, while significant, still has a long way to go, and we live in a world of declining real aid flows. Given these financing constraints, the tension between the respective objectives of macro-stability and the needs of economic reconstruction will continue for the foreseeable future.

## External Debt

As a result of very large aid inflows over the last decade, Mozambique is one of Africa's most indebted countries; the debt stock was US$5.3 billion in 1995, most of which is owed to bilateral and multilateral donors (GOM, 1997). Of the US$5.3b debt stock, US$1.2b represents arrears of principal and interest to bilateral creditors. Mozambique is one of the 32 countries classified by the World Bank as a Heavily Indebted Poor Country (HIPC). The Bank calculates that if a country's present value of debt stock to exports is greater than 200 per cent then repeated debt rescheduling is almost inevitable since export earnings will not, under reasonable assumptions, grow fast enough to service the HIPC's debts (World Bank, 1994b).[4] The median value of the debt-to-export ratio in the HIPC group is 438 per cent, while Mozambique's ratio is 1,155 per cent; this is the highest ratio of any HIPC which has a reform programme in place.

The very high debt-to-export ratio reflects not only inflows of aid loans but also the depression of Mozambique's foreign-exchange earnings as a result of war. This is highlighted if we compare

Mozambique's situation with those of Tanzania and Zambia which are also major aid recipients but which have not had to contend with a loss of export earnings resulting from war. While Tanzania's debt stock (US$6.7b) exceeds that of Mozambique, the present value of debt-stock to exports of Tanzania is, at 791 per cent, much lower. Zambia's debt-stock to export ratio is 444 per cent (World Bank, 1994b: 18).

Debt creates a number of well-known macro-economic problems. The two most important are the cash-flow problem (debt takes such a high proportion of foreign exchange earnings that it threatens the import of essential goods) and the debt-overhang problem (high debt-to-GNP and debt-to-export ratios discourage domestic and foreign investment, and therefore reduce economic growth). A third problem is the potential for debt-service to crowd out other components of public expenditure, most importantly basic social services and rural infrastructure investment, both of which are crucial for poverty reduction (Addison, 1996a; Oxfam, 1996; Plank, 1993).

Despite its very high debt, Mozambique does not face a cash-flow problem as long as it maintains its reform programme, and therefore as long as new flows of concessional lending are sufficient to meet the import bill. But Mozambique certainly does have a very large debt-overhang, which can potentially discourage foreign investors if they see it as a sign of future macroeconomic difficulties. So far this does not seem to have happened; foreign investment has increased since 1994. But investor sentiment can quickly change if, for example, relations with the donor community deteriorate, thereby creating a cash flow problem that threatens the repatriation of profits.

Reduction of the debt overhang is therefore essential. Debt relief has been agreed five times since 1984 and debt relief of US$664m was agreed (on Naples terms) at the 1996 Paris Club meeting. This relief represents the cancellation of bilateral debts (the retrospective conversion of loans into grants), and relief of bilateral debt has facilitated the continued servicing of multilateral debts, an outcome which is common across the HIPC group (ODI, 1995). Since 1994 the bilateral donors have provided grants rather than loans. Grants from IDA and bilateral donors have financed a buy-back of 64 per cent of commercial debts.

Further reduction of debt increasingly depends on reducing multilateral debt which now amounts to US$1.6b or nearly one-third of the total debt stock (GOM, 1997). The World Bank is the largest multilateral creditor (IDA loans account for 55 per cent of the multilateral debt total) followed by the African Development Bank (19 per cent) and the IMF (13 per cent). Given the fiscal and servicing burdens of its debts, Mozambique is eligible for multilateral debt relief under the HIPC Debt Initiative (World Bank/IMF, 1996). To be eligible a country must have pursued reform under an IMF ESAF for at least six years, and Mozambique has now achieved this; it has one of the longest records of adjustment among the HIPC group. On this basis the Government has appealed to donors to accelerate debt relief, and for grants of US$207m to cover debt-servicing over 1997–99, until multilateral debt relief is granted (GOM, 1997).

## 8.4 MARKET LIBERALIZATION

### Liberalization Policies

At the start of the ERP in 1987 the metical in the parallel market was trading at a premium of 2,100 per cent over its official rate. Foreign exchange provided at the official rate by the Central Bank was rationed to essential imports such as fuel and 'priority' users such as SOEs. In January 1997 the metical was devalued from Mt. 39/$1 to Mt. 202/$1 and the parallel-market premium fell to 200 per cent. This large one-step devaluation was followed by further devaluations, which became monthly in 1989. In 1990 a secondary foreign-exchange market was introduced, in which the rate was market determined. This was followed by a further devaluation, and the unification of the official and secondary markets in 1992 (for a while a separate window applied to donor import funds). By 1992 the parallel market premium had fallen to 15 per cent, and with the metical's depreciation in the market over 1992–94, the premium fell to three per cent by early 1996. This decline in the parallel market premium indicates that the metical's over-valuation has been largely eliminated.

The currency depreciation has stimulated exports, and the value of exports increased from 15.9 per cent of GDP in 1990 to 28.5 per cent in 1996. However, imports have risen strongly, and their growth must accelerate if reconstruction is to proceed at its planned pace. As a consequence the trade balance has steadily worsened. The current account deficit before grants rose from 53.1 per cent of GDP in 1990 to 70.7 per cent in 1994 (and after grants from 22 per cent to 24.6 per cent). The trade deficit has been US$900–1000m since 1993, and this has been covered mainly by balance of payments support from bilateral and multilateral donors.

Trade reforms accompanied the foreign exchange reforms. In 1987 the number of goods controlled by the state trading monopolies was reduced, and enterprises were allowed to export and import directly. The system of import licences was cut back with the introduction of the secondary foreign-exchange market in 1990. The tariff structure was simplified in 1991 from one with 34 rates to one with five rates (with rates from five to 35 per cent), and in 1993 the tariff on imported inputs was cut to five per cent. The revenue impact of the tariff reduction has been partly offset by the rise in import volume, although the Government has lost a great deal of potential tariff revenue through smuggling and poor customs procedures.

Price controls were a feature of the socialist planning system prior to 1986. Price control became increasingly ineffective as a vibrant parallel market in controlled goods developed, stimulated by the increasing shortages of war time (Sahn and Desai, 1994). The prices of controlled goods were increased by 100–500 per cent at the start of the ERP in 1987, and in 1988 the prices of rationed staple goods were increased by 400 per cent. Abolition of price controls accelerated from 1988 onwards, and the system of price controls came to an end in 1996 when the last controls, those on wheat and bread, were eliminated (Lopez and Sacerdoti, 1991).

Financial reform began in earnest in 1991 when the commercial and central banking functions of the Bank of Mozambique were separated. This transformed the BOM from an organization whose main function was to provide credits to cover the losses of the SOE sector to a central bank which exercises indirect control over interest rates and the volume of credit by the use of market-based monetary instruments. The state-owned banking system has been restructured to enforce stricter lending practices to reduce the level of bad debts and new commercial banks have begun to operate.

## Agricultural Policy

Until the late 1980s the state marketing board, AGRICOM, dominated maize marketing. AGRICOM purchased maize from farmers through licensed rural stores and wholesalers (Tarp, 1990; World Bank, 1990). Unlicensed traders expanded during the 1992 drought. By 1992 AGRICOM was purchasing only 15 per cent of national maize output (Addison and McDonald, 1995). Most of the maize marketing system is now run by private traders. A public company, the Institute of Cereals (ICM), with a buyer of last resort objective, was set up in 1994 out of the remnants of AGRICOM. However, its purchases are limited by its inability to borrow significantly from the banking system; the prices that Government obliges ICM to pay do not enable it to fully service its debts. In effect the Government has mandated ICM to pursue a social goal – to provide an alternative buyer for smallholders especially in marginal areas – without the resources to achieve it.

The rural road network is still being rebuilt and therefore the movement of maize between regions is still constrained. There is a vigorous and competitive trade transporting maize into Maputo, the main national market, and the district capitals. But in many areas, private marketing activity is limited, and barriers to entry into marketing such as transport difficulties and a lack of credit lead to monopsonies, which are to the detriment of smallholders (Addison and McDonald, 1995). The quality of the marketing system available to small-holders is a very important input into poverty reduction. At present, the Institute of Cereals does not have the capacity to offer small-holders an extensive alternative to private traders, in the way that Zimbabwe's Grain Marketing Board continues to operate in that country's liberalized grain market (Addison, 1996b; Hanlon, 1996). Assistance to community projects that market and sell produce should also be increased. The 'Green Zones' around Maputo are one example of initiatives by women micro-entrepreneurs in food marketing (Addison and Ribe, 1996).

The way in which food prices are determined is also changing, with major consequences for the welfare of consumers and small-holder producers. Large amounts of food aid delivered during the war significantly lowered real food prices (Alderman *et al.*, 1991; Tschirley *et al.*, 1996). The much reduced role of state marketing and its accompanying stable (but often low) producer prices, has led to larger seasonal price fluctuations, and difficulties for food-deficit rural households which must purchase at high-prices before harvest, a time when their own food stocks are depleted. Moreover, farmers supplying Maputo and the south, as well as consumers, will be faced with widely fluctuating prices depending on the level of maize output in South Africa, the region's largest maize producer (Coulter, 1995).

The currency's depreciation, and therefore the improvement in border prices for export crops, has not been fully translated into improvements in real producer prices, but has instead been absorbed by the marketing system to the detriment of small-holders. The slowness in liberalizing export-crop marketing as compared to food crop marketing has been common throughout sub-Saharan Africa (World Bank, 1994a).

The cashew sector is a case in point. Marketed production peaked at 216,000 tonnes in 1972 but declined to only 35,000 tonnes in 1993. (Addison and McDonald, 1995). While conflict disrupted production, pricing and marketing have also disadvantaged smallholders. There is a tax on the export of raw cashew nuts; in 1995 the tax was 25 per cent and before that there were quantitative restrictions amounting to a near-total export ban. During the period 1987 to 1993, the farm gate price was about 35 per cent of the world price, and it fell to about 15–20 per cent for the 1993/94 season.[5] The cost of the export tax has therefore been borne by small-holders. The main beneficiary – in the short term – is the cashew processing industry, which gets its inputs 20 per cent more cheaply than under full liberalization. If the export tax is reduced to zero in the next four years as the Government has undertaken to do, the favourable impact on small-holders – most of whom are poor or near poverty – could be considerable.

Agricultural growth and rural poverty reduction are both dependent on the supply response of small-holders. During the war, smallholder output was depressed by their vulnerability to attack, landmines, difficulties in accessing markets and buying inputs, together with the absence, for most of them, of normal Government services such as extension and credit. These constraints are now being reduced as roads are rehabilitated and mines cleared and as donor and NGO projects start up, although the pace of recovery is very uneven across the regions, reflecting differences in the scale of destruction but also large regional variations in local administrative capacities. The increased availability of consumer goods in rural areas, which was severely restricted during the war, also improves smallholder incentives, and their supply response. In general the estimated supply response for food crops is higher than for export crops, reflecting the greater dependence of the latter on inputs, infrastructure, and agricultural services (see Azam *et al.*, 1991, and Kyle, 1991, for estimates of supply response in Mozambique).

Public works programmes to rebuild rural infrastructure have been under way since the late 1980s (World Bank, 1989). Well-designed public works are critical to raising agricultural supply response, and provide valuable non-farm income. Investments in extension services – especially for women who are the main producers of food – and in crop research for pro-poor crops and farm technologies, should be prioritized in public expenditure allocations. A new response system for drought and other natural disasters is also essential now that the emergency system for food relief has ended (Addison and McDonald, 1995).

Investing in rural livelihoods through projects will, however, be worth nothing if the rights of access of smallholders to land and other natural resources such as forests and fisheries are not secured (Addison and Ribe, 1996). Before the war ended, and increasingly since 1992, very large concessions of some of the country's best agricultural land have been made to commercial interests, including foreign interests. There is considerable confusion in land rights, with many overlapping claims (Myers, 1993). Protection of community rights will require revision of the existing land laws. Unless these rights are secured, the future pattern of agricultural growth will be inequitable, and social tensions will be created.

## 8.5 FUTURE PROSPECTS

On the basis of the very imperfect national accounts data, GDP growth averaged six per cent over 1985–89 and over 1990–94 (World Bank, 1996). This hides immense annual variation: from – 2.3 per cent growth in 1986 to 14.7 per cent in 1987, and from –0.8 per cent in 1992 to 19.3 per cent in 1993. Growth is estimated to have been six per cent in 1996. How much economic reform contributed (either positively or negatively) to these trends, and its impact relative to that of war, drought, and Cyclone Nadia in 1994 is still open for debate (Kyle, 1994; Hanlon, 1996).

At US$76, GDP per capita in 1996 was far below the level of 1978 (US$200). Given population growth of 2.6 per cent per year, six per cent GDP growth per year will restore GDP per capita to its 1978 level in about 20 years. This would still leave Mozambique as poor as Malawi and Uganda are today. The challenge is therefore to accelerate growth beyond six per cent, but also to ensure that the growth process is environmentally sustainable and one in which the poor participate.

The economy does have the potential to achieve more than six per cent growth annually, and the eight per cent recently achieved by Uganda is possible. Diversification is crucial to raising the long-run growth rate. At present the economy is over-concentrated on primary commodity exports, the three most important sources of export earnings being prawns (43 per cent), cotton (12 per cent) and cashews (9 per cent). The economy has more potential for diversification than the typical sub-Saharan African case, specifically in transport services, minerals, energy, and tourism.

The rehabilitation of port, railway, and storage facilities, mainly through joint ventures with foreign investors, is facilitating the resumption of Mozambique's traditional earnings as a transit port for international trade to the landlocked countries of Southern and Central Africa, and for South Africa's exports. Large-scale mining and energy projects have begun, including the resumption of coal exports (which the war closed down in the mid-1980s) and the start of off-shore gas projects. The export of power to the traditional markets of South Africa and Zimbabwe has resumed following the reconstruction of power lines from Mozambique's Cahora Bassa hydro-electric dam, and the servicing of the dam's US$1.7b debt will resume in 2000. There is significant foreign investment in tourism, and Mozambique is set to resume its pre-independence role as major tourist destination for South Africans.

These new investments provide considerable potential for the growth of non-agricultural income, which is essential for reducing both urban poverty (through the creation of service sector and manufacturing employment) and rural poverty reduction (through remittance flows, and reduced vulnerability to drought). But all of these investments require careful management of their environmental impacts to preserve the country's rich natural resource base on which livelihoods depend (GOM, 1994). There is much disquiet about the environmental impact of tourist and mining developments in particular, and rigorous and transparent mechanisms for the environmental evaluation of projects are essential to secure sustainable growth.

## 8.6 CONCLUSIONS

Mozambique's reform programme has now been sustained for a decade. While there have been interruptions along the way, the Government has shown a greater degree of commitment to the reform process than many other African governments. Some observers would say that the Government had no choice given the scale of the balance of payments support to run an economy at war, and the dependence of the budget on aid flows. While it is true that Mozambique has had no option but to accept policy conditionality, it is also evident that there is a high degree of commitment within Government to the liberalization process, not withstanding the difficulties of its implementation. The IMF and the World Bank have been key actors in driving the reform process, but the bilateral donors have been influential as well, in particular keeping the donor community focused on the need for social reconstruction.

Economic reform is a difficult enough business without having to engage in economic reconstruction as well. War has hit hard Mozambique's agriculture, the most critical sector for growth and poverty reduction, and the costs of rebuilding and running economic and social infrastructure are enormous in relation to the meagre revenues available. It is easy to be pessimistic about Mozambique's prospects. There are many constraints to achieving economic and social progress, not least the scarcity of human capital and the associated weakness of central and local governments in implementing policies and programmes. And while elections have taken place, Mozambique's democracy is fragile. However, Mozambique has not gone the way of Angola, and the transition from war to peace has been a rare success for the UN. South Africa, the region's pre-eminent power, can also play a major stabilizing role.

Mozambique's prospects for economic recovery are relatively good, given the depths to which the economy has fallen over the last fifteen years. Rural communities are rebuilding their lives. Modest, but significant, foreign investment is now occurring, and there is potential to create more employment in its tourist sector and possibly a labour-intensive export manufacturing sector linked to the South African market.

There are fewer grounds for optimism regarding poverty reduction. While the recovery of subsistence agriculture will do much to improve food-security, and to provide a growing non-farm rural economy, the fundamental problems of raising the productivity of rain-fed smallholder agriculture remain. Moreover, growing inequality in access to land and natural resources will, if it goes unchecked, exacerbate rural poverty. The Government's targets for expanding primary education and basic health are laudable, but clearer expenditure priorities and more debt relief are essential if they are to be achieved. Mozambique's economic and social recovery will therefore continue well into the next century.

## Notes

1. A first draft of this paper was presented at the fourth workshop of the Structural Adjustment Forum, University of Nottingham, 5–7 January 1995. Versions of the paper were also presented at seminars in ISS (the Hague) in March 1995 and Queen Elizabeth House, Oxford in November

1996. We are grateful to Robert Cassen, Carlos Nuno Castel-Branco, Jaiki Desai, Sue Fleming, Iolanda Fortes, Assa Guambe, Lucia Hanmer, Bridget O'Laughlin, John Knight, Ian McDonald, Oliver Morrissey, Graham Pyatt, Helena Ribe, Frances Stewart and Howard White for comments and discussion on these issues. Errors and omissions remain our own.

2. For differing perspectives on reform in Africa see Easterly and Levine (1995), Helleiner (1989), Ndulu (1991), World Bank (1994a). For evidence on the impact of policies see Rouis, *et al.* (1994). On the poverty impact see Sahn (1995) and Stewart (1996). On the role of the state see Harrold *et al.* (1996) and Mosley *et al.* (1991).
3. Abrahamsson and Nilsson (1995), Hanlon (1991) and Newitt (1995) provide comprehensive discussions of Mozambique's economic and political history.
4. The present value measure takes into account both the profile of debt servicing payments and the concessionality of the debt structure by discounting the stream of future debt servicing payments.
5. The low price received by smallholders was due to the export ban and the minimum pricing arrangements, which, although they were intended to help farmers achieve higher prices, sometimes ends up penalizing them because the traders, who are in a stronger bargaining position, succeed in turning the minimum price into a fixed price (Addison and Ribe, 1996).

## References

Abrahamsson, H. and A. Nilsson (1995), *Mozambique: the Troubled Transition*, London: Zed Books.

Addison, T. (1996a), 'The Poverty Impact of Programme Aid: a Framework for Evaluation', in H. White (ed), *Evaluating Programme Aid: Proceedings of a Workshop held at the Institute of Social Studies: Volume I*, The Hague: Institute of Social Studies, pp. 78–142.

Addison, T. (1996b), 'Zimbabwe: The Impact of Economic Reform on Livelihoods and Poverty', University of Warwick (processed). Paper presented at the *1996 Development Studies Association Annual Conference*, University of Reading.

Addison, T. (1997), 'Debt Sustainability and Human Development', Department of Economics, University of Warwick. Report prepared for UNCTAD (January).

Addison, T. and C. de Sousa (1997), 'Reducing Rural Poverty in Post-War Mozambique', Department of Economics, University of Warwick (Processed).

Addison, T. and I. McDonald (1995), 'Rural Livelihoods and Poverty in Mozambique', Maputo: Poverty Alleviation Unit, Ministry of Planning and Finance, Government of Mozambique (Processed).

Addison, T. and H. Ribe (1996), 'Reducing Rural Poverty in Southern Africa: Meeting the Challenge', Washington, DC: World Bank Paper for the SADC/IFAD/World Bank Workshop on *Approaches to Rural Poverty Alleviation in SADC Countries*, Cape Town, South Africa, 19–22 February.

Alderman, H., D.E. Sahn and J. Arulpragasam (1991), 'Food Subsidies and Exchange Rate Distortions in Mozambique', *Food Policy*, 16:5, pp. 395–404.

Azam, J.-P., J. Berthelemy and C. Morrison (1991), 'L'Offre de Cultures Commerciales en Economie de Pénurie', *Revue Economique*, 3, pp. 553–573.

Colletta, N., M. Kostner and I. Wiederhofer (1996), *The Transition from War to Peace in Sub-Saharan Africa,* Washington, DC: The World Bank.

Coulter, J.P. (1995), 'Maize Marketing and Pricing Study – Mozambique', Processed. Chatham: Natural Resources Institute (April) (Proceed).

Easterly, W. and R. Levine (1995), 'Africa's Growth Tragedy: A Retrospective, 1960–89' *Policy Research Working Paper 1503*, Washington, DC: The World Bank.

Finnegan, W. (1992), *A Complicated War: the Harrowing of Mozambique*, Berkeley: University of California Press.

Government of Mozambique (GOM) (1994), 'National Environmental Management Programme', Maputo: Comissão Nacional do Meio Ambiente.

Government of Mozambique (GOM) (1995a), 'The Poverty Reduction Strategy for Mozambique', Paper presented at the Donor Consultative Group.

Government of Mozambique (GOM) (1995b), 'Establishing the Basis for Economic and Social Development: Key Policies', Maputo: Report Prepared for the Meeting of the Consultative Group for Mozambique (March).

Government of Mozambique (GOM) (1997), 'Debt Strategy for Mozambique', Maputo: Ministry of Finance.

Hanlon, J. (1991), *Mozambique: Who Calls the Shots?*, London: James Currey.

Hanlon, J. (1996), *Peace without Profit: How the IMF Blocks Rebuilding in Mozambique*, Oxford: James Currey and Heinemann.

Harris, L. (1980), 'Agricultural Cooperatives and Development Policy in Mozambique', *Journal of Peasant Studies*, 7:3, p. 338.

Harrold, P., M. Jayawickrama and D. Bhattasali (1996), 'Practical Lessons for Africa from East Asia in Industrial and Trade Policies', *World Bank Discussion Paper 310*, Washington, DC: The World Bank.

Helleiner, G. (1989), 'The IMF, the World Bank, and Africa's Adjustment and External Debt Problems: an Unofficial View', *World Development*, 20:6, pp. 779–792.

Kyle, S. (1991), 'Economic Reform and Armed Conflict in Mozambique', *World Development*, 19:6, pp. 637–649.

Kyle, S. (1994), 'Structural Adjustment in a Country at War: the Case of Mozambique', in D.E. Sahn (ed) *Adjusting to Policy Failure in African Economies*, Ithaca: Cornell University Press, pp. 234–259.

Lopez, P. and E. Sacerdoti (1991), *Mozambique: Economic Rehabilitation and the Poor*, Washington, DC: International Monetary Fund, Working Paper 91/101.

Mosley, P., J. Harrigan and J. Toye (1991), *Aid and Power: the World Bank and Policy-Based Lending*, 2 vols, London: Routledge.

Munslow, B. (1984), 'State Intervention in Agriculture: the Mozambican Experience', *Journal of Modern African Studies*, 22:2.

Myers, G.W. (1993), 'Confusion, Contradiction and Conflict: Land Access in Mozambique in the Post-Peace Period, Four Cases from Manica, Sofala, Gaza, and Inhambane Provinces', University of Wisconsin-Madison, Land Tenure Centre (Processed).

Ndulu, B.J. (1991), 'Growth and Structural Adjustment in Sub-Saharan Africa', in A. Chhibber and S. Fischer (eds), *Economic Reform in Sub-Saharan Africa*, Washington, DC: World Bank, pp. 287–302.

Newitt, M. (1995), *A History of Mozambique*, London: Hurst.

O'Laughlin, B. (1996), 'Through a Divided Glass: Class and the Agrarian Question in Mozambique', *Journal of Peasant Studies*, 23:4.

Overseas Development Institute (ODI) (1995), *Poor Country Debt: A Never-ending Story?*, London: Overseas Development Institute, Briefing Paper No. 1.

Oxfam(1996), *Multilateral Debt: the Human Costs*, Oxford: Oxfam Position Paper (February).

Plank, D. (1993), 'Aid, Debt, and the End of Sovereignty: Mozambique and its Donors', *Journal of Modern African Studies*, 31:3, pp. 407–30.

Rouis, M., W. Razzak and C. Mollinedo (1994), 'The Supply Response to Exchange Rate Reform in Sub-Saharan Africa', *World Bank Policy Research Working Paper 1311*, Washington DC: The World Bank.

Sahn, D.E. (1996), 'Economic Reform and Poverty: an Overview', in D.E. Sahn (ed), *Economic Reform and the Poor in Africa,* Oxford: Clarendon Press, pp. 3–26

Sahn, D.E. and J. Desai (1994), 'The Emergence of Parallel Markets in a Transition Economy: the Case of Mozambique', Washington, DC: *Cornell Food and Nutrition Policy Program Working Paper 53*.

Srivastava, R.K. and I. Livingstone (1983), 'Growth and Distribution: the Case of Mozambique', in D. Ghai and S. Radwan (eds), *Agrarian Policies and Rural Poverty in Africa*, Geneva: International Labour Office, pp. 249–280.

Stewart, F. (1995), *Adjustment and Poverty*, London: Routledge.

Tarp, F. (1990), 'Prices in Mozambican Agriculture', *Journal of International Development*, 2:2, pp. 172–208.

Tibana, R.J. (1994), 'Structural Adjustment and the Manufacturing Industry in Mozambique: some Problems of Transition from Socialist-Type to Free-Market Economy', Oxford: Centre for the Study of African Economies (Processed).

Tschirley, D. and M. Weber (1994), 'Food Security Strategies Under Extremely Adverse Conditions: the Determinants of Household Income and Consumption in Rural Mozambique', *World Development,* 22:2, pp. 159–173.

Tschirley, D., C. Donovan and M. Weber (1996), 'Food Aid and Food Markets: Lessons from Mozambique', *Food Policy*, 21:2: pp. 189–210.

UN (United Nations) (1995), *The United Nations and Mozambique 1992–95*, New York: United Nations, Department of Public Information.

UNDP (United Nations Development Programme) (1996), *Human Development Report 1996*, New York: Oxford University Press for UNDP.

UNICEF (1993), *The Situation of Children and Women in Mozambique – 1993*, Maputo: Government of Mozambique and UNICEF.

World Bank (1989), *Mozambique Food Security Study*, Washington, DC: World Bank Report No. 7963-MOZ.

World Bank (1990), *Mozambique: Restoring Rural Production and Trade*, Washington, DC: The World Bank.

World Bank (1994a), *Adjustment in Africa: Reforms, Results, and the Road Ahead*, Washington, DC: The World Bank.

World Bank (1994b), *Reducing the Debt Burden of Poor Countries: A Framework for Action*, Washington, DC: The World Bank.

World Bank/IMF (1996), 'Debt Sustainability Analysis for the Heavily Indebted Poor Countries', Washington, DC: World Bank, January 30 (mimeo).

Wuyts, M. (1995), *Negotiating and Managing Public Expenditures: Mozambique's Experience with Public Expenditure Reviews*, The Hague: Institute of Social Studies Advisory Service (April).

# 9 Vietnam: An Economy in Transition or In Between?

Karel Jansen

## 9.1 INTRODUCTION

Most of the case-studies examined in this book have looked at the liberalization of predominantly market economies in the 1980s and 1990s. The experience of Vietnam shows many parallels with that of liberalizing developing market economies, but also significant differences. In both cases the direction of reform has been the same, towards less state intervention and more market coordination. But the economic reforms in Vietnam go beyond mere liberalization and are, generally, captured by the term 'transition to the market economy'. The difference is that, whereas other developing countries were liberalizing their economies within a given institutional and legal framework, the reforms in Vietnam implied the creation of an entirely new structure of institutions, within which the freedom of economic agents was considerably increased.

Also the reasons for the economic reforms have been different. In developing market economies, a combination of external shocks, excessive external borrowing, loose fiscal policies and poor export performance led to unsustainable imbalances, as reflected in balance of payments problems and debt crisis, negative growth and high inflation. These problems called for 'structural adjustment' usually assisted by the international financial institutions, the IMF and the World Bank, and by bilateral donors. The direction of structural adjustment reforms has been strongly influenced by the neoclassical paradigm, which has become increasingly dominant in economic academic and policy thinking. Where countries may have been reluctant to follow this paradigm, their growing dependence on IMF and World Bank often forced them to accept it.

The reforms in Vietnam also find their background in disappointing economic performance. After the 1975 victory, the unification of the North and the South implied the forced collectivization of the Southern economy. Resistance against this process led to stagnation and decline in output. The inefficiencies of central control of the very poor economy became increasingly obvious in the 1980s. From the mid 1980s, the turmoil in the Soviet Union and the Eastern European states not only shocked the confidence of Vietnamese central planners, but also cut off Vietnam from its main trading partners and its main sources of foreign assistance.

The response was an initially hesitant but increasingly radical programme of economic reform. The reforms started in 1980, but the real turnaround came with the 6th Party Congress of 1986, which initiated the renovation or *doi moi* policy. The 1986 decision was reflected in reform measures taken in 1987 and 1988 and, particularly, 1989 and later years. Vietnam had to undertake these reforms without significant external assistance. The aid from the Soviet Union was cut off with the collapse of that country, and aid from Western countries and Japan, as well as from the IMF and the World Bank, was blocked by the USA.

## 9.2 LIBERALIZATION AND THE TRANSITION TO THE MARKET

The 1970s and 1980s were a difficult period for most developing countries. In the 1970s severe external shocks (two oil crises) hit the oil-importing developing countries. However, international financial markets were very liquid in these years, so that developing countries could borrow substantial amounts. This external finance was partly used to accommodate the trade shocks and partly to finance increased investment. However, the external borrowing accumulated in rapidly increasing debt burdens, particularly when the international interest rates rose to high levels in the early 1980s. In 1982 came the crunch when Mexico could no longer service its external debt obligations. This crisis made international banks reluctant to go on lending to other developing countries as well. Thus, rather suddenly, the flow of international finance stopped and developing countries could no longer finance their large current account deficits (see Jansen and Vos, 1998).

These events had two important consequences. The first was that, in view of their balance of payments problems, developing countries started to look at ways to increase their exports. The second was that, in view of the reduced access to international private finance, developing countries became more dependent on official financial flows, in particular loans from the IMF and the World Bank. However, such loans come with policy conditions attached to them and, for many developing market economies, these conditions implied a significant change in their economic policies.

The diagnosis of the IMF and the World Bank was that developing countries in the 1980s were suffering from unsustainable macroeconomic imbalances, as reflected in large current account deficits and high debt burdens, fiscal deficits and high rates of inflation. Moreover, excessive government intervention distorted many markets. For instance, trade barriers and overvalued exchange rates created an anti-export bias; public subsidies resulted in inefficient use of resources and in fiscal deficits; controlled financial systems failed to ensure an efficient allocation of investment funds. These distortions undermined the efficiency of resource allocation and resource use and kept the level of output below what could have been achieved (World Bank, 1990). From this diagnosis follows the prescribed cure. Structural adjustment has two main tasks: it must restore macroeconomic stability and it must increase efficiency. Stabilization, which is seen as an absolute precondition for the recovery of economic growth, depends crucially on the success of public sector financial reform.

After the unification of the country in 1975 and for much of the 1980s Vietnam was rather isolated from the events in the world economy as described above. The economy was poor and external trade was only small, most of it took place within the administered framework of the Council for Mutual Economic Assistance (CMEA). Substantial amounts of aid were received from the Soviet Union. With the political changes in the Soviet Union and Eastern Europe, and the subsequent collapse of their economies, the basis for the CMEA trade and aid suddenly disappeared by the end of the 1980s. So, like the developing market economies, Vietnam had rather urgently to look for other sources of export earnings and for other sources of external finance.

The policy reforms that Vietnam put into place to deal with these challenges also contain many elements that are familiar from the structural adjustment experience of developing market economies. There was a combination of stabilization policies (mainly fiscal and monetary policies) and of structural reform policies (price liberalization, trade liberalization). However, underlying these reform policies was a more fundamental reform in the entire institutional structure of the economy. These reforms will be discussed in more detail in the next section.

The reforms in Vietnam have been successful in turning its economic performance around. Vietnam is still one of the poorest countries in

Southeast Asia, but its growth rate over the last five years has been over eight per cent per annum, a rate comparable to other dynamic economies in the region, such as Malaysia and Thailand. Despite the similarity in growth rate and the joint experience of liberalization, it should be pointed out, however, that the Vietnamese economic system remains in many respects fundamentally different from that of other Southeast Asian countries. The role of the state in the economy is still large. All land is owned by the state, most of industrial production takes place in state-owned enterprises, the main commercial banks are state-owned. The role of the market was substantially enhanced over the last ten years, but in many economic decisions non-market arguments continue to play an important part.

## 9.3 A BRIEF HISTORY OF ECONOMIC REFORMS IN VIETNAM

After the end of the war, the unification of the economies of the North and the South implied that the South was to be moulded into the collective model of the North. This reform was, however, strongly resisted, particularly in the agricultural sector. Most of the Southern farming sector was thus collectivized only in name, in fact farming continued to be a household activity. But that did not mean that all remained the same. For instance, land allocation was centralized and farmers could never be certain about their tenure. They had thus little incentive for investment in land maintenance or improvement (Vo-Tong Xuan, 1995).

The outcomes of the first five-year plan after re-unification were very disappointing. Actual performance stayed far behind stated plan targets. Production stagnated in the second half of the 1970s; in 1979 and 1980 industrial output even declined. This was the background for a first round of reforms initiated around 1980.

The Directive 100 of 1981 is usually seen as the first step in agricultural reform. Faced with emerging food shortages and with farmers' unrest, the directive gave more autonomy to individual farmers. Household farms were allocated plots of land to cultivate under contract with the cooperative. Farmers undertook to produce a certain quantity of a crop to be sold to the state at a fixed price. Production beyond the contracted quantity could be used for own use or for free sale. Cooperatives continued to control the distribution of inputs and the marketing of outputs.

The effect of this measure was to increase rice production over the period 1982–87. Still, this reform could not solve the problems of agriculture (Vo-Tong Xuan, 1995). The main problem was the too centralized nature of decision making. The central decision on which crop the farmers had to produce did not always meet the local conditions. Failures of the state to indeed procure the contracted amount or to timely deliver the required inputs undermined the effectiveness of the system and the confidence of the farmers.

The problems were more radically attacked after 1986. The 6th Party Congress of 1986 made the fundamental political decision to go for economic reform. The Resolution 10 of 1988 gave the details of these reforms for the agricultural sector. The property rights of the households were strengthened through longer-term land-use rights contracts. It gave farmers a free choice in which crop to grow, decontrolled prices of crops and of inputs and privatized the distribution of inputs. Later farmers were also released from the obligation to sell contracted amounts of rice to the state. Private trade in output was now allowed. The 1993 Land Law further extended land-use rights, and made such rights transferable, giving farmers more security of tenure.

These reforms have resulted in a private agricultural sector operating on free input and output markets. Cooperatives still exist, but in most places their functions have been reduced to giving advise and, occasionally, in providing credit or jointly purchasing machinery or organizing infrastructural or irrigation facilities. The industrial sector is dominated by the state-owned enterprises. Up to 1980, the policy priority in this sector, in line with the Soviet model, was heavy industry. Ambitious targets were formulated in the subsequent five-year plans for, for instance, electricity, steel, coal and cement production. Around 1980, after substantial failures in meeting these targets, policy priorities shifted to agriculture and to light industries producing consumer goods. At this time there was also a loosening up of the central planning control (Vo Dai Luc, 1994). Firms were given some leeway to produce, beyond their plan targets, for the free market. These reforms led to an acceleration of industrial growth in the early 1980s. But efficiency in the state-owned enterprises remained low and substantial government subsidies were required.

The 1986 Party Congress provided the watershed, also for this sector. The decisions of the Congress shifted priorities away from heavy industry towards agriculture and light industry, with a particular emphasis on the production of food, consumer goods and goods for export. It was decided to move towards a multi-sectoral economy where, next to state-owned enterprises, there would be non-state firms. Firms were to be given more financial autonomy and market coordination would take the place of central planning control. These changes in policy direction were embodied in a series of laws and resolutions that were promulgated in the following years. Of particular interest is the Law on Foreign Investment (1987) and Resolution 16 of 1988 on small-scale and private sector activities. This resolution established the rights of these non-state economic units to operate and the conditions for their operation (Ronnas, 1992). In 1990 this was followed by the issuing of a Company Law and a Private Business Law.

The reform of the state enterprise sector was, however, not just a matter of shifting priorities and moving to a multi-sector economy. The efficiency of the sector had to be enhanced. State enterprises were, at the same time, the main source of government revenue and the main user of government subsidies. The substantial public sector financial imbalances were reflected in very high rates of inflation, over 300 per cent per year during 1986–88. The fight against inflation, that was engaged seriously in 1989, thus included elimination of government subsidies to the state enterprises. The enterprises were given greater financial autonomy and responsibility. Their input and output prices were set free and they were free to decide on procurement of inputs, production and output marketing, investments, hiring and firing of personnel and setting of wages. Government subsidies were terminated but state-owned enterprises obtained preferential access to commercial bank loans.

At the same time, a decree was issued requiring all centrally and locally state-owned enterprises to register anew. This re-registration was used to dissolve some loss-making state enterprises and to merge some others. The outcome was a sharp reduction in the number of state-owned enterprises from about 12,000 to 7,000 (World Bank, 1995). This rationalization involved substantial lay-offs of workers. The reforms of the state-owned enterprise sector had important implications for the role of the financial system. Vietnam used to have the traditional Soviet-type mono-bank system with the large state bank combining central bank and commercial bank functions. After 1988 the State Bank of Vietnam (SBVN) shifted its credit activities to four separate state-owned commercial banks. At the same time new laws set down the conditions under which new banks could be established. By the end of 1995 there were four state-owned commercial banks, 46 joint stock banks, 4 joint venture banks, 18 foreign banks and 71 representative offices of foreign banks (*Vietnam Investment Review*, 5 February 1996). Measured in terms of assets, the four state-owned banks take care of the banking business, they held 86 per cent of all bank assets by the end of 1994 (World Bank, 1995).

Most of the business of the banks is with state-owned enterprises. To some extent, the state-owned commercial banks have taken over from government the task of financing the state enterprises' activities. The access of the private sector to bank loans is still very limited and restricted to some short-term loans. As in other transitional economies, the commercial banks hold a substantial proportion of bad loans (McKinnon, 1993). The World Bank estimated that, by the end of 1994, the non-performing loans may account for 25 per cent of all assets of the state-owned commercial banks (World Bank, 1995).

Financial reform went beyond a mere restructuring of the system. A major change was the increase in the interest rates. Real interest rates were strongly negative in 1986, 1987 and 1988. They turned positive in 1989 both because of the increase in the nominal interest rates and because of the decline in inflation. In 1990 and 1991 the real interest rate turned negative again when nominal rates were reduced and inflation bounced back. Since 1992 real interest rates have been positive. Apart from the negative real interest rate, a further subsidy to the borrowers was that lending rates were held below deposit rates. Only in 1992 was this anomaly turned around (World Bank, 1995, p. 101).

It is clear that under such conditions the financial system cannot work very well. Indeed, financial development indicators are low for Vietnam. The M3/GDP ratio increased sharply in 1989 to 29 per cent, probably due to the fall in inflation and the increase in the interest rates, but declined again in subsequent years. The payment system is still largely based on cash transactions. The role of bank transfers is very small, also because such transfers are very cumbersome to make. The confidence in the banking system is low, partly due to the history of inflation, partly to the poor services provided by banks. A considerable proportion of wealth holdings is in the form of gold or foreign currency. There is a substantial circulation of US dollars, which is widely used in transactions. Another fundamental set of reforms took place in the area of external trade. Under the old system, exports and imports were part of plan targets and were conducted at administered prices. Most of the external trade was within the CMEA network. The economic reforms liberalized trade; importing and exporting now became market decisions. A crucial element in these reforms was the 1989 devaluation of the exchange rate. This decision signaled the fact that the exchange rate had become a 'market' price rather than an artificial accounting price. A major challenge was to find new markets for Vietnamese exports. Around 1990, with the collapse of the economies of the Soviet Union and the East European countries, a traditionally ensured market for Vietnamese exports disappeared.

Existing import tariffs are, on average, not excessively high, but there is a wide dispersion and the regular changes in the tariff structure generate uncertainties. The tariff structure and some import quotas reflect the attempt to protect some local industries, but they do, of course, also imply an anti-export bias. There are reasons to think that the tariffs are not very effective in protecting local industries. The main indication of this is the rampant smuggling that takes place. Estimates suggest that illegal imports account for about 25 per cent of recorded imports. There are furthermore strong pressures on Vietnam to reduce its tariffs. Vietnam's membership of ASEAN implies it had to join its process of tariff reductions, and the application for membership of the WTO further adds to these pressures.

It will thus be increasingly difficult to protect local industries through import tariffs and quota. The exchange rate also does not help very much. Between 1989 and 1991 the nominal exchange rate gradually depreciated, keeping the real exchange rate rather stable. But in the subsequent years (1992 to 1996) the nominal exchange rate remained stable, leading to a substantial appreciation of the real exchange rate. The overvalued exchange rate stimulates imports and undermines the viability of import-competing industries. So far, it has done little to discourage exports, export growth in 1995 is estimated to be 30 per cent (in current dollar terms).

## 9.4 THE OUTCOMES

The results of the economic reforms are clearly visible. Hanoi and Ho Chi Minh City have changed from sleepy towns into bustling cities. In rural areas the growing activity at local markets shows the economic progress. More precise economic assessment of the results of the economic reforms is made difficult by the lack of data and by the unreliability of the data that are available. Indeed, this lack of data dictates that our analysis of the impact of Vietnam's economic reforms largely relies on the sort of before and after comparisons discussed above in Chapter 2. The relevant caveats expressed in that chapter therefore apply to this analysis. Economic statistics used to be collected according to the Material Product system. Estimates of the value of production and income measured according to the UN System of National Accounts (SNA) are available only from 1986 onwards. As the two statistical systems have considerable differences in definitions and coverage, comparison of statistics before and after 1986 is difficult.

Material production stagnated in the late 1970s. The economic reforms that started around 1980 were associated with a growth in material production in the early 1980s, both in agriculture and in industry. Agricultural growth slowed down again in subsequent years, ending up in stagnation around 1987 (Vu Tuan Anh, 1994, p. 48).

Table 9.1 presents economic data based on the SNA system of accounts. Real GDP growth increased from a low level in 1987 to a satisfactory level in 1989. The two years 1990 and 1991 showed a growth recession, but since 1992 the Vietnamese economy really boomed with an average growth rate in excess of 8.5 per cent. Six aspects of the main dimensions of Vietnam's growth experience may be noted from Table 9.1.

First, the high growth rates of the last four years, at more than 8.5 per cent per year, have been achieved with modest levels of investment. The ratio of investment in GDP has been around 20 per cent, implying an incremental capital-output ratio (ICOR) of around 2.3. Such a low ICOR suggests that the high growth originates from a more intensive use of existing production capacity as much as from the creation of new production capacity.

Second, the sectoral breakdown of production growth provides some interesting patterns. Agricultural production had stagnated in the late 1970s, but started to grow after 1980. Between 1980 and 1986 the average annual growth rate of real gross agricultural production was 5.2 per cent (Tran Hoang Kim, 1992, p. 125). Gross output of food crops increased from 14.4 million tons in 1980 to 18.4 in 1986 and 21.5 million ton in 1989. After stagnation in 1990 and 1991, growth resumed to 27.5 million ton in 1995. This rapid growth in agricultural production and incomes is important because the majority of the population depends on the agricultural sector for its income. The rapid rise of agricultural incomes provided a significant stimulus to the rest of the economy.

Gross industrial output had actually declined in 1979/80 and only slowly recovered in the early 1980s. Between 1982 and 1988, however, the industrial sector had shown rapid growth. In 1989 and 1990 the sector was hit by a severe recession. Two reasons can be given. The anti-inflation policy and financial reforms in these years cut off the easy

*Table* 9.1 Selected Economic Indicators, Vietnam

| | 1986 | 1987 | 1988 | 1989 | 1990 | 1991 | 1992 | 1993 | 1994 | 1995 |
|---|---|---|---|---|---|---|---|---|---|---|
| Growth of Real GDP | n.a. | 3.7 | 5.9 | 8.0 | 5.1 | 6.0 | 8.6 | 8.1 | 8.8 | 9.5 |
| Agriculture | n.a. | –0.6 | 3.9 | 6.9 | 1.5 | 2.2 | 7.2 | 3.8 | 3.9 | 4.6 |
| Industry | n.a. | 8.8 | 5.3 | –2.6 | 2.9 | 8.7 | 13.5 | 12.8 | 13.6 | 13.9 |
| Services | n.a. | 5.5 | 9.2 | 18.3 | 10.8 | 8.3 | 7.0 | 9.2 | 10.2 | 10.5 |
| State Sector (% GDP) | 36.7 | 35.8 | 32.5 | 33.2 | 32.5 | 33.3 | 36.2 | 39.2 | 40.2 | 42.2 |
| Investment (% GDP) | 11.7 | 10.9 | 14.4 | 11.6 | 12.6 | 15.0 | 17.6 | 20.5 | 24.2 | 27.1 |
| Domestic Savings (% GDP) | –2.4 | –2.1 | –2.4 | 5.0 | 6.8 | 10.0 | 13.8 | 14.8 | 16.6 | 19.0 |
| Exports ($USm) | 494 | 610 | 733 | 1320 | 1731 | 2042 | 2475 | 2985 | 4054 | 5300 |
| Foreign Investment[a] ($USm) | – | – | 366 | 539 | 596 | 1288 | 1938 | 2777 | 3705 | 7200 |
| Inflation (CPI, %) | 774.7 | 223.1 | 393.8 | 34.7 | 67.5 | 67.6 | 17.6 | 5.2 | 14.4 | 12.7 |
| Government Revenue (% GDP) | 14.0 | 13.2 | 11.3 | 13.9 | 14.7 | 13.5 | 19.0 | 22.3 | 24.3 | 23.9 |
| Government Expenditure[b] (% GDP) | 20.0 | 17.9 | 18.3 | 21.4 | 20.5 | 15.0 | 20.7 | 27.1 | 26.2 | 24.7 |
| Government Budget Deficit (% GDP) | 6.0 | 4.7 | 7.0 | 7.5 | 5.8 | 1.5 | 1.7 | 4.8 | 1.9 | 0.8 |

[a]: Total capital of approved projects; includes equity and debt financing and contribution of local partners.
[b]: Current and capital expenditure, including interest payments.

government subsidies on which many industrial firms had come to depend. Moreover, exporting firms were hit by the loss of their markets in the Soviet Union and Eastern Europe. By 1992 the sector had overcome these problems and over the years 1992–95 annual growth of real production averaged 14 per cent.

Services has only recently become important. The activities of the services sector were incompletely covered by the earlier Material Product statistics and, indeed, the development of the services sector was not encouraged under central planning. The liberalization of the economy and the increased opportunities for private sector initiatives led to a rapid growth of the services sector. Many small-scale, household-based, firms emerged as shops, restaurants, traders. The development of tourism invited the establishment of many new hotels and tourist agencies. Tourist arrivals increased from 280,000 in 1990 to more than 1.6 million in 1995. The financial reforms led to the establishment of new local and foreign banks. In the period 1987–91 growth of the services sector sharply exceeded overall income growth, suggesting that the services sector was catching up.

It is relevant to analyze another sectoral breakdown, according to ownership. The reforms since 1986 have aimed at making Vietnam a multi-sector economy. The sectors that are distinguished are the state sector, the collective sector, and the private sector. The overall share of the state sector in GDP declined from 38 per cent in 1986, to 33 per cent in 1990, after which it started to increase again up to 40 per cent in 1994. The ups and downs of the state sector are determined mainly be the patterns of growth of the productive sectors. The share of the state sector in the agricultural sector is negligible. In the industrial sector the state accounts for over 60 per cent of all value added and in the services sector for about 50 per cent. The fall of the share of the state sector in GDP between 1986 and 1990 is due to the declining share of the industrial sector in these years. Since 1990 the industrial sector, where the share of the state is high, is booming and also the services sector growth rapidly, while growth in the agricultural sector is much more modest. Moreover, the share of the state sector in industrial production is increasing since 1990. As a result the share of the state sector in overall GDP is rising.

It should be noted that most direct foreign investment takes the form of joint ventures with state-owned enterprises and is thus counted as part of the state sector. The foreign investors feel more secure with the network of contacts that their local partners bring. The non-state sector consists of the collective sector, which is now very small, and the private sector. Private enterprises are all very small, only a handful of them reach middle-size (Ronnas, 1992). They lack the capital required to grow. Private firms have only limited access to bank credit as state-owned enterprises have a preferential claim on available bank resources.

The continued prominent role of the state sector reflects the policy of the Vietnamese government and of the communist party. Recent statements by high-ranking officials confirm that the state sector is the leading sector in the economy and that non-state firms can operate where it is allowed. It seems fair to state that the private sector outside agriculture is tolerated rather than stimulated.

The third aspect emerging from Table 9.1 relates to the decisive success of the reforms with respect to the rapid growth of exports and the opening up of new export markets. Total merchandise exports increased from less than US$500 million in 1986 to more than US$5,000 million in 1995. The average annual growth rate of exports, measured in current dollar values, has been around 30 per cent per year. Every year again shows impressive growth of exports, this despite the gradual and substantial appreciation of the real exchange rate since 1992.

This rapid growth was assisted by the fact that oil exports, the exploration for which had started long ago, came on stream. The exports of crude oil increased from a negligible level in 1986 to more than one quarter of total merchandise exports in recent years. The strong performance of the agricultural sector is reflected in the rapid growth agricultural exports. Exports of rice, rubber, tea and coffee increased from negligible levels in 1986/87 to 22 per cent of total merchandise exports in 1995. Another main new export item is the aqua products and there is also an emerging export of industrial goods, led by clothing and footwear. It is also relevant to note that foreign exchange earnings from tourism have sharply increased. The predominance of bulk goods like oil, coal and agricultural commodities in Vietnam's exports also made it easier to find new markets. Trade with the former CMEA countries almost disappeared. By 1995 Vietnam's major trading partners were the Asian countries, such as Japan, Singapore, Hong Kong, Korea, China, Taiwan and Indonesia.

Fourth, Table 9.1 also shows foreign investment commitments. The figures listed are an exaggeration for two reasons. The first is that the figures do not reflect direct foreign investment. They are the total investment amount for the projects, including the contribution by the local partner in the case of joint ventures, and any loan finance foreseen for the project. The second is that there is a wide gap between the projects that are signed and approved (as listed in Table 9.1) and the actual implementation. It is estimated that of the total amount of over 18 billion dollars approved between 1988 and the end of 1995, about one third has been actually invested. The gap between commitments and realization is due to the time consumed in bureaucratic procedures, even after project approval, but also to the 'wait and see' attitude of some foreign investors. Even accounting for these factors, the inflows of foreign investment funds are large relative to the local economy. In recent years, actually invested foreign investment funds (both equity and loan finance) may well account for about one quarter of total domestic capital formation. Foreign investment has concentrated on the oil industry, on hotels and tourism and on construction and property development.

The main sources of foreign investment are nearby Asian countries, such as Taiwan, Hong Kong, South Korea and Japan; all in all 70 per cent of foreign investments come from Asian countries. Thus both through its trade and through foreign investment, Vietnam is becoming a part of the Southeast Asian region. This trend was underlined by Vietnam's becoming member of ASEAN in 1995.

Fifth, Table 9.1 shows the substantial investment–savings gap. The savings ratio has increased since its negative level in the late 1980s, but it remains low and domestic savings are insufficient to finance the high level of investment required for rapid growth. The government estimates that from 1996 to the year 2000 Vietnam would to need to invest about 42 billion US dollars to maintain the current high growth rate. About half of that amount is expected to come from domestic sources with the other half being provided by aid and foreign investment. It is not clear which calculations lay behind these figures. Assuming an ICOR of 3 and a desired growth rate of 10 per cent, the investment ratio should be 30 per cent of GDP. The present recorded savings rate is less than 20 per cent of GDP (see Table 9.1) and thus sufficient to finance half of the required investment.

To cover the other half it is assumed that official development assistance (ODA) will provide between six and seven billion dollars and foreign investment about 13–14 billion. At the donor consultative group meeting end November 1995, donor countries pledged US$2.3 billion in aid. This came on top of pledges of US$2 billion at the 1994 meeting and US$1.8 billion at the 1993 meeting. There appear thus to be enough aid commitments but the actual disbursements are much lower, mainly due to the low absorptive capacity of Vietnam. For instance, the actual disbursements in 1994 were only US$600 million (United Nations, 1995).

The foreign investment projects approved between 1988 and end 1995 had an accumulated value of over US$18 billion. Of these commitments an estimated US$6 billion has been actually invested. If the presently still outstanding commitments are turned into reality, together with the new investment projects that will be approved up to the year 2000, it would appear that the target of V14 billion of foreign investment could be attained.

The dependence on foreign funding implies a rapid accumulation of external debt. At the end of 1994 the external debt, in convertible currencies, was US$4.5 billion, of which about one billion is debt to commercial creditors. Outstanding official debt was rescheduled in 1993. On top of this is a debt in non-convertible currency of 9.8 billion roubles, which depending of the exchange rate used, can be valued at between US$2 and US$17.5 billion (United Nations, 1995).

The external financing plans till the year 2000 will substantially add to the external debt. Foreign investment projects typically contain a substantial element of debt financing, on average about 50 per cent of total investment (*Vietnam Economic Times*, March 1996). Also the greatest part of aid comes as loans rather than grants. The financing plans as outlined above would thus certainly lead to a rapid growth of external debt by the year 2000. Most of the aid loans come at highly concessional terms but, with the growing role of debt-financed foreign investment, the share of commercial debt, at higher interest rates, in total external debt will sharply increase. The external debt/GDP ratio by the year 2000 would then be around 65 per cent, and the external debt/export ratio between 150 and 200 per cent, depending on the rate of growth of exports. This would lift these ratios to levels that generally are considered dangerous (see Cline, 1995). On top of the debt service requirements will come the profit remittances by foreign companies in Vietnam. Export earnings will thus have to increase very rapidly to ensure the supply of foreign exchange to service these investment income payments.

Sixth, and finally, the 1980s were characterized by high levels of inflation. The dual system of plan targets and free markets for output beyond the plan quota turned the repressed inflation of the controlled market into open inflation of the free market. In 1981 and 1985 price reforms were necessary to bring official prices closer to market prices, but such price reforms in themselves became the source for further inflation as the subsidies required by state enterprises increased. By the late 1980s inflation was out of control. The anti-inflation campaign of 1989 was almost immediately successful. Three elements of the campaign can explain this success. Firstly, a sharp increase in nominal interest rates turned real interest rates positive. There was an immediate response in the form of a sharp increase in deposits. The M2/GDP ratio increased from 19 per cent in 1988 to almost 30 per cent in 1989 (see Dollar, 1993).

The increased demand for money helped to reduce demand pressures at commodity markets. And the supply of commodities increased. The high interest cost induced firms to move out of anti-inflation hedges, such as hoarded inventories of goods (Vo Dai Luoc, 1992). The trade liberalization and the devaluation of the currency led to a sharp increase in exports and imports. The new attitudes towards non-state activities also led to a sharp increase in production. All these factors resulted in an increased availability of goods and helped to reduce excess demand and inflation. A third element contributing to the success of the anti-inflation campaign was the reform of the state enterprises. The termination of government subsidies and the liberalization of prices forced state enterprises to increase their efficiency and production so as to avoid losses. After 1989 inflation rebounded in 1990 and 1991 as the real interest rate fell back, supply increases stagnated and the budget deficit remained high (see Dollar, 1993).

As Table 9.1 showed, the fiscal deficit declined in the early 1990s after its high levels in the 1980s. Government revenue increased rapidly. The inflationary pressures since 1993 may therefore be more due to the demand pressures associated with the high levels of capital inflows. Stability concerns shifted from inflation to the trade balance. The trade gap is very wide, certainly when smuggled imports are taken into account. However, policy measures are much less drastic than in 1989. The interest rate is kept relatively low and the devaluation of the exchange rate is strongly resisted for fear that it would fuel inflation. The overvalued exchange rate encourages imports. Credit controls are imposed to avoid too great an instability. It could be suggested that the 1989 experience showed that a more market-conform approach, working through prices such as the interest rate and the exchange rate, would be more effective.

The six points analyzed above can be summarized as follows. The economic reforms that began around 1980 did invite an increase in production, both in agriculture and in industry. The main characteristic of these early reforms was that firms in agriculture and industry were allowed to undertake activities on their own account beyond the contractual plan quota. A dual system emerged with free market transactions and prices existing next the central planning system. The opportunities of the market system invited a strong response from producers. But the existence of the two systems next to each other also created problems. For instance, in 1981 and 1985 major price reforms were undertaken to bring state prices closer to the free market prices. Unfortunately, the large and growing fiscal deficits and the regular price reforms resulted in rampant inflation.

Inflation was already high in the years 1981–85, but really exploded in 1986 to 1989. The radical reforms of the late 1980s were, therefore, as much an attempt to stabilize the economy as to reform it. The late 1980s saw a combination of:

(i) stabilization policies to reduce inflation. A major element of these policies was a sharp reduction of subsidies to state enterprises.
(ii) economic reform measures that brought a substantial liberalization of the economy. Prices were set free and also the exchange rate was devalued and liberalized.
(iii) considerable external shocks. With the changes in the Soviet Union and Eastern Europe, Vietnam suddenly lost its traditional trading partners and its source of foreign aid. It shows the strength of the Vietnamese economy that, despite these external and policy shocks, growth was maintained although it fell to a low level.

The stabilization policies were successful in reducing inflation. The initial reaction to the price liberalization and devaluation was an moderate acceleration of inflation in 1990 and 1991, but after 1991 inflation came down to modest levels. Once the economy was stabilized and had adjusted to the external shocks, the growth momentum came on full steam in the early 1990s.

## 9.5 EVALUATING THE REFORMS

In evaluating the effects of the reforms on economic performance it is useful to distinguish between policy measures that remove barriers (institutional reforms) and measures that shift incentives (price reforms).

Institutional reforms that remove barriers open up opportunities for economic activities that were previously prohibited and illegal. For instance, the 1980 reforms made production for the market, beyond the plan quota, legal for farm households and for state firms. After the 1988 Resolution and the 1990 law, private sector firms had a legal basis to exist and to operate. The 1987 law on foreign investment opened the country to foreign investors. These institutional reforms were accompanied by policies of price liberalization, rationalization of the exchange rate and so on, which shifted incentives among various economic activities. The removal of barriers can be expected to lead to a sharp rise of previously repressed activities. Indeed, the institutional reforms of 1980 led to an increase in production in the agricultural and industrial sector. The number of registered private businesses increased sharply after the 1988 Resolution, and foreign investment inflows increased rapidly since 1988.

However, much of this rapid growth may be just realizing opportunities that were missed before. Clearly, the reforms led to a more intensive and more efficient use of existing production capacity. Production in agriculture and industry increased sharply without much new investment. The reforms also opened the way for new activities. That was, for instance, observed above for the services sector. Activities in this sector are typically repressed under central planning. It is also a sector where small-scale private firms can make a substantial contribution. It is not surprising, therefore, that when the planning controls were lifted and private sector initiative was given more leeway, the growth in the services sector accelerated strongly. As noted above, over the period 1987–91 the growth rate of the services sector was significantly above the overall economic growth rate. Since 1992 the growth rate of the services sector stays closer to the overall growth rate, suggesting that the catching-up process is near completion and that in the future the services sector will follow the general growth trend.

It is conceivable that a similar process of consolidation may be occurring in foreign investment. When it opened for foreign investment, many foreign companies came to explore the new market. Many contracts were signed and approved and, although the gap between approved contracts and actual investment remains unusually large, actual investment inflows have steadily increased. However, the mood is clearly changing. The international media described in the early 1990s Vietnam as the investors' hot spot, but the tone now is different. One prominent local English-language paper (*Vietnam Economic Times*) carried on the cover of its March 1996 issue the question 'Why are you still here?', addressed at foreign investors. Also other publications carry stories with the worries of foreign investors about the Vietnamese bureaucracy and about the high cost of production. Officials have indicated that they expect foreign investment activities to stabilize in 1996 after years of exponential growth (*Vietnam Investment Review*, 18 March 1996). One could raise the question whether this is another case of catch-up completed or whether it is just a lull before the next boom.

Of course, this 'catching up' growth is real growth and can be attributed to the reforms undertaken. In evaluating the impact of reforms it is, however, more useful to assess the longer-term growth potential that has been created by the reforms. The catching up that has taken place over the last few years may overestimate the longer-term growth effects of the reforms. The debate about the effectiveness of economic reforms in transition economies has concentrated on comparing the 'big bang' or shock therapy approach to a more gradual approach to economic reform. The main example for the gradual approach is China, while the former Soviet Union and some East European countries (such as Poland) provide example for the shock therapy. The big bang is described to consist of (see Woo, 1994):

(i) Immediate and complete price liberalization.
(ii) Full liberalization of trade, involving a devaluation of the exchange rate and a removal of trade barriers.
(iii) The adoption of anti-inflationary macro policies, such as cutting subsidies to state enterprises, reducing the budget deficit, increases in the interest rates and credit controls.
(iv) The legislation of private sector activities and giving autonomy to state enterprises in their production, pricing and investment decisions. The intention to privatize state enterprises is announced, although the actual implementation may take some more time.

The gradual approach takes things easier. Liberalization of production and pricing is partial, with firms being allowed to produce for the free market beyond their plan quota. For most products there will be dual prices, one official price and one free-market price. The more gradual approach to economic reform in China has been associated with high rates of growth and moderate rates of inflation, while the shock therapy has been associated with economic contraction and macroeconomic instability. However, the conclusion that therefore the gradual approach is superior is too easy. There are many differences between China and the European countries that all may have a bearing on the outcomes. The following reasons for the Chinese success have been suggested (Woo, 1994; McKinnon, 1994).

First, China is, and certainly was at the beginning of the reform period, still a predominantly agricultural economy. The early liberalization in agriculture provided new incentives to farm households and the response to these new opportunities was strong. Thus the supply of agricultural goods and the income of a large segment of the population increased at the outset of the reform process, providing impulses to other sectors of the economy. The reforms had a far less positive impact in the industrial sector where the state-owned enterprises could increase their production but not their efficiency. Their deficits remain a main drain for public funds.

Second, the rapid growth of rural incomes is one of the reasons behind the rapid growth of the non-state sector in China. One crucial element in the rapid growth of the Chinese economy has been the emergence of the so-called 'Town and village enterprises' (TVEs), local non-agricultural firms usually financed from the surpluses of rural communities.

Third, the political situation in China was more stable than in European countries in transition. The central government maintained control over the economy that it used, for instance, to combat inflationary pressures.

Fourth, a main factor behind the high rate of investment and growth and the moderate rate of inflation is the high savings ratio of China. The high savings were deposited with banks and could be used to finance the deficits of the government and of the state enterprises.

Fifth, and finally, China became the main destination of foreign investment, providing a further boost to the economy. A very large proportion of these investments came from overseas Chinese. On all these points the contrast between China and Russia and the other East European countries is great. In the European countries the economic reforms took place under conditions of political instability. The European countries were industrialized, with only small agricultural sectors. The savings ratios were much smaller and insufficient to finance the public sector deficits; this made inflationary financing inevitable. With the collapse of communism, also the CMEA which had organized the international trade between the Soviet Union and the Eastern European countries (and Vietnam) disappeared, disrupting the trade flows. Given the political and economic instability it is not surprising that the European transition economies invited little foreign investment.

It could be suggested that the contrasts listed above are more important in explaining the difference in performance than the different approaches to reform policies. It is often suggested that Vietnam has followed a pattern of reforms similar to that of China, but there are significant differences. The reforms that Vietnam started around 1980 can be characterized as a gradual approach. Production in agriculture and by industrial state enterprises increased, but the co-existence of the plan system and the free market led to unmanageable problems, which were reflected in hyper-inflationary conditions by the mid-1980s. Vietnam lacked the high savings that provided the anti-inflationary cushion in China.

The subsequent round of economic reforms in 1989 carry many of the characteristics of the big bang approach. Prices were completely liberalized, the exchange rate was liberalized and devalued, barriers to external trade were removed, the real interest rate was sharply increased and state enterprises could no longer count on subsidies from the government budget. The impact of these measures was a slowdown of economic growth, particularly industrial state enterprises had difficulties in adjusting to the new conditions. Moreover, during these years the collapse of the CMEA disrupted Vietnam's external trade and cut off the source of substantial amounts of foreign aid. But the slowdown of growth was only temporary, by 1992 the growth rate settled above eight per cent and has remained there in the following years.

It is therefore justified to use Vietnam as a case to show that the shock therapy can work. The reform policies introduced around 1989 led, after a short period of adjustment, to rapid growth, a slowdown of inflation, strong export performance and an influx of foreign investment. The basis for this success has been, like in China, the rapid growth of agricultural incomes and, later on, the upsurge in foreign investment inflows. The other factors, listed above as explaining China's success, seem less applicable to Vietnam. There was growth of the non-state sector, but not on the scale experienced in China and domestic savings in Vietnam remained relatively low. By 1996 it can be concluded that Vietnam has almost completed its transition from a planned to a market economy. But it has not progressed much on the transition from a state to a private sector economy and from recent policy statements is appears that Vietnam is also not pressing this second transition. It could be argued that the Vietnamese economy is not in transition but in between. It is situated in between the extremes of a state planning economy and a private market economy.

The role of the state sector is smaller than in some other transition economies. For instance the contribution of the state sector to non-agricultural GDP was 67 per cent in Poland in 1992 and the contribution to non-agricultural NMP was 51 per cent in China in 1991 (Woo, 1994). In Vietnam the contribution to non-agricultural GDP in 1994 was 55 per cent in Vietnam. But, whereas in the other countries the share of the state sector was declining (for instance, in China from 74 per cent in 1978 to 51 in 1991), in Vietnam the share of the state sector is rising – from 45 per cent of non-agricultural GDP in 1990 to 55 per cent in 1994.

The relative decline of the state sector in the other countries is the result of (i) rapid growth of the non-state sector and (ii) privatization of state enterprises. In Vietnam there is less movement on both these tracks. The non-state sector is growing, but not rapid enough to push the state sector aside. The non-state sector has two components: the cooperatives and private enterprises. The number of cooperatives has fallen sharply since the reforms of 1989, they could no longer compete in the market economy. Private enterprises consist of household firms and of larger firms using wage labour. Their number has grown rapidly, but all of them are very small and remain small. The growth is obstructed by lack of capital and by lack of active government support. Life is not easy for private enterprises. Access to land is more difficult, and more costly, than for state enterprises and the same holds for access to bank credit. The trade in many items that they may need as inputs is controlled by state enterprises. Moreover, private enterprises are subject to endless regulations and licensing requirements (*Far Eastern Economic Review*, 29 February 1996). It is not surprising that foreign investors give preference to joint ventures with state enterprises that can provide cheaper land and have better government access.

There are plans to privatize, or equitize, state enterprises. Some time ago 40 enterprises were listed as candidates for privatization under a pilot scheme. Up until mid-1996 only five have been successfully equitized, all of them rather small firms. Further progress on the route appears stalled by resistance of workers and management of enterprises to be privatized, by the lack of clarity about the procedures and by the lack of government commitment both at central and at local levels. Recent pronouncements by leading political figures suggest the same. For instance, Dao Duy Tung, a conservative member of the Politburo, mentioned in an interview:

> We are building an economy that is . . . not based on the dominance of private ownership . . . The state-run economic sector plays the leading role in paving the way and supporting the development of

> other economic sectors. It represents a tool of material strength with which the state can regulate and navigate the market economy. (*Vietnam Economic Times*, October 1995).

Other political leaders have made similar statements about the leading role of the state-owned sector. Can Vietnam achieve rapid growth with the state sector as the leading sector? State enterprises in Vietnam are not noted for their efficiency. There are roughly 7,000 state enterprises, most of them small- or medium-size firms run by local governments. The reforms have rationalized the state sector, closing down many loss making firms. Still, a World Bank report mentioned that by the end of 1993 still about 20 per cent of the state enterprises were making losses (World Bank, 1994). Now that the pressures of external shocks and of macroeconomic instability have eased somewhat, there is an apparent reluctance to further rationalize the state sector.

The production of the state enterprises is increasing rapidly, assisted by their easy access to cheap credit and by their joint ventures with foreign investors. Studies in China showed that the production of state enterprises increased after the reforms but that their profitability declined in the face of increased competition. It was established that total factor productivity growth was negligible in state enterprises, but positive and high in the TVEs. In state enterprises the share of labour in total value added increased sharply as workers and management claimed a larger share of income. The labour share in the value added of the TVEs has remained constant (Woo *et al.*, 1994). There are some indications that similar processes may be occurring in Vietnam with profits of state enterprises being spent on higher compensations and other perks for management and workers or being diverted into side-line businesses (*Asian Business*, October 1995).

Other observers conclude that Vietnamese industrial corporations had, by the mid-1990s, become remarkably efficient and capable of competing with imports and on export markets (Fforde and Goldstone, 1995, p. 91). The actual situation is most likely a mix, with some state companies, with dynamic leadership of in joint venture with foreign firms, doing quite well, while others stay behind. Some scholars hold the view that state enterprises cannot survive the reforms. Kornai (1995) calls the combination of state ownership and market coordination artificial and likely to be pushed aside by bureaucratic coordination which more naturally relates to state ownership. He argues that ideology, bureaucratic intervention and the absence of legal protection of private ownership will make private entrepreneurs uncertain and unwilling to invest in business expansion; 'there cannot be a smoothly operating market without a predominance of private ownership' (Kornai, 1995, p. 212). He also argues that the process of privatization is inherent to the strength of capitalist production. The private sector will see new firms emerging while the state sector will decline through stagnation, privatization and theft (Kornai, 1995). The Vietnamese government clearly does not agree with Kornai, as reflected in the statement quoted above. There are now plans to group the state enterprises in a small number of large conglomerates for various industries, along the lines of Korea's *chaebols*, so as to create the size and dynamism necessary for international competitiveness (see *Far Eastern Economic Review*, 26 October 1995).

Others have emphasized more practical problems. The reforms during the transition period imply that ownership rights and control rights get confused. Generally, the role of central state agencies declines while that of local government, management and workers increase. These changing rights and the large number of agencies involved lead to unclear decision making and low efficiency (see Shleifer and Vishny, 1994, for Russia, and Berg, 1994, for Poland). This ambiguity also exists in Vietnam (Nguyen Tien Hung, 1995). It is thus conceivable that Vietnam would end up with the worst of two worlds. With the unclear and dispersed control over state enterprises leading to low profits and low accumulation and with uncertainly and lack of confidence undermining private accumulation. To avoid this fate seems to bathe main policy challenge of the years to come.

## 9.6 CONCLUSION

Vietnam is a country in economic transition. Developing countries in transition and developing countries under structural adjustment have many things in common. In both government intervention is being reduced and the market is being given a greater role in coordinating economic activity. The significant difference is, however, that countries in transition have to go through a much more extensive process of institutional reform. In the case of Vietnam central planning has been abandoned and almost all prices are now free. In that sense it is now a market economy; the transition from planned to market economy has been completed.

However, the transition in terms of ownership is far less decisive. In the agricultural sector collective farming has given place to farming by individual households. The farmers do not own their land but they hold long-term land-use contracts, giving them security of tenure. A dynamic private sector has emerged in trade, services and industry. However, all of that private sector remains small-scale. There are hardly any middle-sized private firms in Vietnam. Middle-sized and large firms in industry, trade, services, banking are all still state-owned. Privatization schemes for state-owned enterprises have progressed very slowly and are, in fact, put on hold. Recent statements by political leaders re-affirm that the state should play the leading role in the economy. The prospects for economic development of Vietnam thus depend on whether a market economy with the state as leading sector can deliver rapid growth. In theory there is no reason why state-owned enterprises cannot be dynamic and efficient and, in fact, there are many examples of successful state enterprises. Still, there are also many instances of bureaucratic meddling and lack of accountability that turn state enterprises into obstacles to growth.

## References

Berg, A. (1994), 'The Logistics of Privatization in Poland' in O.J. Blanchard, K.A. Froot and J.D. Sachs (eds), *The Transition in Eastern Europe*, Chicago: The University of Chicago Press.

Cline, W.R. (1995), *International Debt Reexamined*, Washington DC: Institute for International Economics.

Dollar, D. (1993), 'Vietnam: Successes and Failures of Macroeconomic Stabilization', in B. Ljunggren (ed), *The Challenge of Reform in Indochina*, Cambridge , MA: Harvard University Press.

Fforde, A. and A. Goldstone (1995), *Vietnam to 2000: Advancing of all fronts*, Research Report, The Economist Intelligence Unit, London.

Jansen, K. and R. Vos (1998), *External Finance and Adjustment, Failure and Success in the Developing World*, London: Macmillan.

Kornai, J. (1995), *Highway and Byways; Studies on Reform and Post-communist Transition*, Cambridge, MA: MIT Press.

McKinnon, R. (1993), 'Macroeconomic Control in Liberalizing Socialist Economies: Asian and European Parallels', in A. Giovannini (ed.), *Finance and Development: issues and experience*, Cambridge: Cambridge University Press.

McKinnon, R. (1994), 'Financial Growth and Macroeconomic Stability in China, 1978–1992: Implications for Russia and Other Transitional Economies', *Journal of Comparative Economics*, 18:3, pp. 438–469.

Nguyen Tien Hung (1995), *Vietnam: Reforming the State Enterprises, towards an agenda for Privatization*, Bangkok: Post Books.

Ronnas, P. (1992), *Employment Generation through Private Entrepreneurship in Vietnam*, ILO (ARTEP), Geneva.

Shleifer and Vishny (1994), 'Privatization in Russia: First Steps', in O.J. Blanchard, K.A. Froot and J.D. Sachs (eds), *The Transition in Eastern Europe*, Chicago: The University of Chicago Press.

Tran Hoang Kim (1992), *Economy of Vietnam: Review and Statistics*, Hanoi: Statistical Publishing House.

United Nations (1995), *Development Cooperation Report: Vietnam 1994*, Hanoi: United Nations.

Vo Dai Luoc (1992), *Curbing Inflation and the process of economic renovation in Vietnam*, Hanoi: Social Sciences Publishing House.

Vo Dai Luoc (1994), *Vietnam's Industrial Development Policy in the Course of Renovation*, Hanoi: Social Science Publishing House.

Vo-Tong Xuan (1995), 'Rice Production, Agricultural Research, and the Environment', in B.J.T. Kerkvliet and D.J. Porter (eds), *Vietnam's Rural Transformation*, Boulder, CO: Westview Press.

Vu Tuan Anh (1994), *Development in Vietnam: Policy Reform and Economic Growth*, Singapore: Institute of Southeast Asian Studies.

Woo, Wing Thye (1994), 'The Art of Reforming Centrally Planned Economies: Comparing China, Poland and Russia', *Journal of Comparative Economics*, 18: 3, pp. 276–308.

Woo, Wing Thye, When Hai, Yibiao Jin and Gang Fan (1994), 'How Successful Has Chinese Enterprise Reform Been? Pitfalls in Opposite Biases and Focus', *Journal of Comparative Economics*, 18:3, pp. 410–437.

World Bank (1990), *Report on Adjustment Lending II: Policies for Recovery of Growth*, Document R 90–99, World Bank

World Bank (1994), *Vietnam: Public Sector Management and Private Sector Incentives. An Economic Report*, Washington, DC: The World Bank.

World Bank (1995) *Vietnam Financial Sector Review: An Agenda for Financial Sector Development*, Washington, DC: The World Bank.

# 10 Market-Oriented Policy Reforms and Manufacturing for Export in Sri Lanka

Prema-chandra Athukorala

## 10.1 INTRODUCTION

An important element of economic liberalization has been trade policy reform, notably the removal of the bias against exports with the intention of increasing the efficiency of the economy and facilitating export-led growth (see Chapter 3 of this volume). There is empirical evidence that a number of liberalizing economies (LEs) have experienced improvements in export performance, with significant increases in manufactured exports (Helleiner, 1994 and 1995; Weiss, 1992; Arslan and van Wijnbergen, 1993; Joshi and Little, 1996). Many of these observers believe that such export success, in particular the expansion of manufacturing output and employment, has been the major contributor to the sustainability and success of economic reforms in these countries. Sri Lanka has witnessed successful export-led growth. Was this due to liberalization or, more precisely, which elements of liberalization generated such success? The driving forces behind rapid export expansion remain a matter of debate.

The key issues in this debate include: Did manufacturing for export develop *de novo* in response to new incentives or was it simply a 'switching' of sales from industries established during the import-substitution era? What has been the relative importance of accompanying macroeconomic policies (including exchange rate policy) and trade policy reforms in generating the export push? Within the trade policy mix, what role did export subsidies play? What influence did policy towards foreign direct investment have upon the export orientation of domestic manufacturing? Answers to these and related questions are important in understanding why policy reforms in many other developing countries failed to achieve the anticipated export breakthrough. They also have a direct bearing on the choice of appropriate policy configurations in designing liberalization reform packages.

This chapter contributes to this debate through a case study of the Sri Lankan experience with liberalization reforms over the past two decades. Given the decisive policy shift in 1977 and policy continuity during the ensuing years, Sri Lanka provides a valuable laboratory for the study of these issues. After almost two decades of policy reforms, Sri Lanka is now one of the most open and market-oriented countries in the developing world. In the new policy environment, the manufacturing sector in Sri Lanka has become increasingly export oriented. The share of exports in total manufacturing output increased from less than 5 per cent in the late 1980s to over 60 per cent in 1995 and more than half of the total manufacturing work force is now employed in export-oriented firms. The share of manufactured goods in total merchandise exports was over 75 per cent in 1995, up from a mere two per cent in the early 1970s.

The structure of the chapter is as follows. The following section traces the evolution of trade and industry policy in Sri Lanka since independence, discusses the key elements of the market-oriented reforms initiated in 1977, and examines the pattern of overall incentives for manufactured exports. Section 10.3 presents an overview of trends and patterns of manufactured export expansion with emphasis on the pivotal role played by export-oriented foreign direct investment in transforming a classical primary commodity-dependent economy into a 'new exporting' country. Section 10.4 undertakes an econometric analysis of the determinants of manufactured exports. A novelty of the analysis is the emphasis placed on the effect of the presence of foreign firms in export-oriented manufacturing on the nexus between the real exchange rate and export performance. Section 10.5 summarizes the main findings of the study and draws policy inferences.

## 10.2 EVOLUTION OF ECONOMIC POLICY

Sri Lanka's industrialization strategy during the post independence period until 1977 was a classic example of 'forced' import substitution (IS). Quantitative import restrictions (QRs), introduced in the late 1950s to try to keep the negative trade balance under control, soon turned out to be the key instrument in directing private sector activities in line with (perceived) national priorities. Following a hesitant and mild liberalization attempt during 1968–70, the period from 1970 to

1977 was marked by further government intervention in the economy under the guise of creating a 'socialist society'. By the mid-1970s Sri Lanka had become one of the most inward-oriented and regulated economies, excluding those that were centrally-planned, characterized by stringent trade and exchange controls and pervasive state interventions in all areas of economic activity.[1]

Policy-makers in Sri Lanka, like their counterparts in many other developing countries, expected the growth of IS industries to reduce the heavy dependence on imports. The reality was quite different, however (Athukorala, 1981). While consumer goods imports were reduced substantially, this was at the expense of increased reliance on imported capital goods and raw materials, resulting in an even more rigid dependence on imports. Given these structural features, the growth of the newly established industrial sector tended to follow the fortunes of the traditional export industries, and unanticipated import contraction brought about by foreign exchange scarcity turned out to be the main constraint on industrial expansion since the late 1960s. In most states with IS policies, rapid expansion of domestic industry continued until the 'easy' import-substitution opportunities (e.g. meeting domestic demand in textiles and other light labour-intensive activities) were used up. It was only then that the cost of additional investment in new IS activities began to rise and growth slowed down (Krueger, 1992: 43–4). However, in Sri Lanka, a limit was set on the growth of industry by the balance of payments constraint well before the completion of the easy IS phase.

Some policy initiatives were taken from the mid-1960s to promote manufacturing and other non-traditional exports. These included import duty rebates, export-performance related import entitlements, multiple exchange rates and new incentives for export-oriented foreign investment. These attempts largely failed because, reflecting the cumulative impact of macroeconomic instability, stringent trade controls, high export taxes and the overvalued exchange rate, the overall incentive structure of the economy continued to be characterized by a significant anti-export bias (Cuthbertson and Athukorala, 1991). Moreover, during the period from 1970 to 1977, widespread nationalization measures and threats, coupled with various economic controls, effectively marginalized the private sector in the economy.

As a reaction to the dismal economic outcome of the inward-looking policy stance, in 1977 Sri Lanka embarked on an extensive economic liberalization process, becoming the first country in the South Asian region to do so. The first round of reforms, carried out during 1977–79, included significant trade liberalization, revamping the foreign investment approval and monitoring process with new incentives for investors, a significant interest rate reform and opening of the banking sector to foreign banks, limits on public sector participation in the economy and exchange rate realignment. Despite major macroeconomic problems, political turmoil and the ongoing ethnic conflict from 1983, market-oriented reforms have been sustained and broadened over the years. In 1990 a 'second wave' liberalization package was announced. This included an ambitious privatization programme, further tariff cuts and simplification of the tariff structure, and removing exchange controls on current account transactions. Following almost two decades of significant reforms, Sri Lanka today stands out as one of the most open economies in the developing world (Dornbusch, 1992). This basic policy orientation looks set to continue in the foreseeable future. Indeed, the most dramatic change in the Sri Lankan political landscape in recent years has been the convergence in broad economic policies among the major political parties and groupings; achieving greater openness and liberalization is now a bipartisan policy in Sri Lanka. With this background we now discuss the key elements of the reform process which have a direct bearing on export performance.

### Trade Policy

Trade policy was the key element of liberalization reforms in Sri Lanka. In November 1977 the near universal QRs were supplanted by a revised system of tariffs, retaining only 280 items under licence. This far reaching change was accompanied by the removal of most price controls on domestic trade. While many of the tariff changes involved a gazetted increase in the rate, the tariffication typically involved a sharp reduction in the degree of protection compared to the stringent QR regime. In practice, the retention of licensing for some imports has not been a significant protective barrier; except for imports covered by health and security considerations, licences have been issued freely. In the process of fine-tuning tariff rates, some imports with a 'damaging' impact on state-owned enterprises (SOEs) were returned to the licensing list. There have also been moderate across-the-board revenue-oriented duty increases in some years. These limitations notwithstanding, and despite the fact that the pace of trade reforms slackened until a new stimulus was given with the second wave of liberalization a decade later, there has been no major reversal of the reforms. Indeed, subsequent trade policy initiatives have reinforced the role of tariffs as the central instrument regulating Sri Lanka's merchandise trade. The tariff regime has also become less distortionary and currently relies on a structure with three rates of 10, 20, and 35 per cent. In 1994, the unweighted average, across 6,050 tariff items, was in the order of 20 per cent and the ratio of actual duty revenue to imports was about 11 per cent (WTO, 1995: 35).[2]

A wide range of export promotion schemes was introduced under a newly established Export Development Board (EDB). These included an all-encompassing duty rebate scheme with flexible operational procedures, direct cash subsidies, manufacturing-in-bond, provision of equity and working capital to firms with export potential, and various measures aimed at product and market development. Steps were also taken to streamline and improve fiscal incentives for export production at successive stages, finally limiting tax holiday concessions to export ventures only. A scheme of manufacture-in-bond for importing material to re-export as a part of a finished good, a cash grant scheme based on annual export increments, and concessionary credit for exporters were among other EDB incentives. A five-year tax holiday was introduced in the 1978 Budget Speech for export-oriented companies.

**Foreign Investment Policy**

The most important aspect of the new foreign investment policy was the setting up of the Greater Colombo Economic Commission (GCEC) in 1978 with wide-ranging powers to establish and operate Export Processing Zones (EPZs). The investment promotion policy package offered by the GCEC to EPZ investors included allowing complete foreign ownership of investment projects; a tax holiday for up to 10 years with complete tax exemption for remuneration of foreign personnel employed, royalties, and dividends of shareholders during that period; duty exemption for the importation of inputs and assistance with customs clearances; industrial services at subsidized rates and unlimited access to foreign-currency credit at interest rates prevailing in world financial markets. Steps were also taken to enter into Investment Protection Agreements and Double Taxation Relief Agreements with the major investing countries. A guarantee against nationalisation of foreign assets without compensation was provided under the Article 157 of the new Constitution of Sri Lanka adopted in 1978.

The *Investment Policy Statement* in 1990 announced several important changes to the foreign investment policy framework in line with the increased outward orientation of the economy. These included abolition of various restrictions on the ownership structures of joint-venture projects outside EPZs, providing free-trade-zone status to export-oriented foreign ventures in all parts of the country (in addition to the area demarcated by the original GCEC Act), and reformulating institutional procedures with a view to speeding up investment approval within a unified policy framework applicable to both import-substituting and export-oriented investors.

**Macroeconomic Policy and Export Profitability**

Trade liberalization was accompanied by a significant exchange rate reform: the dual exchange rate system introduced in 1968 was abolished, and the new unified rate was placed under a managed float. This resulted in an initial devaluation of almost 80 per cent. The exchange rate was to be adjusted daily to reflect changes in foreign exchange market conditions. In order to sustain improved international competitiveness achieved through the exchange rate reforms, it was imperative to supplement the reform package with sound macroeconomic management. The policy initiatives in this direction included a significant interest rate reform and attempts to reduce the budget deficit (which had been the major source of macroeconomic imbalance) through significant cuts in food and fertilizer subsidies, restraints on budgetary transfers to SOEs and limits on inflationary financing of the budget deficit. But the focus on fiscal prudence was short lived, and government policies soon resulted in the generation of inflationary pressures. The government's attitude to SOEs was a contributory factor; while a few loss making public enterprises were either shifted to the private sector or closed down, most continued to operate despite dismal performance and ongoing dependence on budgetary transfers. These transfers soon outweighed the expenditure reduction resulting from subsidy cuts and aggravated the budget deficit. But the chief source of macroeconomic instability and pressure on the real exchange rate in the early post-reform period was a massive public sector investment programme (Athukorala and Jayasuriya, 1994). To make matters worse, from about 1979, the Central Bank started using the nominal exchange rate as an anchor for inflation control, intensified its intervention in the foreign exchange market and eventually abandoned (in November 1982) the practice of determining the exchange rate daily.

Estimates of the real exchange rate (RER) for manufactured exports are plotted in Figure 10.1 to shed light on the cumulative effects of trade

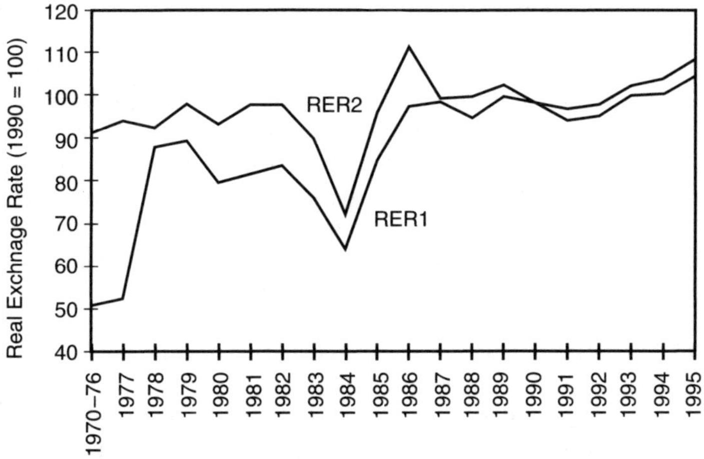


*Figure* 10.1 Real Exchange Rate Indices (1990 = 100) for Manufacturing Exports, 1975–95

*Notes:* RER1: Real exchange rate estimated as the ratio of export price index (domestic currency, rupee) to domestic wholesale price index of manufactured goods.

RER2: Real exchange rate measured as the ratio of export price index (in rupee) adjusted for export subsidies to domestic wholesale price index of manufactured goods.

*Source:* Compiled by the author; details available on request.

policy reforms and the developments in the macroeconomic front for the relative profitability of manufacturing for exports.[3] Two separate sets of estimates for the real exchange rate (RER1 and RER2) are presented in order to help understand the role of direct subsidies in determining relative profitability. RER1 measures the changes in domestic-currency (rupee) price of exports (world-market price of exports adjusted by nominal exchange rate) relative to changes in the respective domestic market price. Thus it can be interpreted as an indicator of the relative profitability of exporting over selling in the home market ('the home market bias' or 'anti-export bias'). According to the particular construct adopted here, an increase in the index implies an improvement in relative profitability of exporting (a reduction in home market bias). The only difference between RER1 and RER2 is that the latter captures export subsidies as an additional component of local-currency receipts from exports.

The RER1 series point to a dramatic improvement in relative export profitability during the immediate aftermath of the 1977 reforms, but the improvement is mild in terms of RER2. This is because the liberalization reforms involved the abolition of the premium exchange rate and import entitlements enjoyed by the exporters of manufactured (and other non-traditional) goods. More importantly, both indices indicate a significant deterioration in profitability during the first half of the 1980s, when the public-sector investment boom was in full swing. A comparison of RER1 and RER2 suggests that subsidy policies have had a noticeable, though mild, impact on export profitability until about the late 1980s, after when the annual changes in the series have been negligible. In the early 1980s, when exchange rate policy ceased to provide a stimulus for exports, the EDB resorted to strengthening various financial incentives to restore export profitability. However, this indirect approach largely failed in subsequent years because of severe financial constraints on the operation of the EDB brought about by an aggravated fiscal situation.

The adjustment programme implemented as part of the second-wave liberalization during 1989/90 provided a brief period of relative macroeconomic stability, with steps being taken to bring the fiscal deficit under control and to maintain a more realistic exchange rate under a crawling-peg system. Commitment to a policy of flexible exchange rate management in order to restore international competitiveness was another key element of the reform package. Reflecting the new policy, the Sri Lankan rupee depreciated *vis-a-vis* the US dollar, the intervention currency, by 17.4 per cent in 1989 (based on an end-of-year comparison). Following this, the Central Bank has continued to adjust the exchange rate daily, taking into account developments in the foreign exchange market.

The rate of nominal exchange rate depreciation under the managed-float exchange regime in the 1990s has more than compensated for the negative effects of the overall macroeconomic policies that fuelled domestic inflation. In other words, the Central Bank pursued a sufficiently flexible exchange rate policy to improve the international competitiveness of the traded goods sector. However, in recent years a massive surge in defence expenditures, to seven per cent of GDP in 1996, has placed major constraints on sound fiscal management, and made it extremely difficult to maintain an environment conducive to investment and growth. In sum, liberalization reforms since 1977 included a significant opening of the Sri Lankan economy to foreign trade and investment. However, with the exception of relatively short periods, the economy did not have the benefit of macroeconomic policies that complemented the trade reforms.

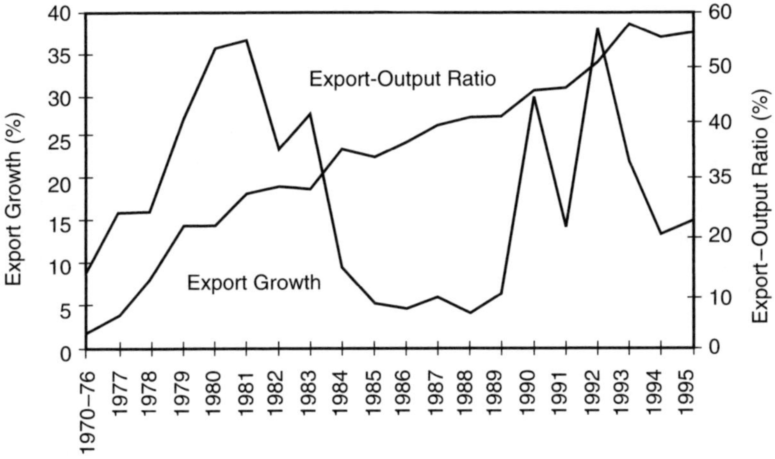


*Figure* 10.2 Growth of Manufactured Exports and Export-Output Ratio of Domestic Manufacturing*
*Notes:* * Export growth is in current SDR terms. In calculating the export-output ratio, FOB export values were converted to producer-price basis using data on trade and transport margin obtained from the Input-Output Table – 1991 (Ministry of Finance and Planning).
*Source:* Compiled using data from Central Bank, *Annual Report* (various issues)

## 10.3 TRENDS AND PATTERNS OF MANUFACTURED EXPORTS

Export response to liberalization was swift (Figure 10.2): the average annual growth rate of manufacturing exports during 1978–95 was over 18 per cent (24 per cent when 1984–89, a period of intense political turmoil, is excluded) compared to eight per cent growth during 1970–76. During 1980–94, Sri Lanka was among the top five low-income countries in terms of both the average annual growth in earnings from manufactured exports and the increase in manufacturing share in total merchandise exports (UNCTAD, 1995). Export orientation of manufacturing, as measured by the export coefficient (ratio of exports to gross manufacturing output) increased rapidly, from 0.03 in the mid-1970s to 0.55 in 1995 (Figure 10.2) and export expansion was the most important source of growth between these two years.

Table 10.1 demonstrates that Sri Lanka was dependent on agricultural commodities, notably tea and rubber, for 95 per cent of exports in the pre-liberalization period (represented by 1970–71).

*Table* 10.1 Export Structure of Sri Lanka (%)

| | 1970–71 | 1980–81 | 1993–95 |
|---|---|---|---|
| Agricultural exports | 94.6 | 61.6 | 22.4 |
| Tea | 55.5 | 35.1 | 13.8 |
| Rubber | 22.0 | 14.7 | 2.3 |
| Coconut | 14.5 | 7.0 | 2.2 |
| Other # | 3.1 | 4.8 | 4.1 |
| Manufactured exports | 1.7 | 31.2 | 73.2 |
| Textiles and garments | 0.4 | 10.3 | 48.8 |
| Petroleum products | 0.9 | 17.7 | 2.6 |
| Mineral exports | 0.8 | 4.5 | 2.7 |
| Unclassified (including re-exports) | 3.9 | 2.7 | 1.7 |
| Total (%) | 100 | 100 | 100 |
| Value (SDR million) | 686 | 873 | 2141 |

*Notes:* All figures relate to two-year averages.
# The other products in this category include coffee, pepper, nutmeg, cardamom, betel leaves, essential oils, cashew nuts, areca-nuts (beetle leaves), papain, vegetables and fruits.
*Source:* Compiled from data reported in Central Bank, *Annual Report* (various issues).

Following liberalization and within ten years, agricultural exports had fallen to less than two-thirds of the total and manufacturing had risen to almost a third. By 1993–94, manufactures accounted for almost three-quarters of exports, with textiles and garments being almost half, while agriculture's share had fallen to 22 per cent, with tea the only significant commodity export. Consistent with the early outward orientation experience of most countries, manufactured exports from Sri Lanka initially showed a strong reliance on standard labour-intensive consumer goods (Table 10.2), with the garment industry being dominant. However, since the late 1980s there has been a noticeable increase in export earnings in other labour intensive product areas such as electronics (included under the category 'machinery'), footwear and diamond cutting.

Foreign direct investment (FDI) has undoubtedly been the engine of manufactured export growth over the past two decades. During 1967–77, a total of 82 foreign manufacturing firms were set up in Sri Lanka of which only 12 were export-oriented (Athukorala, 1995). In contrast,

*Table* 10.2 Composition of Manufactured Exports, 1970–95 (%)

| Products | 1970 | 1977 | 1980 | 1985 | 1990 | 1995 |
|---|---|---|---|---|---|---|
| Food, beverages and tobacco | 14.1 | 33.4 | 13.1 | 5.1 | 3.4 | 3.6 |
| Textiles, clothing and footwear | 77.2 | 48.2 | 76.9 | 77.7 | 69.7 | 72.3 |
| Fabrics | ... | 0.6 | 0.26 | 1.2 | 0.3 | 1.8 |
| Clothing | 63.1 | 45.0 | 76.5 | 73.9 | 64.7 | 59.5 |
| Footwear | 9.6 | 1.9 | 0.1 | 1.3 | 1.01 | 1.7 |
| Wood products | 8.4 | 2.3 | 0.3 | 0.8 | 1.3 | 1.0 |
| Chemicals and rubber goods | ... | 6.9 | 3.9 | 4.9 | 6.0 | 7.0 |
| Rubber goods | ... | 0.6 | 0.1 | 1.5 | 3.2 | 5.0 |
| Non-metallic minerals | 0.3 | 8.4 | 5.4 | 2.1 | 11.8 | 8.1 |
| Ceramics and wall tiles | 0.3 | 8.4 | 5.4 | 0.9 | 1.9 | 2.1 |
| Diamonds | ... | ... | ... | 3.0 | 9.8 | 6.0 |
| Machinery, metal products | ... | 1.6 | 1.3 | 3.0 | 6.3 | 4.2 |
| Total Manufactures | 100 | 100 | 100 | 100 | 100 | 100 |
| Value (SDR millions) | 13.2 | 86.8 | 25.5 | 51.8 | 72.5 | 16.48 |

*Notes:* All figures relate to year.
... denotes zero or negligible
*Source:* Compiled from Central Bank, *Annual Report* (various issues).

during 1978–95 the Board of Investment (BOI, formerly GCEC) signed contracts (under the special incentive scheme for export-oriented firms) for setting up 1,136 firms of which 835 were in operation by early 1995. In addition, some 125 export-oriented ventures were established with foreign capital participation under general incentive provisions.

During the post-reform period until about the late 1980s, the garment industry continued to be the major area of attraction to foreign investors, encouraged by avoiding quota restrictions under the Multi-Fibre Arrangement (MFA). However, since the late 1980s there has been a noticeable increase in the number of foreign firms entering into other labour intensive product areas. Investors have been attracted to Sri Lanka as a lower-cost export base in terms of both the availability of cheap and trainable labour and the favourable investment climate. Sri Lanka's overseas investment promotion campaign has placed heavy emphasis on courting assembly production in high-tech industries, and the number of such firms increased during the 1980s.

Data on the relative contribution of foreign firms to manufactured exports are given in Table 10.3. There is a close correlation between the growth of manufactured exports and the share of foreign firms in these

*Table* 10.3 Foreign Firms' Contribution to Manufactured Export Expansion, 1976–92 (three-year averages).

| | Manufactured Exports* | Foreign Firms' Contribution to Manufactured Exports (as % of ) | |
|---|---|---|---|
| | US $m | All foreign firms # | FTZ firms |
| 1975–77 | 24.8 | 23.2 | n.a. |
| 1978–80 | 102.7 | 30.2 | n.a. |
| 1981–83 | 234.9 | 43.7 | 30.6 |
| 1984–86 | 421.2 | 47.4 | 35.5 |
| 1987–89 | 653.5 | 58.2 | 43.5 |
| 1990–92 | 1083.1 | 65.8 | 47.6 |
| 1993–95 | 1949.5 | 78.2 | 49.1 |

*Notes:*
* Excluding petroleum products.
\# Combined export share of GCEC and Non-FTZ firms.
n.a. Not applicable.
*Source:* Athukorala (1995).

exports. The share of foreign firms in total exports of manufactures increased from 23 per cent in 1977 to almost 80 per cent in the mid-1990s. The contribution of foreign firms to the total increment in manufactured exports has increased from 46 per cent between 1978 and 1985, to 85 per cent between 1985 and 1995. Apart from this 'direct' contribution, there is evidence that the presence of foreign firms generates significant positive effects on the export success of local export producing firms (Athukorala, 1995).

A crucial issue in the contemporary trade and industrial policy debate in developing countries is whether an import-substitution phase is a precondition for the successful transition to export orientation. In Sri Lanka, there is no evidence of a direct link between recent export growth and output expansion during the earlier IS period. As in other countries such as Taiwan, Malaysia, and Chile, manufactured exports emerged *de novo* in response to the creation of new incentives (Helleiner, 1994 and 1995; Riedel, 1993). Most of the new exporting firms developed initially as exporting ventures independently of the industrial base laid down in the earlier period. In the garment industry, some firms established during the IS era have successfully ventured into export business, but their new operations are largely based on know-how, managerial inputs and to some extent even capital, obtained through foreign collaboration and/or marketing links established through international buying groups which came to the country following the trade policy reforms. During the pre-reform 1970s, a significant portion of manufactured exports came from a handful of import-substituting subsidiaries of multinationals in food and beverages, pharmaceutical and chemical industries which temporarily diverted some of their domestic sales to the world market in order to become eligible for import entitlements under the convertible rupee accounts scheme. Most of these exports disappeared after the 1977 trade liberalization (Athukorala and Jayasuriya, 1994: 102).

## 10.4 DETERMINANTS OF MANUFACTURED EXPORTS

The purpose of this section is to undertake an econometric analysis of the supply response of Sri Lankan manufacturing exports. An attempt is made to shed light on the link between export incentives (as measured by the real exchange rate) and export performance, while allowing for the impact of the overall shift in trade policy in favour of greater market orientation and the promotion of foreign direct investment. Note that the use of a supply function (instead of a full demand-supply system) as the basis of our empirical analysis is based on the implicit assumption that foreign currency prices faced by Sri Lankan exporters are determined exogenously (the small-country assumption). This is not a restrictive assumption given the nature of manufactured goods exported by Sri Lanka (largely undifferentiated light manufactures) and Sri Lanka's small world market share in these product categories (Athukorala and Riedel, 1996; Riedel and Athukorala, 1995).

The estimated export supply equation is of the form:

$$QX = F(RER, PLBD, PCAP)$$

where

*QX* real exports,
*RER* real exchange rate,
*PLBD* a pre-liberalization dummy variable which takes value 1 for the years 1968–77 and 0 otherwise, and
*PCAP* production capacity.

The regression coefficient of *PLBD* is expected to be negative, others positive. All variables except (*PLBD*) are measured as indices with 1990 as the base year. The rationale behind the choice of explanatory variables is the following. As discussed, the *RER*, the key explanatory variable in the model, measures changes over time in the relative profitability of exporting and selling domestically (we use RER2, but comparable results are obtained with RER1). It brings together changes in the nominal exchange rate, the effective value of financial incentives, and domestic and world market prices. It is therefore a composite indicator of relative export profitability.

The *RER* is expected to influence only the changes in real exports resulting from movement along the production possibility curve triggered by relative price changes. In practice even if *RER* remain unchanged, exports would still change depending on shifts in the country's production capacity. The net effect of changes in the *RER* on exports can therefore be meaningfully delineated only if the latter changes are taken into account. On these grounds, we use the average of real manufacturing output in the three previous years as a proxy to account for the impact of the expansion of domestic production capacity on export expansion. The third explanatory variable *PLBD* is included to capture the distinction (if any) between pre- and post-trade liberalization periods with regard to export performance which are not expressed in the *RER*. The literature suggests that the favourable impact of trade liberalization on export performance is not limited to relative price aspects (which are captured in the *RER*). Various institutional changes embodied in the liberalization package (such as access to imported inputs, increased flexibility in the exchange control mechanism, and a relatively more conducive atmosphere for private sector activity) may also contribute to improved export performance.

The model was estimated separately for total manufacturing goods (TMF), clothing exports and non-clothing manufacturing exports (total manufacturing exports less garments). In the latter category exports by non-GCEC firms are treated as a separate category. Clothing exports are treated as a separate category in order to allow for 'special' market conditions faced by garment exporters throughout the period due to the market quota system under the MFA.

The distinction between GCEC and non-GCEC firms within non-garments exports is made for the following reasons. The GCEC firms (of which over 90 per cent have FDI participation) are 'exporters by decree' and the factors that induce such firms in export decisions can be different to those governing other firms (see Athukorala, Jayasuriya and Oczkowski, 1995). Various special incentives accorded to the GCEC firms (such as duty free concessions and subsidized infrastructure) are not captured in our RER estimates. Moreover, there are reasons to believe that foreign investors who set up plants in free trade zones generally place relatively more (or perhaps sole) emphasis on fundamentals governing international relocation of production bases (such as the availability and relative cost of labour and political and policy certainty) than on the nominal exchange rate and other domestic financial incentives. With regard to the cost of labour – a major consideration in international relocation of production – one can argue that perhaps the most important aspect is the relative wage *level* rather than the relative annual *changes* in wages. In the presence of vast wage differentials across investment locations, even a quite substantial increase in wages over time in a given investment location may not receive much weight in investment relocation decisions. For these reasons we expect exports by non-GCEC firms to be more sensitive to changes in the RER than the GCEC firms.

In estimating an export supply function, it is necessary to allow for possible time lags involved in the hypothesized relationships. For this, we make use of the error-correction method (ECM) which is considered a highly appropriate dynamic specification when one works with relatively short time series (Hendry, 1995).[4] Under the ECM method, the long-run (steady state) relationship being investigated is embodied within a dynamic specification including lagged dependent and independent variables, in order to minimize the possibility of estimating spurious relationships. It is important to guard against the possibility of uncovering spurious relations when working with variables (real exports and production capacity in our case) which seem to have a strong trend component. The ECM procedure has the added advantage of separating long-run relationships from the short-run impact in the estimated equation.

The estimation procedure starts with an autoregressive distributed lag (ADL) specification of an appropriate lag order:

$$Y_t = \alpha + \sum_{i=1}^{m} A_i Y_{t-i} \sum_{i=0}^{m} B_i X_{t-i} + \mu_t \qquad (10.1)$$

where $\alpha$ is a constant, $Y_t$ is a $(n \times 1)$ vector of endogenous variables, $X_t$ is a $(k \times 1)$ vector of explanatory variables, and $A_i$ and $B_i$ are $(n \times n)$ and $(n \times k)$ matrices of parameters.

Equation 10.1 is then reparameterized in terms of differences and lagged levels so as to separate the short-run and long-run multipliers of the system.[5]

$$\Delta Y_1 = \alpha + \sum_{i=1}^{m-1} A_i^* \Delta Y_{t-i} + \sum_{i=0}^{m-1} B_i^* \Delta X_{t-i} + C_0 Y_{t-m} + C_1 X_{t-m} + \mu_t \tag{10.2}$$

where

$$C_0 = -\left(I - \sum_{i=1}^{m} A_i\right) \qquad C_1 = \left(\sum_{i=0}^{m} B_i\right)$$

and the long-run multipliers of the system are given by $C_0^{-1}C_1$.

Equation 10.2 constitutes the *maintained hypothesis* of our specification search. This general model is *tested down* (using OLS), by dropping statistically insignificant lag terms, and imposing data-acceptable restrictions on the regression parameters. The testing procedure continues until a parsimonious error correction representation is obtained which retains the *a priori* theoretical model as its long-run solution. To be acceptable, the final equation must satisfy various diagnostic tests relating to the OLS error process. The sample period is 1968–94. All variables (except of course *PLBD*) are used in log form so that the coefficients can be directly interpreted as elasticities.[6] The results are reported in Table 10.4.

As expected, the real exchange rate (*RER*) is not a significant determinant of clothing exports. These exports are explained predominantly by exports in the previous year and production capacity. The results for total exports are largely dictated by clothing. In this equation, the coefficient attached to the real exchange rate variable suggests an elasticity of 0.77, which does not attain statistical significance even at the 10 per cent level. For non-clothing exports we find a statistically significant real exchange rate elasticity of 1.06 per cent. When GCEC exports are netted from this category, the elasticity coefficient increases to 2.95 with the level of significance shifting from five per cent to one per cent. Thus there is strong statistical support for the hypothesis that non-GCEC manufacturing exports are much more sensitive to changes in overall financial incentives than exports by GCEC firms. This result is consistent with our conjecture that international location decisions of export-oriented production foreign firms are governed by various factors other than the domestic incentive structure of a given host country.

The coefficient on the dummy intercept variable used to represent regime shift (*PLBD*) is statistically significant at least at the ten per cent level (five per cent or better in three cases) with the expected (negative)

*Table* 10.4 Determinants of Manufacturing Exports

---

*Total Manufacturing Exports*

$$\Delta QX_t = -0.68 + 0.27\,RER_{t-1} - 0.27\,PLBD + 0.24\,PCAP_{t-1} - 0.35\,QX_{t-1}$$

(0.65) (0.93) (2.16)** (1.10) (3.17)***

Long-run elasticity of *QX* with respect to *RER* = 0.77 (1.24)

*Adjusted-*$R^2$ = 0.37 $F = 3.11$ $SE = 0.26$ $DW = 2.49$
*LM-F*(1,20) = 1.23 *RESET* (1,20) = 0.11 *JBN* (2) = 44.27
*HSC* (1,24) = 0.04

*Clothing exports*

$$\Delta QX_t = 2.66 - 1.99\,PBLD + 0.23\,PCAP_{t-1} - 0.77\,QX_{t-1}$$

(6.23)*** (6.06)*** (2.24)** (7.57)***

*Adjusted-*$R^2$ = 0.75 $F$ (3,22) = 21.92 $SE = 0.36$ $DW = 1.97$
*LM-F*(1,21) = 0.01 *RESET* = 10.95 *JBN* (2) = 0.23 *HSC* (1,24) = 0.24

*Other (non-clothing) exports*

$$\Delta QX_t = -6.49 + 0.98\,RER_t + 0.75\,RER_{t-1} - 0.32\,PLBD$$

(2.74)* (2.11)** (1.71)* (1.35)*

$$+ 1.39\,PCAP_{t-1} - 0.71\,QX_{t-1}$$

(3.36)*** (3.68)***

Long-run elasticity of QX with respect to RER = 1.06 (1.90)

*Adjusted-*$R^2$ = 0.52 $F = 3.98$ $SE = 0.28$ $DW = 1.76$
*LMS-F*(1,17) = 0.84 *RESET-F*(1,17) = 2.63 *JBN*(2) = 17.93
*HSC* (1,26) = 11.88

*Other (non-clothing) exports by non-GCEC firms*

$$\Delta QX_t = -1.89 + 1.03\,\Delta RER_t + 1.09\,RER_{t-1} - 0.86\,PLBD$$

(1.29) (1.98)** (2.86)*** (2.51)***

$$+ 1.03\,PCAP_{t-1} - 0.37\,QX_{t-1}$$

(1.34)* (3.63)**

Long-run elasticity of *QX* with respect to *RER* = 2.95 (4.04)***

*Adjusted-*$R^2$ = 0.50 F = 4.4 $SE = 0.32$ $DW = 2.01$
*LMS* (1,17) = 0.05 *RESET* (1,17) = 5.52 *JBN*(2) = 15.29
*HSC* (1,22) = 2.44

---

*Notes: t*-ratios in parentheses with the level of statistical significance (one-tailed test) denoted as, * for 10 per cent, ** for 5 per cent and ***for one per cent. *LMS* is the Lagrange multiplier test for serial correlation; *RESET* Ramsey RESET test for functional form mis-specification; *JBN* denotes the Jarques-Bera test for the normality of residuals; *HSC* Test for heteroscedasticity based on squared residuals. Except for *JBN*, based on the $\chi^2$ distribution, all other tests are based of the *F*-distribution.

*Source:* Author's estimates based on data sources discussed in the text.

sign. This result provides statistical support for the view that, quite apart from its impact operating through the incentives captured in *RER*, the liberalization policy package has been instrumental in creating a conducive environment for export expansion. As we have already discussed, the key elements of the policy reform package such as trade liberalization, foreign investment promotion and greater emphasis placed on the role of the private sector in the economy seems to have set the stage for the rapid expansion of manufacturing exports.

## 10.5 CONCLUDING REMARKS

The market-oriented policy reforms initiated in 1977 have led to far-reaching changes in the structure and performance of Sri Lanka manufacturing. The manufacturing sector has become increasingly more export-oriented, and is no longer reliant on the fortunes of the traditional primary export industries to obtain required imported inputs. The view that an import-substitution phase is a precondition for the successful transition to export orientation receives no support from the Sri Lankan experience. We found no evidence of a direct link between recent export growth and output expansion during the earlier IS period: manufactured exports emerged *de novo* in response to the creation of new incentives. Most of the new exporting firms developed initially as exporting ventures independently of the industrial base laid down in the earlier period.

Our findings cast serious doubt on the popular structuralist prescription of using direct subsidies (as a substitute for genuine trade and macroeconomic reforms) an export promotion tool. In the typical developing economy with a weak government revenue base the potential stimulus through subsidies is bound to be rather insignificant in a context of aggravating macroeconomic imbalance.

A key theme running through the chapter is the importance of the concomitant reforms in both trade and investment policy regimes in determining the outcome of liberalization in small trade dependent countries like Sri Lanka. Internationalization of production through FDI participation has been central to the rapid integration of developing countries in the global manufactured goods trade system. In this context there is limited room for a small developing economy to enter manufactured goods trade solely through local entrepreneurial initiatives. Foreign investment not only provides the initial stimulus for a rapid expansion in exports and the associated increase in employment, but is also a vehicle for forging links between local firms and international markets.

The results of our econometric exercise do provide support for the view that maintaining a realistic real exchange rate is important in achieving a broad based manufactured export structure with greater local capital participation (this is consistent with proposing stabilization as a precursor to liberalization). At the same time, there is evidence that the significant role played by foreign firms has contributed to a considerable weakening of the link between the real exchange rate and export performance. There is also strong statistical evidence that, quite apart from its impact operating through the incentives captured in *RER*, the liberalization policy package (including elements such as trade liberalization, foreign investment promotion and greater emphasis placed on the role of the private sector in the economy) has been instrumental in creating a business environment which was conducive for export expansion. Thus the overwhelming (or sole) emphasis placed on exchange rate and incentive policies (as is done in the current policy debate in Sri Lanka) in explaining export performance can lead to misleading inferences, and more attention needs to be paid to factors impacting on the overall investment climate.

## Notes

1. Sri Lanka's post-independence policy history has been well documented. See, for instance, Snodgrass (1966), Rajapatirana (1988), Cuthbertson and Athukorala (1990) and Athukorala and Jayasuriya (1994).
2. The difference between the gazetted rate and the actual rate may be due to the operation of tariff exemptions and waivers and the deterrent effects of high tariffs on trade in the relevant items.
3. Data used in constructing *RER* are from the following sources: Central Bank, *Annual Report* (various issues) for official exchange rate, exchange rate premium and wholesale price index); official records of the EDB for duty rebates, export grants and other subsidies and concessionary finance; and OECD, *Key Economic Indicators* for wholesale manufacturing prices of major importing countries. Nominal exchange rate is measured as a trade weighted index of the rupee versus currencies of the six major destinations for Sri Lankan manufactured exports (USA, Japan, UK, Germany, France and Canada). Export price is proxied by an export-weighted average of wholesale price indices (WPIs) of manufactured goods in these six countries. First, for each country, WPIs at the two digit ISIC level were linked using Sri Lanka's export shares to form a single index

relating to Sri Lanka's exports. Individual country indices obtained in this manner were then linked using the same country weights used in constructing the exchange rate series. Trade weights are for 1990.

4. Consider the simple bivariate model, $Y_t = a + bX_t$. Assuming a one-period lag effect of $X$ on $Y$, this equation can be reparameterized in terms of levels and differences to obtain the following error-correction specification (where $\Delta$ denotes change in value of variable):

$$\Delta Y_t = a + b_1 \Delta X_t + b_2 X_{t-1} - b_3 Y_{t-1}$$

The short-run impact of $X$ on $Y$ is captured by $b_1$. The long-run (equilibrium or steady state) effect is given by, $b_2 / -(-b_3)$, and the standard error (*SE*) of this coefficient can be calculated as, [(*SE* of $b_1$ + *SE* of $b_2$)/*SE* of $b_2$].

5. This method is also known as the Hendry method, or the LSE approach (Hendry, 1995). Given the small sample, there is little to be gained by employing the now-fashionable two-stage approach to the estimation of an error correction model. Recent comparative Monte Carlo studies have identified the original Hendry method as a 'general' estimation technique which has superior small sample properties compared to these alternative techniques (Banerjee *et al.*, 1993, and Inder, 1993).
6. In all cases the log-linear specification was preferable to linear specification in terms of the Ramsey RESET test for functional form misspecification.

## References

Adhikari, R. (1993), 'Policy Reforms and Export Performance in Sri Lanka: Some Observations', in R. Adhikari, C. Kirkpatrick and J. Weiss (eds), *Industrial and Trade Policy Reforms and Experience in Developing Countries*, Manchester: Manchester University Press, pp. 186–197.

Arslan, I. and S. van Wijnbergen (1993), 'Export Incentives, Exchange Rate Policy and Export Growth in Turkey', *Review of Economics and Statistics*, 75(1), pp. 128–133.

Athukorala, P. (1981), 'Import Substitution, Structural Transformation and Import Dependence: A Case Study of Sri Lanka', *Developing Economies*, 19(2), pp. 119–142.

Athukorala, P. (1995), 'Foreign Direct Investment and manufacturing for Export in a New Exporting country: The Case of Sri Lanka', *World Economy*, 18(4), pp. 543–564.

Athukorala, P. and S. Jayasuriya (1994), *Macroeconomic Policies, Crises and Growth in Sri Lanka, 1969–90*, Washington, DC: The World Bank.

Athukorala, P., S. Jayasuriya and E. Oczkowski (1995), 'Multinational Firms and Export Performance in Developing Countries: Some Analytical Issues and New Empirical Evidence', *Journal of Development Economics*, 46, pp. 109–122.

Athukorala, P. and J. Riedel (1996), 'Modelling NIE Exports: Aggregation, Quantitative Restrictions and Choice of Econometric Methodology', *Journal of Development Studies*, 33(1), pp. 81–98.
Banerjee, A., J. Dolado, J.W. Galbraith and D.F. Hendry (1993), *Co-integration, Error Correction, and the Econometric Analysis of Non-stationary Data*, Oxford: Oxford University Press.
Cuthbertson, A. and P. Athukorala (1991), 'Sri Lanka', in D. Papageorgiou, M. Michaely and A. Choksi (eds), *Liberalizing Foreign Trade: Indonesia, Pakistan and Sri Lanka*, Oxford: Basil Blackwell, pp. 287–414.
Dornbusch, R. (1992), 'The Case for Trade Liberalization in Developing Countries', *Journal of Economic Perspectives*, 6(1), pp. 69–87.
Greenaway, D. and D. Sapsford (1994), 'What Does Liberalization Do for Exports and Growth?', *Weltwirtschftliches Archiv*, 130(1), pp. 152–174.
Helleiner, G. (1994), 'Introduction', in G. Helleiner (ed), *Trade Policy and Industrialization in Turbulent Times*, London: Routledge.
Helleiner, G. (1995), *Manufacturing for Exports in the Developing World: Problems and Possibilities*, London: Routledge.
Hendry, D. (1995), *Dynamic Econometrics*, Oxford: Oxford University Press.
Inder, B. (1993), 'Estimating Long-run Relationships in Economics: A Comparison of Different Approaches', *Journal of Econometrics*, 34(2), pp. 359–382.
Joshi, V. and I. Little (1996), *India's Economic Reforms 1991–2001*, Delhi: Oxford University Press.
Krueger, A. (1992), *Economic Policy Reforms in Developing Countries*, Oxford: Basil Blackwell.
Krueger, A. and B. Tuncer (1982), 'Growth of Factor Productivity in Turkish Manufacturing Industries', *Journal of Development Economics*, 11(2), pp. 307–325.
Little, I., R. Cooper, W. Corden and S. Rajapatirana (1993), *Boom, Crisis, and Adjustment: The Macroeconomic Experience of Developing Countries*, Oxford: Oxford University Press.
Riedel, J. (1993), 'Vietnam: On the Trail of the Tigers', *World Economy*, 16(4), pp. 401–423.
Riedel, J. and P. Athukorala (1995), 'Export Growth and the Terms of Trade: The Case of Curious Elasticities', in D. Vines and D. Currie (eds), *North-South Linkages and International Macroeconomic Policy*, Cambridge: CUP, pp. 29–45.
Rodrik, D. (1992), 'The Limits of Trade Policy Reforms in Developing Countries', *Journal of Economic Perspectives*, 6(1), pp. 87–106.
Rajapatirana, S. (1988), 'Foreign Trade and Economic Development: Sri Lanka's Experience', *World Development*, 16(10), pp. 1143–1157.
Snodgrass, D. (1966), *Sri Lanka: An Export Economy in Transition*, Homewood, Ill: Richard D. Irvin.
Thomas, V., J. Nash and Associates (1991), *Best Practices in Trade Policy Reforms*, New York: Oxford University Press.
UNCTAD (1995), *Trade and Development Report – 1995*, Geneva.
Weiss, J. (1992), 'Export Response to Trade Reforms: Recent Mexican Experience', *Development Policy Review*, 10(1), pp. 43–60.

World Bank (1993), *The East Asian Miracle: Economic Growth and Public Policy*, New York: Oxford University Press.
World Bank (1995), *Sri Lanka: Non-plantation Crop Sector Policy Alternatives*, Agriculture and Natural Resource Division, South Asia Region, Washington, DC: The World Bank (mimeo).
World Trade Organization (WTO) (1995), *Sri Lanka Trade Policy Review*, Geneva: WTO.

# Index

*Note*: 'n.' after a page reference indicates the number of a note on that page.